DATE	ISSUED TO
MAR 2 9 1985 - 5312	
NOV 1 8 1985	DEC - 5 1993
DEC 1 3 1985	APR - 5 1994
OCT 2 9 1986	FEB. 2 5 1996
DEC 1 9 1986	DEC 5 1997
JAN 2 8 1987	
DEC 1 6 1988	
FEB 2 5 1990	
MAR 1 2 1990	
APR 1 8 1990	
MAR 2 9 1992	
JAN - 4 1993	
MAR 1 2 1993	

Sexual Assault

by

Christine L.M. Boyle

LL.B., LL.M.
of the Inn of Court of Northern Ireland,
Barrister-at-law,
member of the Nova Scotia Bar
Professor of Law, Dalhousie University

THE CARSWELL COMPANY LIMITED
Toronto, Canada
1984

Canadian Cataloguing in Publication Data

Boyle, Christine, 1949–
  Sexual assault

Includes index.
ISBN 0-459-36720-X

1. Sex crimes - Canada.   2. Rape - Canada.   3. Child molesting - Canada.   4. Sex and law - Canada.
I. Title.

KE8928.B69   1984   364.1′53′0971   C84-098918-0

Copyright © 1984
The Carswell Company Limited

For my parents
Norah and Leslie Boyle

Preface

This book is primarily intended to provide the legal practitioner and academic with a guide to the concept of sexual assault, which is new to Canadian criminal law. It is hoped that it will also be of assistance and interest to others with a knowledge of the reality and law of rape and curiosity about the recent reform. The subject is one which attracts a great deal of attention among non-lawyers, probably because of its highly political nature and the impact that the fact and fear of sexual assault have on everyday life. The process of law reform extended over a lengthy period of time, so that it was possible for the public interest, which was largely responsible for the initiation of the process, to snowball. It seemed desirable that some clear statement of the results of that process should be made and the necessary assessment begun.

The concept of sexual assault was introduced in January 1983, in response to concerns that the emotional and political baggage carried by the term rape was a serious impediment to the reporting of, and conviction for, the crime of rape. The Criminal Law Amendment Act, S.C. 1980-81-82, c. 125, also contained other significant reforms. These, and the change in terminology, were and still are highly controversial. It is vital that research now be carried out on the question of whether these changes in the law are producing any corresponding changes in behaviour and the practice of law enforcement. In the meantime it is important to know precisely what the law now is.

The scope of this book includes both adults and children as victims. Thus its concerns are broader than the reforms introduced in the Criminal Law Amendment Act, since the law as it relates to children has not yet been the subject of completed law reform. The Code provisions covered can therefore be found in various places, the new sexual assault sections having been placed in Part VI, Offences Against the Person and Reputation, while the old offences against children and other vulnerable persons remained in Part IV, Sexual Offences, Public Morals and Disorderly Conduct, where the repealed offences of rape and indecent assault used to be. Since these crimes against children are not couched in terms of assault, it might be thought that they do not fall within the ambit of this book. However, it is the view of this writer that they

v

are conceptually and politically in the class of sexual assault and that reform recognising that view is inevitable. The subject of sexual assault would therefore not be comprehensively covered if offences against children were omitted. This approach is discussed in more detail in Chapter 5 entitled "Offences Against Children and Other Vulnerable People." I ought to confess that I am beginning to consider that crimes relating to prostitution ought also to be classified under sexual assault, but I have not attempted that analysis here for pragmatic reasons. I hope to return to that topic at a later stage.

The organisation of the book is probably self-explanatory. Since the subject to a very great extent is quite new, it seemed necessary to include some historical and constitutional information as a necessary back-drop. That is to be found in Part I. The substance of the new sexual assault offences as well as the old remaining offences is discussed in Part II, while evidentiary, procedural and sentencing matters are covered in Part III. Readers who wish to concentrate on the present law should therefore direct their attention to Parts II and III.

With respect to matters of style, sections referred to are sections of the present Code, unless it is necessary to refer to the actual sections of the Criminal Law Amendment Act or other statutes. A difficulty arose with respect to references to "old" offences such as rape, now repealed, and "old" offences such as seduction, which still remain in the Code. I have attempted throughout to utilise the term "old" to refer to offences which no longer exist and hope that the context will prevent confusion if any "olds" have slipped in elsewhere.

The primary stylistic difficulty related to pronouns, since I was reluctant to obscure reality by calling accused persons and complainants "he or she." I ultimately decided to refer to accused persons and sexual assaulters as male and complainants and victims as female, while referring to other persons in some gender-neutral way. The sensitive subject of gender neutrality in the law is discussed in Chapter 2 entitled "The Constitutional Setting."

A further practical difficulty arose because of the immense body of research and writing on the subject. This is essentially a legal book, yet the law cannot be studied in isolation. I have tried to refer to research in other areas where this throws light on, or leads one to question, established legal doctrine. I am very aware of the fact, however, that it has not been possible to give a complete sense of the richness and diversity of the literature in the field within the scope of this book. Readers, who have not already done so, may well wish to consult other sources.

Probably the best-known popular discussion of rape is contained in Susan Brownmiller's book, *Against Our Will: Men, Women and Rape* (1975). It contains an impressive survey of the history of rape and an analysis of its significance today, leading to the controversial conclusion which is used on the jacket cover of the Penguin edition.

> From prehistoric times to the present, I believe, rape has played a critical function. It is nothing more or less than a conscious process of intimidation by which *all* men keep *all* women in a state of fear.

Brownmiller suggests that this process is supported by the law which can appear reasonable on paper but, to a great extent in practice, operates in response to a fear of false accusations.

The very least that can be said of Brownmiller's work is that it is a forceful reminder of the fact that it is not fruitful to consider the law in a social and economic vacuum. An analysis of sexual assault which ignored the fact that our law operates in a world in which men and women occupy very different positions would be of limited usefulness. The new sexual assault offences which are, in part, the subject of this book are, on paper, gender-free, but it is important to remember that sexual assault is almost completely a crime committed by men against women. The fact that complainants are women and accused persons are men must have enormous significance in a society in which women suffer various forms of social, economic and legal discrimination. It seems reasonable to suppose that the men who have created our law in this context would, if they tried to do so, find it enormously difficult to think about the matter from the perspective of a woman. What has happened in the past, and is still largely true, is that men have had to formulate laws to deal with an issue in which it was a certainty that members of their sex would play either of two roles, that of accused or relative/friend of the victim. They could rarely be the victim in any direct sense. An attempt is made in Chapter 1 to explore the implications of this fact, which relates to sexual assault and no other area of criminal law.

Any discussion of sexual assault would be incomplete without reference to another major influence in our thinking about rape, a work that is cited whenever this subject is discussed, that of Lorenne Clark and Debra Lewis. Their book, *Rape: The Price of Coercive Sexuality*, published in 1977, contained an important empirical study of rape in Toronto and the now-familiar property analysis of the crime as well as the practices surrounding it. On the basis of their findings on which rape complaints proceed through the criminal justice process and which are "filtered" out, they conclude (p. 124):

> Rape laws were never meant to protect all women from rape, or to provide women with any guaranteed right to sexual autonomy. Rape laws were designed to preserve valuable female sexual property for the exclusive ownership of those men who could afford to acquire and maintain it.

This study of Toronto, later duplicated in Vancouver, showed that it was only those women who had some property value who were in practice protected by the law. That is, not "open territory" victims who had transgressed the norms of acceptable female behaviour, those who were drunk, separated, divorced or living in a common-law relationship, mentally-ill or sexually "promiscuous." Even apparently "respectable" women have been treated as suspect and their evidence tested to determine if they had been taking risks with their sexuality and to ensure that they were not making false accusations.

There is no doubt that this analysis and the recommendations for law reform which flow from it, gave considerable impetus to the political commitment to the change from rape to sexual assault which is the subject of this book. One has only to read the chapters entitled "Rape as an Assault" and "Recommendations" to identify at least one source of the reasoning which has lead to the removal of rape (including attempted rape and indecent assault) from Part IV of the Criminal Code, Sexual Offences, Public Morals and Disorderly Conduct, to its new home in Part VI, Offences Against the Person and Reputation. This is not at all to suggest that Clark and Lewis would approve of all the changes made to the Code, but merely to acknowledge their considerable influence.

Other writers have offered varying analyses, some overtly political, others lacking an express political orientation. An example of the latter can be found in the work of Tony Honoré, who suggests, in his book *Sex Law in England* (1978), that the law discriminates in favour of women in order to protect women against "male aggression." He emphasises the quality of violence in sexual assault, not in the sense that it is an act of violence in itself, but that it is committed by men who are prepared to use violence to get what they want. He perceives the law as a means of discouraging certain methods of obtaining sex.

A more sophisticated, and overtly political analysis, also in the context of the English law of sexual offences, is offered by Susan Edwards, in a recent book in the impressive Law in Society Series, called *Female Sexuality and the Law* (1981). While she shares a little common ground with Honoré in her view that "[f]rom within the boundaries of statutory law, it is the sexual behaviour of men that immediately appears as the primary object of control," she goes on to argue that it is an "erroneous belief that it is men rather than women that are the objects of legal control." She develops a theory of fundamental paradox in the law, in that statute law incorporates the notion of female sexual passivity while case law and procedural rules are based on a belief in female precipitation, so that women are oddly seen both as potential victims of men and victimisers of them, thus establishing a need to divide women into two classes, chaste and unchaste. It was this classification of women that provided the vehicle of control of female sexuality. Edwards states (p. 56):

> The unchaste woman especially, then, was subject to legal and ideological controls. On the legal front she was the object of direct legislation, as in the regulation of prostitution, and of indirect informal ideologies, as in the experience of rape trial procedures.

The book is a significant contribution to the literature which has done so much to raise public consciousness about the objectionable aspects of our sexual offences laws.

The theme of conflict in the law recurs in the literature. Camille LeGrand writes in her article "Rape and Rape Laws: Sexism in Society in Law" (in D. Chappell, R. Geis and G. Geis, eds., *Forcible Rape* (1977), p. 80):

> The fear of the maniac and the genuine desire to protect chaste, totally innocent women . . . clash mightily with the fear of convicting innocent men. As a result, we have on one hand harsh penalties for rape; on the other, however, we have few convictions and a myriad of laws and attitudes that tend to protect men from conviction except when the complainant is a chaste, mentally healthy woman who reports the attack promptly and who is willing and able to undergo the horrors of rape trial.

One other way of thinking about the law is what I would term the puritan view, that is, that the function of the law is to discourage us from engaging in immoral sexual acts. This view is not so tenable in Canada as in the States, since no attempt is made in this country to punish such acts as adultery, fornication and homosexual acts between consenting adults. However, incest between consenting adults, bestiality and gross indecency remain crimes. Professor Mewett has suggested that one significant thread that ran through our law was "the horror of anything ... which is not 'normal'—even between females and males." (See "Sexual Offences in Canada" (1959-60), 2 Crim. L.Q. 21 at 27.) The view that it might be appropriate to classify crimes equivalent to rape and indecent assault in this way is probably no longer of significance, since there seems to be increasing if not general acceptance of the emphasis on the violence of sexual attacks. This certainly appeared to be the prevailing view during the Parliamentary Debates on the introduction of the new sexual assault provisions. The view was perhaps best summed up in the statement by Mr. Ron Irwin, Parliamentary Secretary to the Minister of Justice and Secretary of State for Social Development:

> Above all, the law must recognise the element of violence. . . . Bill C-53 would place the new crimes replacing rape and indecent assault in the part of the Code dealing with offences against the person and reputation. This change would separate violent sexual attacks from the concept of sexual morality.

(See Parl. Debs. H.C., Vol. X, at 11300, 7 July 1981 on the second reading of Bill C-53.)

There are a number of people whose help and encouragement I am delighted to acknowledge. I would like to thank Mark Greenberg for spending a summer on research, and Dalhousie Law School for making that financially possible. A student and friend, Isabel Grant, read most of the book in draft form, making many helpful and tactful comments. Colleagues at Dalhousie who have read sections are Tom Cromwell, Bruce Archibald and Toni Laidlaw. I am particularly grateful to Joel Pink for taking time out of his busy practice to read the chapter on sentencing. I must also acknowledge the various forms of assistance of Tom Kemsley. Monique Dancause and Lynn Ferguson were kind enough to type the manuscript on their word processor. Lastly, it is always a pleasure to work with Ruth Epstein and indeed everyone at the Carswell Company. Any errors or infelicities of style are my own.

I have tried to state the law as of January 1984.

Halifax, Nova Scotia   Christine Boyle
January, 1984

Table of Contents

Table of Cases

Part I

The Background to Reform

Chapter 1

The Historical Setting

A complete understanding of our present law of sexual assault cannot be achieved without at least a superficial knowledge of its historical context. In this chapter the legislative, and to a lesser extent the judicial, history of rape and other sexual offences which form the subject-matter of this book is described and analysed.

It may be that in fact there is no basic organising principle behind the development of our sexual offences law,[1] but some conceptual framework is necessary to facilitate an awareness of the significance of the evolution of our law. What follows, therefore, is not a comprehensive chronological account of the legislative and judicial history of our law, but an attempt to explain why it developed in the way that it did.

A number of writers have discussed the law in terms of inherent contradiction, of paradox and of conflicting values.[2] This is crucial if one is not to see it in an aridly positivistic way, as if it were a set of value-free rules and neutral standards. At any one time, the law has not demonstrated a commitment to any particular goal or value, but has displayed ambivalence, a shifting compromise between the values perceived, either consciously or unconsciously, as important. What is attempted in this chapter is an elucidation of the values which are perceived as having shaped the evolution of the law, and the tension among these values. It is thus possible to suggest what was of most significance to our law-makers at any particular time. This chapter provides the background against which it will be possible to see our new sexual assault law in relief. In this way some assessment

---

1 As the Law Reform Commission indicated in its Working Paper 22, *Sexual Offences* (1978), 2, "the Code embodies a variety of historical developments and has few clearly discernible organising principles."

2 See, *e.g.*, S. Edwards, *Female Sexuality and the Law* (1981).

can be made as to whether the new law constitutes a radical departure in terms of values, or whether it is simply the result of a shift in the tension among the same old competing values.

What have these old competing values been? It is submitted that our law at any particular time can be analysed in terms of the interplay of the law-makers' various self-perceptions or, more accurately, their perceptions of their potential. It is to state the obvious that the people who have created our sexual assault law (until this latest reform) have almost exclusively been male, and it is important to explore the significance of this fact. It would seem reasonable to suppose that, in carrying out any rule-making function, a rule-maker would try to imagine himself as one of those affected by a possible rule in order to reach some opinion of the fairness and efficacy of the rule.[3] But since the ability to put ourselves in someone else's shoes is limited by our imagination, education, sex, class, age and many other factors, all of our law is deeply influenced by this limitation.[4]

Examples can be found in the criminal law wherein laws exist to punish those who kill in the course of a number of serious offences.[5] It seems safe to assume that many, if not all, of our law-makers simply cannot imagine finding themselves in the position of having accidentally killed someone in the course of robbery.

---

3 I am not suggesting that this is always or often a conscious process, but that it is part of the process that makes us reach an intuitive decision that something is fair or unfair.

4 This is a commonplace idea in other disciplines, and a great deal of work has been done on the limitations of gender. The following are examples only. Psychology: C. Gilligan, *In a Different Voice: Psychological Theory and Women's Development* (1982); J.B. Miller, *Toward a New Psychology of Women* (1976); M.B. Parlee, "Psychology" (1975), 1(1) Signs 119; N. Weisstein, "Psychology Constructs the Female, or the Fantasy Life of the Male Psychologist" in M.H. Garskoff, ed., *Roles Women Play: Readings Towards Women's Liberation* (1971), at 68-83. History: A.D. Gordon, M.J. Buhle and N.S. Dye, "The Problem of Women's History" in B.A. Carroll, ed., *Liberating Women's History: Theoretical and Critical Essays* (1976), at 75-92; J. Kelly-Gadol, "Did Women Have a Renaissance?" in R. Blumenthal and C. Koonz, eds., *Becoming Visible: Women in European History* (1977), at 137-64. Anthropology: E. Ardener, "Belief and the Problem of Women" in S. Ardener, ed., *Perceiving Women* (1975), at 1-27; M.Z. Rosaldo, "Women, Culture and Society, A Theoretical Overview" in M.Z. Rosaldo and L. Kamphere, eds., *Women, Culture and Society* (1974), at 17-42. Sociology: M. Eichler, "Sociology of Feminist Research in Canada" (1977), 3 (2) Signs 409; D.E. Smith, "Women's Perspective as a Radical Critique of Sociology" (1974), 44 Sociological Inquiry 7.

5 See s. 213, especially s. 213(d).

Likewise, the Criminal Code contains a provision to punish negligent murder.[6] Yet Parliament has refrained from creating an offence of negligent sexual assault, or, as yet, from taking any effective action to ensure that the severe penalties for drunken driving which exist on paper, exist in practice also. The "there but for the grace of God go I" syndrome can be seen at work in our legislative, judicial and criminal law enforcement systems. Normally this allowed the law-maker to see himself straight-forwardly as a potential victim, particularly in the context of crimes of violence and against property. In that context it seems unlikely that he ever imagined himself in the dock. Where that possibility was obvious, it has had a real impact on law-making and enforcement behaviour.[7]

In the context of sexual assault, it is submitted that the law reveals that the law-maker has seen himself in various guises and not always as a potential victim. He has seen himself very vividly in the shoes of the accused, and hence the victim of a false complaint, and also in the shoes of a man who is close to the woman assaulted, as husband, father, brother, and hence as victim of the assault.[8] It seems to have been extraordinarily difficult, however, for him to cross the sexual barrier and put himself in the position of an assaulted woman. Hence our law, in the balancing exercise

---

6 Section 212(c).

7 A further example can be found in the development of the law of criminal procedure, with its evident commitment to crime control values. In discussion of these in class, I have observed the tendency in many of my students to think of the accused as someone else (unless the accused is a police officer) while the victim is potentially oneself. This is different from the argument that law is created and enforced to further the interests of the dominant group. Rather it is an assertion that one simply sees the world from the perspective of the group/class/sex to which one belongs. The only danger in this is, of course, that one may fall into the trap of thinking that one's perspective is a universal perspective. For a brief review and comment on various theories of crime, see W.J. Chambliss, "Toward a Radical Criminology" in D. Kairys, ed., *The Politics of Law* (1982), at 230.

8 His potential victimisation could be perceived in various ways, *e.g.*, as the result of interference with his property interest in the woman, as suggested by various writers, most notably by Lorenne Clark and Debra Lewis in Canada, or as distress caused by the contemplation of harm to a loved one, or both. Constance Backhouse quotes a nineteenth-century writer in (1862), 8 Upper Canada Law Journal 309. "Nothing is so destructive of domestic comfort and earthly happiness as the ruin of a fond daughter or a loved sister. The contemplation or miseries which arise from this cause cannot be computed." See "Nineteenth-Century Canadian Rape Law 1800-92" in D.H. Flaherty, ed., *Essays in the History of Canadian Law*, Vol. II (1983), at 200.

between competing values, has attached little if any weight to the simple goal of protecting women from assault. This should not be overstated. It may well have happened that some women have been protected indirectly, in the process of protecting the male as husband, father and brother. Certainly individual men may have been able to make the imaginative leap and see the world from a female perspective but, overall, our law does not reveal that much importance has been attached to the protection of women in their own right, as human beings with a right to sexual autonomy.

This assertion will be supported by detailed discussion and illustrations at a later stage, but two examples might be helpful at this point. Firstly, there is no doubt that law-makers, both legislators and judges, were haunted by the spectre of the innocent accused, the victim of a false charge. It was feared that innocent, perfectly respectable men (that is, like them), could suddenly be caught up in the criminal justice system. This was not a fear that was prevalent with respect to other crimes, and special rules had to be developed to protect the falsely-accused person in this context alone. This throws an interesting sidelight on the faith which our law-makers had in the system, which could be trusted to detect untruth and acquit the innocent in other contexts.[9] Until very recently, our law displayed an uncritical acceptance of the idea that a rape complainant was inherently suspect, an idea perhaps best embodied in the words of a famous American writer on the law of evidence.

> Modern psychiatrists have amply studied the behaviour of errant young girls and women coming before the courts in all sorts of cases. Their psychic complexes are multifarious, distorted partly by inherent defects, partly by diseased derangements or abnormal instincts, partly by bad social environment, partly by temporary physiological or emotional conditions. One form taken by these complexes is that of contriving false charges of sexual offenses by men.[10]

Wigmore's conclusion was that charges of sexual offences should not "*go to the jury unless the female complainant's social history and mental make-up have been examined and testified to by a qualified physician.*"[11]

---

9 Perhaps we should listen to what judges have been saying: if they do not feel confident that they can distinguish between truth and untruth, and if proof beyond a reasonable doubt is not sufficient protection for an accused, then this has profound implications for the criminal justice system.

10 J.A. Wigmore, *Evidence in Trials at Common Law*, rev. ed. (1970), §924a, p. 736.

11 *Ibid.*, p. 737 (emphasis in original).

A number of special legal rules could be traced to this type of distrust and suspicion, most significantly those relating to corroboration and questioning about past sexual history. One very important aspect of the new law of sexual assault, discussed in Part III of this book, is the movement away from these special rules. It is interesting to note, in this context, that a devastating exposé by L.B. Bienen of Wigmore's manipulation of his authorities has recently been published.[12] Since Wigmore is the single most influential exponent of the idea that girls and women lie about sexual assault, this new research both vindicates the recent law reform and reveals the unfortunate perspective of lawmakers in the past.

One example from Bienen's article will provide the flavour of how Wigmore utilised his authorities. Wigmore relied heavily on a monograph entitled *Pathological Lying, Accusation and Swindling,*[13] in which there were case studies of female juvenile delinquents labelled as pathological liars by the authors. One might consider it odd to base generalizations about the whole female population on cases specially selected for a work about lying, but the cases themselves hardly justify the label they were given. In addition, Wigmore removed facts which pointed to the conclusion that the girls were in fact telling the truth. One case study involved a girl of seven who was simply described in the monograph as making a "false charge of sex assault against a boy. She is later found to be an excessive liar and to steal. Causative factors: (a) atrociously immoral home environment, (b) early sex experiences, (c) local irritation due to active gonorrhea."[14] Bienen reveals that "Wigmore edited out three separate references to the fact that this seven-year-old child was suffering from a diagnosed, confirmed case of gonorrhea at the time of the report."[15] Wigmore's work may be discredited,[16] but information and law reform alone may not eradicate the idea that accusations of sexual assault are to be regarded with deep suspicion.

---

12 L.B. Bienen, "A Question of Credibility: John Henry Wigmore's Use of Scientific Authority in Section 924a of the Treatise on Evidence" (1983), 19 Cal. West L.R. 235.
13 W. Healy and M. Healy (1915).
14 *Ibid.,* p. 195.
15 Note 12, above, at 252.
16 The article itself should be consulted for further detailed comparisons between Wigmore's sources and the use he made of them. It is an extraordinarily factual article in tone, but it is shocking to think of the unknown number of children

A second illustration of the perspective of past law-makers can be found in the doctrine of the husband's immunity, which survived until 1983. The removal of this provision was one of the most significant of the recent reforms.[17] Until January 1983, a husband could have sexual intercourse with his wife without her consent, and not be guilty of rape.[18] Here the identification with the rapist was extremely strong, as was the fear of false accusations out of spite or ill-will. Conversely, the identification with the aggrieved husband-figure was non-existent, since there was no appropriate male to feel victimised. It is also crystal clear that the protection of the woman's right to sexual self-determination was not a significant factor, indeed it was not a factor at all, since the rule bluntly denied that she had any such right.

Marital rape is unusual in that the issue was resolved in an entirely one-sided way, there being no competing values from a male perspective. In other areas of sexual assault law there was a balancing of different interests, and the law at any particular time did not present a uniform resolution of these conflicting interests. The various possible "shapes" to the law are presented in the following diagram.

---

who said they were being sexually assaulted and who were not helped because disbelieved. Bienen's evidence of Wigmore's attitude toward women is devastating. Wigmore quotes H. Gross, *Criminal Psychology* (1911), p. 30, in *The Science of Judicial Proof* (1937), pp. 336-7: "With [women's] hypocrisy we have, as lawyers, to wage constant battle. Quite apart from the woman's ills and diseases which women assume before the judge, everything else is pretended; innocence; love of children, spouses and parents; pain at loss and dispair at reproaches; a bleeding heart at separation; and piety — in short, whatever may be useful." A moment's reflection will reveal the significance of this in a world in which Wigmore was regarded as the leading exponent of the law of evidence and is still routinely cited as such. California, however, has recently banned the introduction of psychiatric evidence in this context. See J.C. Bangle and L.A. Haage, "Psychiatric Examinations of Sexual Assault Victims: A Reevaluation" (1982), 15 U.C.D.L.R. 973.

17 For a discussion, see Chapter 3.

18 See the old s. 143 of the Criminal Code, now repealed 1980-81-82, c. 129, s. 19. See now s. 246.8. This statutory immunity had its roots in the English common law, since Lord Matthew Hale, writing in the seventeenth century, made a bare assertion that a wife gives a general consent to intercourse on marriage, a consent that she is not permitted by law to retract. See *Pleas of the Crown*, p. 629. For some recent discussion see J.A. Scutt, "Spouse Assault: Closing the Door on Criminal Acts" (1980), 54 Aust. L.J. 720, and G. Geis, "Rape in Marriage: Law and Law Reform in England, the United States and Sweden" (1978), 6 Ade. L.R. 284.

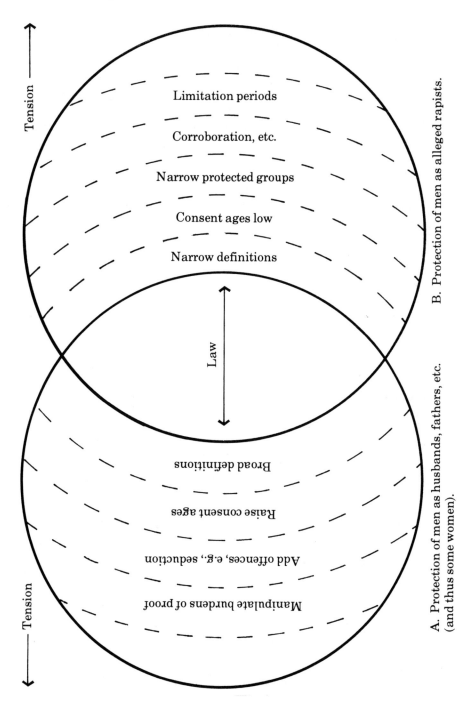

Tension →

Limitation periods

Corroboration, etc.

Narrow protected groups

Consent ages low

Narrow definitions

Law

Broad definitions

Raise consent ages

Add offences, e.g., seduction

Manipulate burdens of proof

Tension

B. Protection of men as alleged rapists.

A. Protection of men as husbands, fathers, etc. (and thus some women).

In A, the man-as-husband-figure circle, we find traces throughout the law of increasing protection for certain women (for example, chaste adolescents), particularly in the form of punishment for consensual intercourse and rules of evidence which are negative from the perspective of the accused (for example, reverse onus clauses). We even find elements of absolute liability where the *mens rea* requirement for a certain element of the offence is removed entirely.

In B, the man-as-accused circle, we find recurring traces of narrow definitions, tightening of protected groups either in the law itself or in tolerance of that practice, as well as rules of evidence and procedure which make it difficult to secure convictions. In this context one would be extremely surprised to find any elements of protection for women, while there might, in effect, be some overlapping of protection of women with protection of the male as husband.[19] (But it is stressed that this would only be protection for *some* women, that is, not those without an associated male to be victimised.)

It is submitted that this analysis is useful because it highlights the dilemma that law-makers have suffered. They were not caught in any simple conflict between their own interests and those of women (in the sense of potential rape victims). They were caught in a dilemma with respect only to their own interests. In crude terms, they simply did not know what was best for themselves, with the result that our law has displayed the ambivalence, the inherent contradictions that a number of writers have identified.

What other evidence can be found in the legislative and judicial histories of our sexual assault laws to support the above hypothesis? What follows is an outline of the most significant legislative and judicial events with respect to the old offences of rape and indecent assault as well as the various seduction offences and offences against children.[20]

---

19 See the text accompanying note 23 below.

20 Our knowledge of the Canadian history of this area of law has increased considerably since the publication of Professor Backhouse's article, "Nineteenth Century Canadian Rape Law 1800-92", note 8 above, and published by the Osgoode Society in the second volume of their essays on the history of Canadian law. This summary is therefore based on her account, to the extent that it relates to the period and offences that she covers.

1. RAPE

In 1800 the legislature of Upper Canada passed legislation adopting the criminal law of England, as it stood in 1792. Although some changes were made in the interim, the next crucial date was 1841, when the first session of the first provincial Parliament of Canada consolidated the existing provincial statutes relating to offences against the person. Although rape was not defined, it merely being enacted that "every person convicted of the crime of rape, shall suffer death as a felon,"[21] it is submitted that the statute tilted noticeably toward protection of the husband/father victim in the section on penetration, which stated as follows:

> And whereas upon trials for the crime of buggery, and of rape and of carnally abusing girls under the respective ages hereinbefore mentioned, offenders frequently escape by reason of the difficulty of proof which has been required of the completion of those several crimes; for the remedy thereof, be it enacted that it shall not be necessary, in any of those cases, to prove the actual emission of seed in order to constitute a carnal knowledge, but that the carnal knowledge shall be deemed complete upon proof of penetration only.[22]

Professor Backhouse argues that this provision was evidence of a significant departure from the view of rape as a crime against male property since that type of analysis "required that the woman's reproductive capacity be impaired; thus ejaculation and the potential of pregnancy were critical to the definition of the crime."[23]

Professor Backhouse's position is not entirely convincing, since the provision might also point to the over-protection of property *ex abundanti cautela.* Further reasons for scepticism are that there had never been any consistent requirement of ejaculation and that the crime of rape extended to all women, or at least there was no denial of protection on the basis of reproductive capacity. In addition, cases in which proof was required that ejaculation did occur could be explained as devices for avoiding the death penalty where judges chose to look for some reason to justify this. It would certainly not be surprising to find uneven and

---

21 An Act for Consolidating and Amending the Statutes in This Province Relative to Offences against the Person, S.C. 1841, c. 27, ss. 16, 17.

22 *Ibid.*, s. 18.

23 Backhouse, "Nineteenth-Century Canadian Rape Law 1800-92" in D.H. Flaherty, ed., *Essays in the History of Canadian Law*, Vol. II (1983), at 205.

irrational developments in the law relating to crimes punishable by death. It is doubtful, therefore, whether a great deal can be read into modified notions of the physical act required. A broadening of the act may simply have been an attempt to provide more efficient protection for certain women, that is those attached to a male, whether husband, father or son. Any sexual interference with such women would surely have been seen as harmful, whether there was the potential for pregnancy or not.[24] However, any over-simplification is no doubt dangerous, and thus it is probably safest to conclude that a complex combination of feelings, fears and prejudices, both conscious and unconscious, led the legislators to enact provisions such as this, that penetration without more is enough. Whatever view one takes of it, section 18 of the 1841 Act would appear to be the ancestor of the latest provision in the Criminal Law Amendment Act, which has the effect of doing away with the requirement of penetration altogether.[25]

The next significant date was 1869, which saw consolidation in the form of the Offences Against the Person Act,[26] modeled upon, but certainly not slavishly following, the equivalent English Act of 1861.[27] The Act left the rape provisions virtually unchanged, and, unlike England, retained the death penalty for rape (as well as for statutory rape of a girl under the age of ten). The political significance of the retention of the death penalty is not at all clear. At first glance it would appear that it was a harsh measure designed to protect the interests of husband victims but it can just as easily be viewed as a deterrent to convictions. One politician of the time acknowledged this. In 1877, life imprisonment was substituted for the death penalty with respect to statu-

---

24 This is not to suggest that a forced pregnancy, whether resulting from rape or not, is not a serious and distinctive harm, but is an argument that the male interest in the sexual integrity of "his" woman goes far beyond this possibility, hence the crime of indecent assault, for example. The best analogy that I can think of is the feeling of a person who has been burgled. There is the loss associated with the theft of certain objects, but there is also a sense of victim-isation arising from the fact that another person has touched and looked at one's private possessions, the emphasis here being on harm to feelings of privacy and security.

25 The new crime of sexual assault is now defined in s. 244 and s. 246.1. It covers all types of sexual touching. Penetration of the vagina by the penis would therefore simply be one way in which the offence could be committed.

26 S.C. 1869, c. 20.

27 An Act to Consolidate and Amend the Statute Law of England and Ireland Relating to Offences against the Person, 1861 (24 & 25 Vict.), c. 100.

tory rape of girls under ten years of age. Professor Backhouse refers to the explanation given by the Minister of Justice, Edward Blake, who stated that the intent was to lower the penalty in order to secure more convictions. The capital penalty in his view prevented the obtaining of convictions, even though few offenders were actually hanged.[28] Other sentencing provisions, such as the requirement of a minimum sentence of two years for statutory rape of a girl over ten and under twelve years,[29] would appear to share the same ambivalent quality. The death penalty for rape was not to disappear until 1954.[30]

In 1890, legislation was passed extending whatever protection the law offered to women who submitted because of fraud, in the form of personation of the victim's husband.[31] This provision seems clearly to emphasise the interests of the husband victim, since otherwise personation of any lover would surely have been included.

In 1892 our first Criminal Code provided a much more well-defined crime of rape. It was not significantly different from the familiar version that was recently repealed to make way for the new crime of sexual assault in its various forms.[32]

In 1921 the punishment for rape was altered by including the sanction of whipping along with the other options of death or imprisonment for life.[33] Whipping was an option until as recently as 1972,[34] when it was dropped from the Code. Otherwise there were only minor changes, which resulted in the modern but now repealed form of rape:

A male person commits rape when he has sexual intercourse with a female person who is not his wife,
  (a) without her consent, or
  (b) with her consent if the consent
    (i) is extorted by threats or fear of bodily harm,
    (ii) is obtained by personating her husband, or
    (iii) is obtained by false and fraudulent representations as to the nature and quality of the act.[35]

28 Backhouse, note 23 above, at 211.
29 S.C. 1869, c. 20, ss. 49, 51 and 52.
30 S.C. 1953-54, c. 51.
31 An Act to Further Amend the Criminal Law, S.C. 1890, c. 37, s. 14.
32 Criminal Code, S.C. 1892, c. 29, s. 266(1).
33 S.C. 1921, c. 25, s. 4.
34 S.C. 1972, c. 13, s. 70.
35 R.S.C. 1970, c. C-34, s. 143 [repealed 1980-81-82, c. 125, s. 6].

The history of the offence of rape was therefore one of a very gradually broadening substantive offence, accompanied by the *possibility* of extremely severe penalties. It might appear on a superficial level, that the law displayed a determination to punish offenders. Judge-made law and enforcement practices, however, ensured a concentration on the need to protect men from false accusations and narrowed the scope of protection to certain women who had not infringed judicial and societal norms about what was appropriate behaviour and life-style.

Three judicial glosses, which put sexual offences in a class by themselves with respect to the law of evidence, should be mentioned. One was the recent complaint rule. The general rule was that a victim's complaint that the crime had occurred was inadmissible, but in a prosecution for rape (as well as other sexual offences), evidence of a complaint was admissible to support the credibility of the victim.[36] This sounds innocuous, but the reason for the general rule was that there was no reason to doubt the evidence of the witness, so such evidence would therefore be superfluous. To judges charged with developing the law of evidence with respect to rape complaints, there was every reason to doubt the word of the witness, and thus evidence of immediate complaint was required to rebut the strong presumption of fabrication. The requirements were strict, since, for example, the complaint had to be made at the first reasonable opportunity after the offence.[37] Any delay regarded as unreasonable by the court would result in the exclusion of the complaint, leaving the presumption of fabrication intact. It has recently been recognised by law reformers that a "victim may have a genuine complaint but delay making it because of such legitimate concerns as the prospect of embarrassment and humiliation, or the destruction of domestic or personal relationships. The delay may also be attributable to the youth or lack of knowledge of the complainant or to threats of reprisal from the accused."[38]

The rule has now been abrogated[39] although the practical

---

36 See Sir F. Pollock and F.W. Maitland, *History of English Law*, 2nd. ed. (1968), Vol. 2, p. 606. See also *R. v. Lillyman*, [1896] 2 Q.B. 167, and *Kribs v. R.*, [1960] S.C.R. 400.

37 *R. v. Osbourne*, [1905] 1 K.B. 551; *R. v. Kulak* (1979), 7 C.R. (2d) 304 (Ont. C.A.).

38 See the Federal/Provincial Task Force on Uniform Rules of Evidence (1982), at 301, which contains an account of the rule itself.

39 S.C. 1980-81-82, c. 125, s. 19.

implications of this are as yet unclear.[40] Its obvious effect was to make more difficult convictions for the relevant offences.

A similar doctrine was that which permitted questioning of a complainant about her past sexual history. Until 1976,[41] the judges who developed and applied the common law assumed that an unchaste woman was more likely to be untruthful. Thus a complainant could be cross-examined as to her sexual conduct in the past in order to attack her credibility.[42] The judge had some discretion to protect her from degrading questioning,[43] but it became notorious that the effect of this doctrine was to subject the rape complainant to severe embarrassment, thus causing some concern that it might discourage reporting.[44]

The third principle that was developed at common law as well as incorporated in statutes was the insistence that a jury be warned of the dangers of convicting on the uncorroborated evidence of the complainant. This blossomed into a rule of practice in the early twentieth century, although a requirement of corroboration (as opposed to a warning) had already been introduced in statute form with respect to certain offences such as seduction, discussed below. Examples can be found in *R. v. Ellerton*,[45] *R. v. Mudge*[46] and *R. v. Galsky*.[47] The rule of practice was codified in 1955,[48] but was repealed twenty years later.[49] It was the view of some judges that this merely resurrected the common-law rule of

---

40 See Chapter 7.

41 When reforms were introduced by the Criminal Law Amendment Act, S.C., 1975, c. 93. For comment, see C. Boyle, "Section 142 of the Criminal Code: A Trojan Horse" (1981), 23 C.L.Q. 253.

42 This is an illustration only. For a full discussion see the Federal/Provincial Task Force on Uniform Rules of Evidence (1982), at 65 *et seq.*

43 *Laliberté v. R.* (1877), 1 S.C.R. 117 at 130.

44 See, *e.g.,* Law Reform Commission, *Report on Evidence: Study Paper 4, Character* (1971). The Hon. Ron Basford, then Minister of Justice, on moving the Second Reading of Bill C-71 (subsequently the 1976 reform) stated that the "amendments . . . are aimed at minimizing the embarrassment the victim must undergo, thereby increasing the number of rapes that are reported and prosecuted." Parl. Debs. H.C., Vol. IX, at 9204, 1975. For a discussion of the present position see Chapter 7, below.

45 [1927] 4 D.L.R. 1126 (Sask. C.A.).

46 [1930] 1 W.W.R. 193 (Sask. C.A.). The court in this case found that torn clothing and bruises were not corroboration, as they could have meant that the complainant initially resisted and then consented.

47 [1930] 1 W.W.R. 690 (Man. C.A.).

48 S.C. 1953-54, c. 51, s. 134.

49 S.C. 1974-75-76, c. 93, s. 8.

practice.[50] The balance of authority is against this view, although the judge retains a discretion to warn in appropriate cases.[51] Parliament has now forbidden reference to corroboration in sexual assault cases.[52]

It is clear that all three of these rules were expressly designed to provide the accused with special protection from false accusation.

2. INDECENT ASSAULT

Even though the substantive definition of rape gradually broadened, it remained an offence with an extraordinarily narrow focus. This was caused by the fact that only females could be the victims of rape and, moreover, by the concentration on vaginal penetration by the penis. Supplementary offences were therefore required to fill in the large gaps remaining in the legal scheme. These were indecent assault on a female and indecent assault on a male.

The crime of indecent assault on a female was first defined in the 1869 Offences Against the Person Act.[53] No definition of indecent assault was ever provided (as is the case with the new offence of sexual assault). As well it is interesting now to note that in the 1892 Criminal Code, this offence was placed in Part XX (Assaults) as opposed to Part XXI (Rape and Procuring Abortion) or Part XIII (Offences Against Morality) where sodomy, incest, obscenity and seduction were to be found. It stayed there until the 1953-54 revision, when it was moved to Part IV (Sexual Offences). The move has of course now been reversed, with the classification of rape and indecent assault as a form of assault. The old connection of indecent assault with violent attacks rather than sexual

---

50 See *e.g., R. v. P.* (1976), 32 C.C.C. (2d) 400 (Ont. H.C.).

51 See *e.g., R. v. Camp* (1977), 17 O.R. (2d) 99 (C.A.); *R. v. Darnell* (1978), 40 C.C.C. (2d) 220 (Ont. C.A.); *R. v. Riley* (1978), 42 C.C.C. (2d) 437 (Ont. C.A.); *R. v. Firkins* (1977), 39 C.R.N.S. 178 (B.C. C.A.); *R. v. Chenier* (1981), 63 C.C.C. (2d) 36 (Que. C.A.); *R. v. Daigle* (1977), 18 N.B.R. (2d) 658 (C.A.).

52 S.C. 1980-81-82, c. 125, s. 19, enacting s. 246.4 of the Criminal Code, R.S.C. 1970, c. C-34, which also applies to incest and gross indecency. The present position is discussed in Chapter 7.

53 S.C. 1869, c. 20, s. 53. The same section contained the offence of attempted carnal knowledge of a girl under 12, but the two offences were separated in 1890, S.C., c. 37, s. 12.

gratification was underlined in 1909, when a new subsection was added to the then current provision. It read as follows:

> Everyone is guilty of an indictable offence and liable to two years' imprisonment and to be whipped, who . . .
>> (c) assaults and beats his wife or any other female and thereby occasions her actual bodily harm.[54]

The recent emphasis on the assaultive nature of certain types of sexual offence therefore has at least one precedent in Canada. The fact that the offence was, at least for part of its history, classified as assault, may explain why it was not subject to the legislative corroboration requirement.

The crime of indecent assault on a male can also be traced to the 1869 Act, and appears to have originally been associated with the crime of attempted buggery, the "abominable crime."[55] This connection persisted until the crime was abolished by the recent amendments. Up until that time, the provision was in the following form:

> Every male person who assaults another person with intent to commit buggery or who indecently assaults another male person is guilty of an indictable offence and is liable to imprisonment for ten years.[56]

There are a number of interesting aspects to this offence. Firstly, a much higher maximum period of imprisonment was possible than with respect to indecent assault on a female, ten years as compared to five. This may have reflected the moralistic judgment involved — men who attacked women may have been bad but they were not abominable, or it may have reflected a straightforward view that it was not such a serious matter to attack a woman as a man. Secondly, only male persons could commit the offence. This very probably reflected the reality that female attacks on men were simply not a social problem, if they occurred at all.

---

54 S.C. 1909, c. 9, s. 2.
55 S.C. 1869, c. 20, s. 63.
56 R.S.C. 1970, c. C-34, s. 156. The offences of buggery and bestiality remain as s. 155, as does the offence of gross indecency in s. 157. They are not, however, covered in this book, as they do not appear to be assaultive offences, *per se.*

3. OFFENCES AGAINST CHILDREN AND OTHER VULNERABLE PEOPLE

The law relating to offences against children is even more revealing of the perspective of the law-makers, since their values are expressed in the statutes themselves as well as in judicial and enforcement decisions. The significant features of this area of law relate to the age of consent, *mens rea* and the burden of proof.

The crime of statutory rape is of great antiquity. Professor Backhouse points out that an English statute of 1275 prohibited the ravishing of maidens under twelve years, whether they consented or not, and refers to Blackstone's explanation for the prohibition of such sexual relations — "the consent or non-consent is immaterial, as by reason of her tender years she is incapable of judgment or discretion."[57] The policy of protecting young girls from the experience of sexual intercourse has been pursued uninterruptedly until the present day. The main legislative focus has been on the age of consent, which has tended to rise.

The 1869 Offences Against the Person Act included several provisions relating to carnal knowledge of girls under the age of consent,[58] which was twelve years at this time; a lighter sentence was mandated if the girl was over ten and under twelve.[59] By the time these offences were incorporated in the Criminal Code of 1892, the upper age had risen to fourteen.[60] The next significant change came in 1920, when girls between fourteen and sixteen were given a certain measure of protection.[61] These ages have remained unchanged to the present time.

It might appear that the legislation shows a consistent pattern of increasing protection for young women, but the changes in the age of consent were balanced by other factors. This can be demonstrated particularly clearly with respect to the last,

57 W. Blackstone, *Commentaries on the Laws of England*, Vol. IV (1765-9), p. 212. See C.B. Backhouse, "Nineteenth Century Canadian Rape Law 1800-92" in D.H. Flaherty, *Essays in the History of Canadian Law*, Vol. II (1983), at 202.
58 S.C. 1869, c. 20, ss. 51, 52.
59 The death penalty was retained where the girl was under 10, while a 2-7 year prison term was deemed appropriate where the girl was between 10 and 12. The death penalty was repealed in 1877 and a minimum term of 5 years was substituted. S.C. 1877, c. 28, s. 2. By 1886, the maxima were life imprisonment if the girl were under 10, and 7 years imprisonment if over. R.S.C. 1886, c. 162, ss. 39, 40.
60 S.C. 1892, c. 29, s. 269.
61 S.C. 1920, c. 43, s. 8.

biggest change, that to the age of sixteen. The 1920 amendments contained a number of provisions designed to protect the interests of the accused. Section 8 divided for the first time those to be protected into the chaste and the unchaste,[62] only chaste girls between fourteen and sixteen being thought deserving of protection. It also introduced a corroboration requirement, stating that "no person accused of any offence under this subsection shall be convicted upon the evidence of one witness, unless such witness is corroborated in some material particular by evidence implicating the accused."[63] Lastly, section 17 required the court to weigh the relative guilt of the complainant and the accused.

> On the trial of any offence against subsection two of this section, the trial judge may instruct the jury that if in their view the evidence does not show that the accused is wholly or chiefly to blame for the commission of said offence, they may find a verdict of acquittal.

However, the picture was not entirely one of rising ages coupled with substantive and procedural protections for the accused. This area of law is distinctive for its unusual substantive and procedural provisions which were significantly anti-accused. The most dramatic one appeared in 1906, and reduced, effectively completely, the accused's ability to make the argument that he did not have the necessary *mens rea*, the requisite guilty intent. With respect to both carnal knowledge of a girl under fourteen and later of a girl under sixteen, it was stated to be irrelevant whether the accused believed the victim to be of or above the requisite age.[64] In effect this made the crime one of absolute liability, and was a major departure from the normal principle that, with respect to criminal offences, the proscribed act must be accompanied by a guilty intent or knowledge.[65]

Another less unusual and less significant feature was the shifting of the burden of proof to the accused with respect to the chastity of the victim, where this was relevant.[66] It is again trite

---

62 The same distinction had however been used with seduction. See S.C. 1886 (49 Vict.), c. 52, s. 1(1).

63 One wonders why the older the victim became the less reliable her evidence.

64 S.C. 1906, c. 146, s. 301 [am. 1920, c. 43, ss. 8, 17].

65 The roots of this exception can be found in the English common law. See *R. v. Prince* (1875), L.R. 2 C.C.R. 154. For an argument that age is a factor of a "morally indifferent nature," see J.C. Smith and B. Hogan, *Criminal Law*, 4th ed. (1978), pp. 58-9.

66 S.C. 1953-54, c. 51, s. 131(3).

criminal law that normally the Crown has the burden of proving all the elements of the offence, but the shifting of this burden is a familiar device for tipping the scales against the interests of the accused.[67] A related element here was that the accused was not allowed to show the lack of chastity of the complainant by adducing evidence that she had previously had intercourse with him.[68]

This area of law presents the dilemma of the law-makers particularly clearly and the resulting compromises demonstrate the tension between the desire to protect young girls from premature exposure to sexual intercourse and the need to provide a fair trial for accused persons. The *overt* distinction[69] between chaste and unchaste women is particularly important, since it reveals that the legislators were not motivated by a desire to protect all girls, *including those who had already been victimised,* but only those who satisfied the criterion of respectability. As the age of the girl increased, it seems likely that so did the identification of the legislators with the accused. Men who could not imagine themselves in the position of an accused who had had sex with a girl under fourteen, may have felt somewhat uneasy when it came to proscribing sexual relations with older girls. This may provide some explanation of the sudden narrowing of the group to be protected and the additional procedural protections.

This theory of the legislators' dilemma is reinforced by the existence of another form of statutory rape. In 1886[70] it was made a criminal offence to have intercourse with certain mentally-disabled females. Emphasis has since consistently been placed on the need for knowledge on the part of the accused of the victim's mental condition, in contrast to the absolute liability approach to the age factor in other forms of statutory rape. Amendments have focused on variations of the scope of the class of people protected.

---

67 This way of promoting convictions now has constitutional implications. See the Canadian Charter of Rights and Freedoms, Constitution Act, 1982 [en. by the Canada Act, 1982 (U.K.), c. 11, Sched. B], s. 11(d), the presumption of innocence provision.

68 S.C. 1953-54, c. 51, s. 131(4).

69 The fact that it is overt is interesting in itself, and provides a contrast to the crime of rape. There the protection appeared to be extended to all women except wives, while the effective distinctions were left to be made by law enforcement officials and judges developing such rules as those relating to questioning about past sexual conduct and recent complaint.

70 S.C. 1886 (49 Vict.), c. 52, s. 1(2). For a brief discussion, see L.J. Applegarth, "Sexual Intercourse with a Feeble-Minded Female Person: Problems of Proof" (1964-65), 7 Cr. L. Q. 480.

The original class was made up of idiots and imbeciles. Insane persons were added in 1887,[71] and those suffering from the infirmities of deafness and muteness in 1892.[72] Feeble-mindedness was only added in 1922,[73] and a definition of this condition was provided.[74] The 1954 revision of the Code radically reworded the provision, cutting out deaf and dumb persons. This was obviously an improvement, since otherwise non-marital sexual intercourse with such women would have continued to be totally illegal.

The section at this time took on the modern form, retained until the 1983 reforms:

> Every male person who, under circumstances that do not amount to rape, has intercourse with a female person
> (a) who is not his wife, and
> (b) who is and who he knows or has good reason to believe is feeble-minded, insane, or is an idiot or imbecile,
> is guilty of an indictable offence and is liable to imprisonment for five years.[75]

Section 2 contained the definition:

> "feeble-minded person" means a person in whom there exists and has existed from birth or from an early age, mental defectiveness not amounting to imbecility, but so pronounced that he requires care, supervision and control for his protection or for the protection of others.[76]

It can be seen at once that this definition, coupled with the requirement of knowledge (although the "good reason to believe" suggests an objective test) made this offence a particularly difficult one to prove. This may explain why few prosecutions were brought[77] and the offence was abolished in the Criminal Law Amendment Act.[78] It seems simply to have paid lip service to the idea that there is a class of persons, other than children, who will

---

71 S.C. 1887, c. 48, s. 1.
72 S.C. 1892, c. 29, s. 189.
73 S.C. 1922, c. 16, s. 10(2).
74 S.C. 1922, c. 16, s. 10(1).
75 R.S.C. 1970, c. C-34, s. 148 [repealed, 1980-81-82, c. 125, s. 8].
76 R.S.C. 1970, c. C-34, s. 2. This definition appears to have been left untouched.
77 See *R. v. Red Old Man* (1978), 8 Alta. L.R. (2d) 101 (Dist. Ct.). Kerans D.C.J., at 102-3, expressed concern about the purpose of the crime. "Why does Parliament make this a crime? The effect of this legislation is to prevent all simple female persons in Canada from having sexual pleasure with a man!... If Parliament wishes, through the Criminal Code, to engage in genetic engineering, they had better be more explicit than that."
78 See note 75 above.

inevitably be exploited by exposure to sexual activity, since their intellectual disabilities render them unable to consent.[79] In any event, these persons are now covered by the general provisions on sexual assault.

The only other form of statutory rape was originally associated with the seduction offences which are discussed in Chapter 5. This offence was introduced towards the end of the last century. In 1890, the Act Respecting Offences against Public Morals and Public Convenience[80] was amended to include guardian-ward seduction or illicit connection as well as the same activities in an employment context. Both offences seem overtly based on the goal of discouraging the exploitation of dependence or weakness. With respect to the employment category, however, the class of protected persons was narrowed by past sexual experience (previous chaste character) and age (21 years). Even more importantly, there was a corroboration requirement.[81]

Parliamentary debates reveal the perspective of the legislators very clearly, and are discussed in a very useful paper by Jeffrey Hoskins, entitled "The Rise and Fall of the Corroboration Rule in Sexual Offence Cases".[82] Mr. Hoskins' research reveals that the new offences had been introduced at the request of labour organisations, such as the Knights of Labour, who were concerned that women were being taken advantage of by their employers and supervisors. He suggests that the debates reveal a deep-seated distrust of women and produced vigorous opposition to the Bill. The Hon. P. Mitchell said, for example:

> I have never heard of an instance of advantage being taken of a woman who was not pretty willing to accede and I do not think we should place men in charge of factories at the mercy of the female sex, because that is what this Bill is doing.[83]

The Minister of Justice, Sir John Thompson, explained the unusual precautions that were in the Bill to protect men from the women in their employ.

---

79 There is a paradox here in that it seems unfortunate for the law to deprive any adult person of the freedom to engage in sexual activity, but this seems the inevitable result of trying to protect from exploitation those people who are incapable of giving consent.

80 R.S.C. 1886, c. 157 [am. S.C. 1890, c. 37].

81 S.C. 1890, c. 37, s. 4(2).

82 Unpublished paper, Faculty of Law, University of British Columbia.

83 Parl. Deb. H.C., 1890, at 3165, quoted by Hoskins, *ibid.*, at 17.

Under this Bill, the defendant has the right to be a witness on his own behalf, and the plaintiff's evidence requires corroboration, so that the provision of the Act will be surrounded by the necessary safe-guards. The defendant can have the benefit of his own testimony, and the incriminating evidence must be corroborated, which is rarely required in the criminal law.[84]

These offences developed in the standard way, with various rewordings and additions. For example, the defence of marriage was added,[85] as was the comparison of blame device[86] with respect to the employment category, although this was watered down somewhat (from the perspective of the accused) in 1959. Up until then, the accused had to be "wholly or chiefly to blame," while afterwards, he simply had to be "more to blame."[87] In 1954 the provision took on its modern form in that the reference to seduction was dropped and the crime was one of simply having illicit sexual intercourse.[88] It therefore constituted a total prohibition of sexual intercourse, except that the comparison of blame provision seems, if anything, to provide a *defence* of seduction, with respect to the employment category. The modern Code still includes a provision prohibiting intercourse between a male person and his step-daughter, foster daughter or ward, as well as intercourse between a male person and a female employee or subordinate under the age of twenty-one.[89]

The possibility that the scope of the law was influenced by the ability of legislators to see themselves in the position of the accused is reinforced by an examination of the crimes of seduction, which existed as a supplement alongside statutory rape (whether that was intended or not). These crimes differed from statutory rape in that they did not prohibit sexual intercourse *per se*, but instead prohibited forms of pressure to have intercourse, vaguely called "seduction". They represented a half-way house between the prohibition of sexual intercourse under any circumstances, and the prohibition of forcible rape. A series of offences was created in the late nineteenth century, starting in 1872, when an amendment was passed to the Immigration Act,[90] criminalis-

---

84 *Ibid.*
85 S.C. 1892, c. 29, s. 184(2).
86 S.C. 1920, c. 43, s. 17.
87 S.C. 1959, c. 41, s. 10(2).
88 S.C. 1953-54, c. 51, s. 145. The meaning of the word "illicit" is unclear. It may be otiose, or intended to exclude marital sex. See the discussion of this offence in Chapter 5.
89 R.S.C. 1970, c. C-34, s. 153.
90 S.C. 1872, c. 28, s. 11.

ing the seduction of female passengers on vessels by the master or
any other employee. The forms of seduction listed are interesting
and comprehensive — seduction "under promise of marriage, or
by threats, or by the exercise of authority, or by solicitation, or the
making of gifts or presents. . . ." The 1892 Criminal Code incorporated this provision.[91] It was somewhat amended in the 1953-54
version[92] and survives to the present day in that form. The present
provision reads:

> Every male person who, being the owner or master of, or employed on board a
> vessel, engaged in the carriage of passengers for hire, seduces, or by threats
> or by the exercise of his authority, has illicit intercourse on board the vessel
> with a female passenger is guilty of an indictable offence and is liable to
> imprisonment for two years.[93]

The other seduction offences have a more obvious connection
to the offences against children discussed above, in that they
related to the protection of chaste women under certain ages. In
1886, the offences of seduction of a chaste female between twelve
and sixteen and seduction under promise of marriage were introduced in An Act to Punish Seduction and Like Offences, and to
make further provision for the Protection of Women and Girls.[94]
Seduction under promise of marriage has survived until the
present day, the significant changes being the raising of the age
to twenty-one,[95] the placing of the burden of proof with respect to
unchastity on the accused,[96] and the addition of what was to
become the ubiquitous requirement of corroboration.[97] One other
addition that should be mentioned provided an unusual protection for the seducers of young women, and that was a limitation
period of one year,[98] which applied to all seduction offences. It will

---

91 S.C. 1892, c. 29, s. 184.

92 S.C. 1953-54, c. 51, s. 146.

93 R.S.C. 1970, c. C-34, s. 154.

94 S.C. 1886, c. 52, ss. 1 and 2.

95 S.C. 1887, c. 48, s. 2.

96 S.C. 1892, c. 29 [am. S.C. 1900, c. 46, s. 3].

97 S.C. 1953-54, s. 131(1). The dangers of this were recognised at the time. John
    Charlton of North Norfolk said that he did "not know of any provision in any
    law in the world that so protects the individual against blackmail as this does.
    In fact, I fear that the provisions made for his safety are so great that they
    render it almost impossible to procure a conviction." Louis Davies of Queen's,
    P.E.I., agreed that the corroboration requirement would be "simply to nullify
    the Bill altogether." Parl. Deb. H.C., 1886, at 706.

98 *Ibid.*, s. 133.

be seen later that, while the offences have survived, some of these special provisions have not.

The offence of seduction of females between the ages of twelve and sixteen was the subject of a certain amount of legislative tinkering with respect to the ages, as well as the addition of a requirement of corroboration. The lower age of twelve became fourteen in 1890[99] and sixteen in 1920. At the same time the upper limit became eighteen and a requirement was added that the accused be over that age.[100] In the 1953-54 revision of the Code, the crime took its modern form.

> Every male person who, being eighteen years of age or more, seduces a female person of previously chaste character who is sixteen years or more but less than eighteen years of age is guilty of an indictable offence and is liable to imprisonment for two years.[101]

The effect of all of this was to produce the structure in the present Code. Any intercourse with a girl under fourteen is criminal. Intercourse with a chaste girl under sixteen is criminal. Putting the kinds of pressure that we label seduction on a girl between sixteen and eighteen is criminal, but sexual activity absent such pressure is legal. With respect to young women between eighteen and twenty-one the only pressure that is criminal is the promise of marriage. All of these persons are of course entitled to the protection of the general law of sexual assault.[102]

The last related offence is that of incest. This offence shares the characteristic of the protection of youth and weakness discussed above but in addition goes far beyond that by proscribing consensual sexual relations between certain adults. Insofar as incest can take the form of an assaultive act, although it may not necessarily do so, it is relevant to the subject-matter of this book. The crime was introduced in 1890[103] (so it does not have the ancient origins that one might expect), and continued virtually unchanged[104] until the present.

---

99 S.C. 1890, c. 37, s. 3.

100 S.C. 1920, c. 43, s. 4.

101 R.S.C. 1970, c. C-34, s. 151.

102 See Chapter 4, "The New Offences," and Chapter 5, "Offences Against Children and Other Vulnerable People."

103 R.S.C. 1886, c. 157 [am. S.C. 1890, c. 37, s. 8].

104 The crime became an indictable one in the 1906 revised statutes and the punishment of whipping was removed from the Code in 1972, S.C., c. 13, s. 10.

150. (1) Everyone commits incest who, knowing that another person is by blood relationship his or her parent, child, brother, sister, grandparent or grandchild, as the case may be, has sexual intercourse with that person.

(2) Every one who commits incest is guilty of an indictable offence and is liable to imprisonment for fourteen years.

(3) Where a female person is convicted of an offence under this section and the court is satisfied that she committed the offence by reason only that she was under restraint, duress or fear of the person with whom she had the sexual intercourse, the court is not required to impose any punishment upon her.

(4) In this section, "brother" and "sister", respectively, include half-brother and half-sister.[105]

Although incest is discussed at a later point,[106] it may be useful to note at this stage that it is a distinctive offence in that it is directed at women as well as men. Both parties are guilty, even female children, whom, one might otherwise suppose, the provision was mainly designed to protect.

Since most of the above crimes are still in existence, the judicial activity in this area will be discussed later when the offences themselves are analysed.[107]

It may be helpful at this stage to provide an outline of the relevant sexual offences as they existed prior to the passage of the recent reforms. It can be seen that they fall into three classes. Reference is made after each offence to its present status.

(1) Prohibition of all sexual intercourse:
- (a) Intercourse with girls under fourteen (still in existence);
- (b) Intercourse with chaste girls between fourteen and sixteen (still in existence);
- (c) Intercourse with feeble-minded females (repealed);
- (d) Intercourse with certain other vulnerable persons such as wards and chaste employees (still in existence);
- (e) Intercourse with certain relatives — incest (still in existence).

(2) Prohibition of intercourse preceded by the forms of pressure labelled seduction:
- (a) Seduction of chaste girls between sixteen and eighteen (still in existence);
- (b) Seduction of chaste young women between eighteen and twenty-one (still in existence);

---

105 R.S.C. 1970, c. C-34, s. 150.
106 For a brief discussion of the present law, see Chapter 5.
107 See Chapter 5.

(c) Seduction of female passengers on vessels (still in existence).
(3) Non-consensual sexual activity:
    (a) Rape — non-consensual sexual intercourse (with marital exception) (repealed);
    (b) Attempted rape (repealed);
    (c) Indecent assault on a female (repealed);
    (d) Indecent assault on a male (repealed).

4. THE LATEST REFORM

If one examines the list of sexual offences which existed immediately prior to the recent reform a number of factors are significant in light of the changes.

First, the main classificatory element of the offences was that of intercourse, uniformly interpreted to mean penetration of the vagina by the penis. This was particularly significant as the distinction between rape and assault. In order to prove rape, the Crown had to establish that this particular event had occurred. If anal intercourse, for example, had taken place, then the appropriate offence was indecent assault. Victims of rape were therefore singled out as suffering a peculiarly exclusive type of harm, and they were liable to be questioned closely about the precise nature of the assault they had suffered.

A second factor to be noted is that, with the exception of indecent assault on a male, nearly all offences contemplated that the victim could only be female and the accused male. (In a sense the form that incest took was to deny the existence of a victim.) This was an avoidance of the fact that men could also be assaulted in a range of ways, for example by premature exposure to sexual activity, and no doubt was a product of the stereotypical image of the male as the active participant in sexual relations while the female was passive. Women could be unchaste and more to blame but they could not be the aggressors in any criminal sense. The message in our law was very clear: men victimise women by attacking them sexually, and women victimise men by making false accusations of sexual attack.

The making of false accusations against men relates to the third point, that various legal devices existed to narrow the class of women protected and to protect the falsely-accused male. Statutory devices were the chaste-unchaste distinction, the comparison of blame, the marital immunity and the corroboration requirements. Judicial supplements included the tolerance of questioning about past sexual conduct, the recent complaint doctrine and the judicial corroboration rules.[108]

Lastly, there were a number of other factors to which attention was drawn prior to the passage of the Criminal Law Amendment Act which were not evident from an analysis of the law itself, but which emerged from studies of the practices of law enforcement. The best Canadian source to consult on this issue is Clark and Lewis, *Rape: The Price of Coercive Sexuality*, which contains statistics on the extent to which the law which exists on paper is actually enforced in practice. Rape is significantly under-reported, many reports are classified as "unfounded" by the police and there is a relatively low rate of conviction for those cases which do go to trial. In addition, the law governing our trial procedure was such that victims felt humiliated and embarrassed.

As a response to these factors, impetus developed in favour of a major overhaul of this area of law. Some of the history of the process of law reform is set out in the *Report on Sexual Assault in Canada*, prepared by Dianne Kinnon for the Canadian Advisory Council on the Status of Women, in 1981. She suggests that pressure for reform focused on the need for sexual equality before the law, recognition of the assaultive nature of rape, and more realistic and enforceable penalties.

In response to such pressure, Ronald Basford, then Minister of Justice, introduced Bill C-52 in May 1978.[109] It utilised indecent assault terminology, left the relevant offences in the section dealing with sexual morals rather than classifying them as assault, and limited marital rape to non-cohabiting spouses. Criticism concentrated on these aspects of the Bill and a conference of representatives from the National Action Committee, Women and the Law and the Canadian Association of Sexual Assault Centres demanded significant changes.

Bill C-52 was not passed and was replaced by Bill C-53 in January 1981, under the direction of Justice Minister Jean

---

108 Others include the admission of reputation evidence, discussed in Chapter 7, and the emphasis on the need for resistance to establish absence of consent.

109 The Law Reform Commission also produced a *Report on Sexual Offences* in 1978, proposing new offences of sexual interference and sexual aggression. See Report No. 10.

Chrétien. The explanatory notes summarize the purposes of that Bill:

> The main purposes of these amendments are to replace existing non-consensual sexual offences by the offences of sexual assault and aggravated sexual assault, to amend certain provisions of law that are prejudicial to complainants, to protect young persons against sexual exploitation and to ensure that the provisions of the Criminal Code apply equally to persons of both sexes.

The Bill proposed significant reforms relating to rape, indecent assault and associated evidentiary matters,[110] as well as statutory rape and the seduction offences. This Bill was considered by many to be an improvement over the previous Bill, in that it classified rape and indecent assault as forms of assault. Nevertheless, it was still controversial, some commentators being of the view that the degenderising of the offences and the abandonment of rape was a retrograde step since it might tend to obscure and deny one very serious form of women's oppression. Other criticisms related to the retention of the subjective mistake of fact defence, a very controversial issue since the decision of the Supréme Court of Canada in the *Pappajohn* case.[111] Also, the scope of permitted questioning about past sexual conduct, and the possibility that semantic change might give the appearance but not the reality of improvement in the law were subjects of controversy.

Considerable concern was expressed in debate about the number of matters dealt with in the Bill, and it became clear that, while there was widespread support for the sexual assault provisions, there were reservations about those sections dealing with young persons. The former provisions, with some changes,[112] proceeded in the form of Bill C-127, and were duly passed, as the Criminal Law Amendment Act.[113] It is the contents of that Act, insofar as they relate to sexual assault offences, which form the subject-matter of the next two chapters of this book.

---

110 As well as new offences relating to child pornography, which were somewhat controversial and were therefore dropped for the time being.

111 [1980] 2 S.C.R. 120. See Chapter 4 for a discussion of the mistake of fact defence, and Chapter 7 for a discussion of the *ratio* of *Pappajohn*.

112 Bill C-53 had contained, for example, two tiers of sexual assault offences, while Bill C-127 contained three. The past sexual history provisions were also tightened considerably.

113 S.C. 1980-81-82, c. 125. This Act also contained provisions relating to the parental abduction of children which are not relevant here.

Chapter 2

The Constitutional Setting

One of the objectives of the latest reform of our sexual assault law was the attainment of sexual equality.[1] This concept, of considerable political significance, now has a constitutional aspect since the introduction of the Canadian Charter of Rights and Freedoms.[2] One basic introductory question, therefore, with respect to the present law of sexual assault is its constitutionality. Three sections of the Charter[3] seem to be of obvious relevance, and are the subject of this chapter, which concentrates on the broader issues of sexual equality. Specific constitutional questions with respect to particular sections of the Code are dealt with as they arise in later chapters.

Since any assault law is designed to protect the individual's freedom from physical attack and freedom of movement, section 7 of the Charter should be noted:

> Everyone has the right to life, liberty and security of the person and the right not to be deprived thereof except in accordance with the principles of fundamental justice.

Section 28 adds an important dimension when combined with section 7, with the result that section 7 rights are guaranteed to both sexes equally. It states as follows:

> Notwithstanding anything in this Charter, the rights and freedoms referred to in it are guaranteed equally to male and female persons.

---

1 "[A]n effort has been made to degenderise the Criminal Code provisions . . . in keeping with the equality rights guaranteed in the Charter of Rights. The few remaining references to a male person or a female person will be dealt with when we amend the child exploitation provisions of the Code." Jean Chrétien, Minister of Justice, Parl. Debs. H.C., Vol. 124, No. 395, at 20039, 4 Aug. 1982.
2 The Constitution Act, 1982 [en. by the Canada Act, 1982 (U.K.), c. 11, Schedule B].
3 *Ibid.*, ss. 7, 28 and 15(1).

Lastly, one must make reference to section 15(1), which, unlike section 28, was subject to the three-year delay set out in section 32(2).

> Every individual is equal before and under the law and has the right to the equal protection and equal benefit of the law without discrimination and, in particular, without discrimination based on race, national or ethnic origin, colour, religion, sex, age or mental or physical incapacity.

The existence of the constitutional prohibition against sex discrimination has been acknowledged by Parliament in the creation of a gender-neutral offence of sexual assault. Previously, as is well-known, a rapist could only be a man and a victim only a woman. It is quite possible that this particular change will save the new offences from successful constitutional challenge.

With reference to the matter of challenge, one initial point, minor because obvious, should be made. The unreformed offences, such as intercourse with a female under fourteen, and the various seduction offences, are gender specific on their face, and thus will be subject to challenge when section 15 comes into force, and indeed may already be unconstitutional under section 28.

There is a far more fundamental issue, however, with respect to the constitutionality of all sexual assault offences both reformed and unreformed. It may appear, on a superficial level, that a gender-neutral offence is safe from challenge, but that raises two complex issues: first, whether sameness equals equality and, secondly, whether the Charter imposes positive duties on government not satisfied by simply making existing laws gender-neutral.

It is proposed to address the second issue only here, with a passing reference to the thorny and massive question of when difference amounts to discrimination. Without putting it more strongly than this, there appears to be an argument that the Charter contains positive rights or, in other words, affirmative obligations on government. This is a very uncontroversial proposition at a certain level, since it obviously imposes obligations on state officials, the police having, for example, a duty to inform an arrested person of the reasons for arrest.

The issue becomes much more complex, and correspondingly controversial, when one examines the whole range of "rights" in the Charter. There is a large number of these, some relatively concrete such as the right to counsel and some much more vague, such as the rights to liberty and security of the person, which, it has been submitted, are of relevance here. It is not at all clear what the word "right" means and whether it always means the same thing, even within the one constitutional document.

The basic distinction of significance here is between a right not to be interfered with by the state, and a positive right, a claim to something that someone else (in this case the state) has a duty to supply. For example, if the Charter stated baldly that everyone had a right to education, would it mean that the state had a duty not to interfere with education, or would it mean that everyone had a claim to the positive assistance of the state in obtaining an education? Although it is clear that the Charter contains a number of positive rights, as already suggested, the judiciary may hesitate to label all the things that are called rights as positive. Thus, unless there is a significant switch from the Bill of Rights approach,[4] the right to retain and instruct counsel without delay may not be construed as requiring the state to supply counsel for those who cannot afford it.[5]

Another way of stating the issue would be, with respect to the above examples, whether we have a right to education or are we simply free to obtain an education; do we have a right to counsel, or are we simply free to obtain counsel? This terminology has appealed to a number of judges already. *Re Allman and Commissioner of North West Territories*,[6] was a case involving an unsuccessful challenge to a statute which required three years residence before one could vote in a plebiscite. Mr. Justice de Weerdt compared the freedoms in section 2 of the Charter (including freedom of expression) which only provided a claim to non-interference, and rights, such as the right to vote in section 3, which could provide a claim to state action.

The distinction was stated somewhat differently by Posner J. in *Jackson v. City of Joliet*, an American case[7] involving the failure of police and fire-fighters to try and rescue people in a

---

4 See generally C. Rice "The Right to Counsel" in G.L. Gall, ed., *Civil Liberties in Canada* (1982), p. 191.
5 The U.S. Supreme Court has of course taken a different view in the famous cases of *Gideon v. Wainwright*, 372 U.S. 335 (1963) and *Miranda v. Arizona*, 384 U.S. 436 (1966).
6 (1983), 144 D.L.R. (3d) 467. A similar distinction was drawn in *Seill v. Broadway Manor Nursing Home, Christian Lab. Assn. of Can. and O.L.R.B.*, Ont. Div. Ct., 24 Oct. 1983 (not yet reported).
7 Digested in (1983), 52 U.S. Law Week 2133.

burning car. Posner J. drew a comparison between traditional "negative liberties"—the right to be left alone—and "positive liberties"—the right to receive elementary protective services. Without analysis, he simply asserted that the American Constitution is a charter of negative rather than positive liberties.[8]

The Charter uses the language of rights and freedoms so that it might be supposed simply that the freedoms are negative and the rights positive. However, a consistency of Parliamentary terminology argument seems to pale in significance when set alongside the consequences of construing all rights in a positive sense, as requiring state action. Does the Charter, for example, require state action to ensure that males and females enjoy an equal right to liberty and security of the person, as a combination of sections 7 and 28 would seem to indicate? This would have devastating implications for the law of sexual assault, so that an examination of the consequences of such an interpretation might well lead the judiciary to draw further distinctions between things called rights *per se*. It is possible that some "rights" will be judicially reclassified as freedoms,[9] with the result, in this context, that section 7 will not be used as a means of requiring state action with respect to the social problem of sexual assault.

It may be useful at this stage to consider terminology on a more theoretical level, since discussion of rights and freedoms may bring Hohfeldian analysis to mind for many people. Hohfeld, an American legal philosopher writing towards the beginning of this century, made the now uncontentious point that we use the word "right" to mean a number of different things. He suggested that the use of different words to mean these different things would assist analysis of legal issues.[10] With this in mind, he suggested the following concepts. A right *per se* is the correlative

---

8 This seems to be essentially a conservative view, which would have the effect of preserving the *status quo*, but in any event it is not accurate as, *e.g.*, the right to counsel has been construed positively. See note 5 above. Nevertheless the question is a helpful one.

9 This is in effect what happened with the right to retain and instruct counsel under the Bill of Rights, R.S.C. 1970, App. III, as discussed by Rice in his article cited in note 4 above. He shows that the Bill of Rights was construed in such a way as to deny that everyone had a positive right to counsel. Rather, they were simply free to retain counsel if they wished and were able to. The U.S. Supreme Court in *Miranda v. Arizona*, note 5 above, rejected such an approach. "In fact, were we to limit these constitutional rights to those who can retain an attorney, our decisions today would be of little significance" (at 472).

10 See generally W.N. Hohfeld, *Fundamental Legal Conceptions* (1923).

of a duty, one's affirmative claim against another. Such a right in the Charter would seem to me to be, for example, the right to be told the reasons for arrest. If no duty exists, there is therefore no true right. A right in this sense can be contrasted with a privilege, which might also be called freedom or liberty. One may have the liberty or privilege of hiring a lawyer, but if there is no duty on the state to supply one, then there is no *right* to a lawyer. Privileges seem to be things which the law does not stop us doing. We are familiar with the use of the concept in the context of defamation, and lawyer-client privilege. The lawyer is free not to testify, whereas others have a duty to do so. In that sense privilege is the opposite of duty. It is what is probably meant by freedom in the Charter. We are free to express ourselves.

A third concept is that of power—the ability to affect others in some legal way, for example, a power of appointment. This is mentioned in order to introduce the fourth concept, that of immunity, which means that someone else does not have a power with respect to us, as in diplomatic immunity. This is useful here because when section 7 speaks of the right not to be deprived of liberty, etc., except in accordance with the principles of fundamental justice, what is meant is that we have a limited immunity. The state has no power to deprive us of these things except in a certain way.[11] This is important since if this "right" is an immunity right, then it would be reasonable to argue that the first "right" in section 7, the right to life, liberty and security of the person, is some other type of "right."[12]

This concept gives us the tools to ask the basic question about section 7 (and thus about its potential impact on the law of sexual assault) in a very clear way. Is the right to liberty and the right to security of the person, a true right, in the Hohfeldian sense, or merely a privilege? Presumably, it is obvious that it is not a power

---

11 The interesting question here, of course, is *how* limited is the power of the state, or, in other words, under how much of a disability has the state placed itself. The answer to this question will be found in the judicial interpretation of the concept of "fundamental justice" in s. 7 of the Charter. I do not mean to commit myself here, by reference to the method of deprivation, to the view that procedural justice only is included here. Whatever one's view of the meaning of fundamental justice, the override power in s. 33(1) remains, so that, ultimately, one could take the view that the state has not placed itself under any disability at all.

12 These are all the relevant concepts in this context, but the full spectrum of Hohfeld's jural correlatives are as follows: right/duty; privilege/no-right; power/liability; immunity/ disability.

and the immunity is granted in the second half of the section. Does right here mean an affirmative claim against the state, or does it really mean privilege, that is, another freedom. Should section 7 really read "you are at liberty to have life, liberty and security of the person"?[13] It has quite a different ring to the ears.

Is it possible that the right to life, liberty and security of the person could be construed as a privilege and not be otiose?[14] It is possible in theory. Just because someone is free to do something, it does not mean that others have a duty not to interfere. Freedom of expression could be a good example, in the sense that people are free to say what they like but others do not have a duty to listen quietly. Technically, the added immunity in section 7 (the right not to be deprived thereof except in accordance with the principles of fundamental justice) was necessary in that it took away the state's power. However, the structure of the rest of the Code shows that the drafters were not proceeding carefully with Hohfeld's *Fundamental Legal Conceptions* in front of them. If they had been they would have known that they had to add an immunity to freedom of expression. The other argument is that the immunity, if the first right is only a privilege, is the crucial, the greater, thing. It has the power to control state action, so that it was not necessary to spell out both. So Hohfeldian and contextual analysis would suggest that the right to life, etc., is not simply a privilege. Nevertheless it is possible to read section 7 as saying that one can have as much liberty and security of the person as one can manage to get without interference by others, and the state does not have the power to take that away except in accordance with the principles of fundamental justice. This is very likely to be the interpretation, though for political reasons, rather than those based on the rules and principles of statutory interpretation or theoretical analysis. To illustrate this point, one has only to refer to the consequences of a positive right interpretation of section 7.

In order to reflect on those consequences, one first has to consider the meaning of the terms liberty and security of the person, the relevant concepts in the context of sexual assault. It is not possible to go into their meaning in detail here, but some general comments can be made on their possible scope.

Liberty could be an extremely broad concept. It may be that

---

13 Just as s. 10(c) may be construed to read: "Everyone is free to retain and instruct counsel without delay...."

14 Which is defined as unoccupied, indolent, functionless, futile and superfluous.

the fact that certain liberties are expressly dealt with in the Charter, for example mobility and democratic rights, points in the direction of the term having a very broad meaning, including the freedom to engage in whatever occupation one chooses, and the freedom to live wherever one wants. It is discussed in a famous American case of *Meyer v. Nebraska*, in which it is described as follows:

> Without doubt, it denotes not merely freedom from bodily restraint but also the right of the individual to contract, to engage in any of the common occupations of life, to acquire useful knowledge, to marry, establish a home and bring up children . . . and generally to enjoy those privileges long recognised at common law as essential to the orderly pursuit of happiness by free men.[15]

Liberty was also broadly defined in *Roe v. Wade*:[16] "Autonomous control over the development and expression of one's intellect, interests, tastes and personality."[17] In the same case Justice Douglas referred to liberty in the sense that is most relevant here, as "freedom to walk, to stroll or loaf."[18] Whatever the boundaries of the concept, therefore, it seems clear that it includes the right to move around freely.[19]

European case law tells us that even a limited interference with liberty is unconstitutional. The case often cited for that proposition is *Guzzardi*[20] in which Mr. Guzzardi, who was charged with kidnapping, was obliged to reside on the island of Asinara off Sardinia. The European Court of Human Rights pointed to the smallness of the area, the permanent supervision, the impossibility of social contacts and the length of the enforced stay in deciding that the restriction on his freedom of movement was unconstitutional.

With respect to security of the person, again it could be held to

---

15 262 U.S. 390 at 399 (1923).

16 410 U.S. 113 (1973).

17 *Ibid.*, at 211.

18 *Ibid.*, at 213.

19 S. Trechsel in "The Right to Liberty and Security of the Person—Article 5 of the European Convention on Human Rights in the Strasberg Case-Law" (1980), 1 H.R.L.J. 88, discusses liberty as the freedom "to come and to go." For general discussions of the meaning of s. 7 see M. Manning, *Rights, Freedoms and the Courts* (1983), pp. 227 *et seq.*, and P. Garant, "Fundamental Freedoms and Natural Justice" in W.S. Tarnopolsky and G. Beaudoin, eds., *Canadian Charter of Rights and Freedoms: Commentary* (1983), at 257.

20 (1980) 1 H.R.L.J. 257.

have a very broad meaning, even encompassing economic security, property and privacy rights. MacKay and Holgate, in their recent article on housing,[21] suggest that, taken literally, it could include rights to housing, minimum income and medical treatment. Whatever it means, it must, at the very least, include the right to be free from physical attack. It thus may be of even more significance than liberty in the context of sexual assault.

It can be safely assumed that section 7 says one has a right to walk, to stroll or to loaf and to be free from physical attack. It also must be added at this point that section 28 guarantees these rights equally to male and female persons. It is now possible to consider the implications of an argument that section 7 confers positive rights on everyone. It might appear that it would be a wonderful thing for our constitution to say that we all have an equal right to walk around and pursue all the common occupations of life and be free from attack, subject, of course, to any governmental deprivation of these rights which passed the fundamental justice test, and also subject to the reasonable limits in section 1.[22] But the implications of the acceptance of an argument that the state has positive duties with respect to section 7, in combination with section 28, are considerable. Some obvious results would follow. A child born in prison, for example, would have a constitutionally-protected right to be released, even though the infant had arguably never been "deprived" of freedom. In the context of sexual assault, the state would have an obligation to try to prevent interference with these rights by other individuals, which would broaden the scope of the Charter considerably.[23] Thus, decisions not to enforce particular laws could be open to constitutional challenge, as well as decisions relating to the allocation of law enforcement resources. It might well be unconstitutional for law enforcement officials to formulate policies which had the effect of minimising enforcement of laws creating offences of which women were primarily the victims.[24] On the contrary, when one

---

21 "Fairness in the Allocation of Housing: Legal and Economic Perspectives" (1983), 7 Dal. L. J. 383.

22 Indeed s. 1 limitations may be necessary to protect other democratic rights and freedoms.

23 As was pointed out by K. Swinton in rejecting the possibility of positive rights, in "Application of the Canadian Charter of Rights and Freedoms (ss. 30, 31, 32)" in Tarnopolsky and Beaudoin, note 19 above, at 44-9.

24 "If the laws go unenforced... the law-abiding citizen then becomes the victim of all sorts of unjustifiable invasions of his interests. His security of person and

takes into account the equality rights, *unequal* resources may have to be directed towards such offences in order to ensure an actual equal right to liberty and security of the person.

This is where the concept of equality becomes of crucial significance. Does equality mean sameness, or is it constitutionally possible for distinctions to be maintained or created in accordance with the realities of the differences between men and women? In other words, if section 7 creates state obligations, does this mean that equal resources have to be directed towards the protection of men and women or should more resources be used to protect one sex where in fact that sex is unequally victimised? Authoritative support can be found for the idea that distinctions should sometimes be made to create equality, the idea being here that more resources should be directed toward the protection of women. Tribe, in his leading work on the American constitution,[25] states that equality can be denied when distinctions are made, but also when "government *fails* to classify, with the result that its rules and programs do *not* distinguish between persons who, for equal protection purposes, should be regarded as differently situated."[26] Maloney puts the difficulty caused by this idea in a nutshell.[27] Since special groups have diverse interests, it follows that:

> equal protection may be at times elusive, for under certain circumstances diverse treatment is the essence of the doctrine while under other conditions diverse treatment is repulsive to the doctrine.[28]

While difficult, equal protection seems a necessary concept, since identical treatment will inevitably have disparate impact on different groups of people.[29] It is therefore arguable that not only do sections 7 and 28 require positive state action but that they

---

property is sharply diminished, and therefore, so is his liberty to function as a member of society." H. Packer, *The Limits of the Criminal Sanction* (1968), p. 158.

25 *American Constitutional Law* (1978).

26 *Ibid.*, p. 993. The example he gives is of voters being required to come to the polls regardless of their physical condition. See also C. Boyle, "Home Rule for Women: Power Sharing Between Men and Women" (1983), 7 Dal. L. J. 790 at 791-2.

27 S. Maloney, "Rape in Illinois: A Denial of Equal Protection" (1975), 8 John Marshall J. of Practice and Procedure 457.

28 *Ibid.*, at 477.

29 Thus, *e.g.*, a mere privilege of retaining a lawyer will have a different effect depending on whether or not the individual can afford it. A distinction between

require greater resources to be directed toward the protection of women so that in fact men and women will equally enjoy liberty and security of the person.

Interpretation of the word "right" in the positive sense is hardly problematic where some specific action is required, although resistance might increase with the prospect of the extensive allocation of state resources, as with a right to counsel. When we come to such extremely vague concepts as liberty and security of the person, then a finding that state action is constitutionally mandated becomes very problematic especially when combined with equality rights, and brings to the boiling point concerns about the appropriate limits of judicial decision-making. And yet on its face, section 7 provides rights to life, liberty and security of the person *as well as* the right not to be deprived of those except in accordance with the principles of fundamental justice. Some additional content should therefore be given to these extra words, since they would be practically, though not theoretically, superfluous if construed to mean an immunity from the power of the state only. Nevertheless, it appears that the recognition of section 7 as containing positive rights would have such dramatic consequences with respect to the allocation of resources and law enforcement decision-making that it may not be taken seriously.

The idea that the Charter requires the re-allocation of state resources toward the protection of women in order to ensure equal liberty and security of the person may be viewed by some as a romantic rather than realistic argument, but at the very least it puts into perspective the change to a gender-neutral sexual offence law. It is uncontroversial that it is overwhelmingly men who commit sexual assaults and women who are the victims of them. One result has been that women are less free "to walk, to stroll or to loaf" than men and to go about the common occupations of humanity. Men, of course, are also the victims of crimes of violence, but the fear and reality of sexual assault is a significant extra limitation on the freedom of movement and bodily security of women.

Women have in fact less security of the person than do men in the context of sexual assault, and yet the Charter states unequivocally that they have an equal right to that security. This is a

---

those who could and those who could not would appear to be necessary in order to create equality in fact, and this inevitably leads to a requirement of positive action by the state.

serious issue with respect to the quality of life of the women of Canada, and of the men who care about them. Two approaches are possible. One is to accept that the appropriate test of constitutionality is whether any sexual assault law, whether new or old, contributes, in some sufficient way, to a world in which men and women are equally at liberty and secure in their persons, or whether we will continue to live in a world in which the fear and reality of sexual assault interferes substantially more with the lives of women than of men. This approach would obviously have profound implications for the substance and enforcement of the law in this area (as in others where male and female behaviour is substantially different).

Another approach seems more likely to be adopted. This is simply to make crimes such as sexual assault gender-neutral, so that theoretical obeisance is made to the value of equality. This has already happened with sexual assault proper and is highly predictable with the unreformed offences such as intercourse with a female under fourteen. It will be ironic if this is the approach taken by Parliament and accepted by the courts since it will mean that the only impact of the Charter is to require the creation of a new crime that women can theoretically commit, without addressing at all the unequal burden of victimisation that women bear in this context.

This seems a classic illustration of Robert Samek's theory of "legal" as opposed to "social" law reform,[30] the latter being concerned with actual social problems and practices, the former concentrating on law as an end in itself. A social law reformer would, it is submitted, ask the question "what can the law do with respect to the problem of men sexually assaulting women?" In constitutional terms this might be "what is the constitutionally mandated response to the reality that women have less liberty and security of the person than men?" The legal law reformer instead changes the words "man" and "woman" into person to give the appearance of equality only.

One can contrast the fact, which should not be ignored, that men can now be charged with sexual assault of other men, for example, in prison. It is submitted that this is a worthwhile reform since it corresponds to an actual social problem.[31]

---

30 See R.A. Samek, "A Case for Social Law Reform" (1977), 55 Can. Bar Rev. 409.
31 Although it could be regarded as a cosmetic change only, since the offence of indecent assault of a male was already in existence.

Whether or not one thinks that section 7 should be construed to require the state to take positive action, it is submitted that, unless the government does more than simply remove all gender specific words from the Code, the equal right to liberty and security of the person will simply be empty words on paper, with no normative power for the state or impact on the way Canadian men and women actually live their lives.[32]

32 Section 7 (combined with s. 28) might more truthfully read "you can have as much . . . liberty and security of the person as you happen to have at any particular time, and if the state deprives you of any it will do so equally and in accordance with the principles of fundamental justice." The implications of insistence on the *status quo* as well as equality in the future are of course obvious.

Part II

The Substantive Law

Chapter 3

The Criminal Law Amendment Act: An Overview

A detailed discussion of the new sexual assault offences can be found in Chapter 4. What follows here is a brief description of the relevant provisions of what was Bill C-127, now the Criminal Law Amendment Act,[1] which was proclaimed in force on the 4th of January 1983.

As mentioned earlier, a number of sexual offences were removed from Part IV of the Criminal Code, dealing with sexual offences, public morals and disorderly conduct. New sexual assault offences were added to Part VI, relating to offences against the person and reputation.[2] The range of assault offences and sexual assault offences is now nearly the same, in that the same gradations are employed, as follows:[3]

1. assault, s. 245	sexual assault, s. 246.1
2. assault with a weapon or causing bodily harm, s. 245.1	sexual assault with a weapon, threats to a third party, or with another person, s. 246.2
3. aggravated assault, s. 245.2	aggravated sexual assault, s. 246.3

---

1 S.C. 1980-81-82, c. 125. Hereinafter referred to as the Act. Section numbers given are from the current Criminal Code, unless indicated otherwise.

2 In the material made available to provincial judges by the Department of Justice, it was stated that the "emphasis of the new provisions is on the violent nature of sexual assault rather than on its sexual nature. This is why such conduct is treated as a subject of the general assault provisions rather than as a special category of criminal conduct."

3 Although there are additional assaults, not relevant here—s. 245.3, unlawfully causing bodily harm and s. 246, assaulting a peace officer.

However, the maximum sentences for the sexual assault range are considerably higher than those for the equivalent assault.[4]

These new sexual assault offences replace the old crimes of rape, attempted rape, sexual intercourse with the feeble-minded, indecent assault on a female and indecent assault on a male.

Three significant aspects of the structure of sexual assault should be noted. First, there is no longer any need, as with rape, for the Crown to prove penetration of the vagina by the penis. This flows from the fact that all the various assault offences now share a common definition of assault contained in section 244(1) which refers in general terms to the application of force or the threat of it. It was no doubt hoped that the removal of penetration as a legally-significant element would go some way towards making the trial more humane for the complainant, in that it will no longer be fruitful for defence counsel to pursue a line of questioning directed at raising a doubt as to whether penetration actually took place.[5] It will still be possible for counsel to question whether any "sexual" touching took place, but establishing the distinction between sexual and non-sexual touching is unlikely to involve questioning on very personal matters. It is likely too that it would often involve a legal matter rather than a factual dispute. It will, of course, remain necessary for the complainant to give evidence as to what occurred,[6] which, in many cases, will inevitably cause some distress.

Secondly, the sexual assault offences are gender-neutral, that is, a person of either sex can commit sexual assault on another person of either sex. One wonders how significant the degenderising of this area of law is. It seems to be of more theoretical than

---

4 Thus, to use the same structure:

1. 5 years	10 years
2. 10 years	14 years
3. 14 years	Life

5 For an example of such a cross-examination, which preceded the withdrawal of the charge, see G.R. Goodman, "Proposed Amendments to the Criminal Code with Respect to the Victims of Rape and Related Sexual Offences" (1975), 6 Man. L.J. 275.

6 P. Nadin-Davis suggests that penetration will still be significant with respect to sentencing. "Making a Silk Purse? Sentencing: The 'New' Sexual Offences" (1983), 32 C.R. (3d) 28 at 34.

practical significance. However, it does have the virtue of providing some consistency of labelling in this area of law and may well protect it from constitutional challenge.[7] No doubt sexual assaults will continue to be committed by men upon women in the vast majority of cases. There may be some educational value in the message that men can be victimised in a similar way, although most of these cases which arise will probably involve male attackers as well as victims, as in the prison system, for example.[8]

The third significant reform is the removal of the spousal immunity in the new section 246.8, which states as follows:

> A husband or wife may be charged with an offence under section 246.1, 246.2 or 246.3 in respect of his or her spouse whether or not the spouses were living together at the time the activity that forms the subject-matter of the charge occurred.[9]

Husbands used to be immune from prosecution for the rape of their wives,[10] although not for other related crimes. It appears that either spouse could have been charged with any of the assault offences, including indecent assault, although the question whether intercourse *per se* would justify a charge of common assault remained untested.[11] If it did, then the criminal law has always in theory offered some protection for wives, even though the label of rape was withheld.[12] Nevertheless, the withholding of that label carried an important message with respect to a husband's rights over his wife's body and, when combined with reluctance to enforce the law of assault in this context, constituted

---

7 See generally Chapter 2, "The Constitutional Setting." It should be noted here that there remain offences which can only be committed by a male, *e.g.*, seduction of female passengers on vessels, s. 154.

8 For a bibliography on homosexual rape, see D. Chappel, R. Geis and G. Geis, eds., *Forcible Rape* (1977), p. 363. Previously, these cases had to be dealt with as indecent assault on a male, so the change relates to the label, and possibly sentencing, rather than to substance.

9 S.C. 1980-81-82, c. 125, s. 19. It was an amendment moved, *ex abundanti cautela*, by Mr. Svend Robinson, who took a continuing interest in the passage of the Bill. Parl. Debs. H.C., Vol. 124, No. 395, at 20050, 4 Aug. 1982.

10 Rape occurred where "a male person . . . has sexual intercourse with a female person who is not his wife. . . ." The Criminal Code, R.S.C. 1970, c. C-34, s. 143, repealed by the Criminal Law Amendment Act, S.C. 1980-81-82, c. 125, s. 6.

11 For a discussion of this point, see C. Boyle, "Violence Against Wives—The Criminal law in Retreat?" (1980), 31 N.I.L.Q. 35 at 41 *et seq.*

12 See P. English, "The Husband Who Rapes His Wife" (1976), 126 N.L.J. 1223, for comment on the labelling issue.

a serious embarrassment for Canadian criminal law.[13] The
removal of that embarrassment is no doubt to be applauded,[14] but
attention will now focus on enforcement practices. Only time will
tell whether the law has been changed in practice as well as in
theory.

A number of other changes were made. Section 17 of the Code,
dealing with duress, has been amended. "Assisting in rape" has
been removed as an offence for which duress is not a defence, and
replaced with "sexual assault, sexual assault with a weapon,
threats to a third party or causing bodily harm, aggravated sexual assault."[15] Thus it would appear that, while the actual perpe-
trators are denied the defence, parties to any form of sexual
assault may now argue duress[16] although it was denied to parties
to rape previously.[17] This is supported by the fact that section
246.2(d) (the "gang-rape" provision), which makes participating
in the offence with another the more serious second-tier type of
assault, is not referred to in section 17. However, the heading for
section 246.2(d) is used which could arguably mean that the whole
of the section is being referred to.[18] If that were the case, aiders
and abettors would be guilty of the second-tier assault by virtue of
section 246.2(d) in their own right, and thus might not be allowed

---

13 The change had been recommended by the Law Reform Commission, *Report
on Sexual Offences* (1978), pp. 16-17. For a selection of articles criticising the
immunity, see J. Scutt, "Consent in Rape: The Problem of the Marriage
Contract" (1977), 3 Monash U.L.R. 225; "Note" (1977), 52 N.R.U.L. Rev. 306;
"Comment" (1978), 82 Dick. L.R. 608; G. Geis, "Rape in Marriage: Law and Law
Reform in England, the United States and Sweden" (1978), 6 Ad. L.R. 284;
Mitra, "... For She has No Right or Power to Refuse her Consent", [1979] Crim.
L.R. 558; S. Schultz, "The Marital Exception to Rape: Past, Present and
Future" (1978), Det. Col. of L.R. 261; C. Boyle, "Married Women—Beyond the
Pale of the Law of Rape" (1981), 1 Windsor Yearbook of Access to Justice 192.
For an article supporting the immunity, see N. Morris and A.L. Turner, "Two
Problems in the Law of Rape" (1952-55), 2 Univ. Queensland L.J. 247. For a
comparison with the U.S. position see C.B. Backhouse and L. Schoenroth, "A
Comparative Study of Canadian and American Rape Law" (1983), 6 Can.-U.S.
L.J. 48.
14 As the Hon. Jean Chrétien, Minister of Justice at that time, stated in debate,
"[w]omen are not the chattels of their husbands and sex without the consent of
both parties is as unacceptable within marriage as it is outside of marriage."
Parl. Debs. H.C., Vol. 124, No. 395, at 20039, 4 Aug. 1982.
15 See s. 17 [am. 1980-81-82, c. 125, s. 4].
16 Applying *Paquette v. R.*, [1977] 2 S.C.R. 189.
17 *Bergstrom v. R.*, [1981] 1 S.C.R. 539.
18 This is mildly reinforced by the fact that, in other sections, the heading is used
to refer to the whole section, as in ss. 213 and 214(5). There, however, the section

to plead duress. It seems unfortunate that the *Bergstrom* anomaly has not been clearly removed as there is no apparent reason to distinguish between parties to sexual assault and parties to other offences.[19]

Consequential amendments have been made to section 178.1 (the definition section in Part IV.1, Invasion of Privacy), section 213 (constructive murder) and section 214(5) (first degree murder).

Section 139 has been repealed, with beneficial results. Section 139(1) was a corroboration provision, *requiring* corroboration with respect to the following offences: sexual intercourse with the feeble-minded,[20] incest,[21] seduction of a female between the age of sixteen and eighteen,[22] seduction under promise of marriage,[23] sexual intercourse with a step-daughter or employee,[24] seduction of female passengers on vessels[25] and parent or guardian procuring defilement.[26] Since only the first offence has been repealed, this has considerable evidential significance,[27] but probably, in a practical sense, only in the context of incest, which alone of the above offences is covered by the new section 246.4, forbidding a corroboration warning.[28] The issue of corroboration generally will be discussed more fully at a later point.[29]

Section 139(2) contained a defence of a subsequent marriage between a seducer and the victim. This had been available as a defence for a seducer under promise of marriage,[30] a male who had

---

number is given as well. It would have been safer if some term could have been coined for the middle form of sexual assault. As it is, it is very awkward to refer to. Perhaps the terminology of degrees could have been used, as in murder.

19 And yet the party/perpetrator dichotomy cannot be defended in any event. Why should a person who assists with a particularly violent rape be able to argue duress, while the perpetrator of any form of sexual assault, no matter how minor, cannot?

20 Section 148 [repealed 1980-81-82, c. 125, s. 70].

21 Section 150.

22 Section 151.

23 Section 152.

24 Section 153.

25 Section 154.

26 Section 166.

27 However, it was originally intended to complement the repeal of most of the relevant offences involved. See s. 5 of Bill C-53.

28 It would appear that the change in the corroboration rules have simply preceded the matching substantive changes. One anticipates that this matter will be tidied up when Parliament deals with reform of the law relating to children.

29 See Chapter 7.

30 Section 152.

illicit sexual intercourse with a chaste employee under twenty-one,[31] or a seducer of a female passenger.[32] Technically the repeal of this section means that a male who promises to marry a chaste woman under twenty-one, thereby inducing her to sleep with him, and proceeds to marry her according to his promise, as he intended to all along, is guilty of an indictable offence and liable to imprisonment for two years.[33]

Section 139(3) placed the burden of proving the unchaste character of the complainant, with respect to certain offences,[34] on the accused. The Crown will now have to prove the chaste character of the complainant, a change that is in line with the spirit of the restrictions on evidence of the sexual conduct of the victim. This removes the possibility of a Charter challenge under section 11(d) relating to the presumption of innocence. However, it conveys the unfortunate suggestion that the law assumes young women to be unchaste unless proved otherwise. A moment's reflection on this raises the obvious question of why chastity or the absence of it remains a factor at all. Why, for example, is a fifteen year old who is already a victim (in the sense that she has already had sexual relations which Parliament has determined is harmful whether she consents or not), not accorded the same protection as any other fifteen-year-old?

Lastly, section 139(4) indicated that evidence that the accused had had prior sexual access to the complainant was not evidence of unchaste character. This was obviously to prevent the accused pleading his own wrong as a defence. Otherwise he could only have been charged with the first act of intercourse. What is the effect of its repeal, while the concept of chaste character is retained? It is conceivable that an accused would now be permitted to raise past consensual intercourse as an argument that

---

31 Section 153(b).
32 Section 154.
33 This is not necessarily as startling as one might first suppose. In a society with considerable differences in the poverty levels between men and women, where women do not yet have unhindered access to the workforce, and where some women may still be socialized to believe that marriage is their main avenue to social prestige and economic security, we might easily consider that the offer of marriage is placing unfair pressure on a girl (since she must be under 21) to submit to intercourse.
34 Section 146(2)—intercourse with female between 14 and 16; s. 151—seduction of female between 16 and 18; s. 152—seduction under promise of marriage; s. 153(b)—illicit intercourse with employee.

the Crown had not proved all the elements of the offence,[35] but it is submitted that "previously chaste character" should be construed to mean that the complainant had been chaste before commencing sexual activity with the accused.[36]

The remaining changes relate to procedural and evidential issues, which will be discussed in full in Chapter 7. In brief, they are as follows:

(1) new rules have been introduced limiting the admission of evidence relating to the sexual activity of the complainant;

(2) the new section 246.4 indicates that a judge shall not instruct the jury that it is unsafe to convict without corroboration with respect to certain enumerated offences, including sexual assault and incest;

(3) the new section 246.5 abrogates the recent complaint rule;

(4) the new section 244(4) requires a judge, when reviewing the evidence relating to the honesty of an accused's mistaken belief in consent, to instruct the jury to consider the presence or absence of reasonable grounds for that belief.[37]

---

35 This is supported by the fact that the old s. 139(4) "deemed" evidence of past sexual intercourse between the accused and the complainant not to be evidence of unchastity, thus suggesting it otherwise would have been.

36 Although intercourse sometime before may be irrelevant, as the S.C.C. has accepted the concept of rehabilitation in *Magdall v. R.* (1920), 15 Alta. L.R. 313 (C.A.); affirmed (1920), 61 S.C.R. 88. Thus chaste character is not synonymous with virginity.

37 It is debatable whether this is a change in the law or not and, if so, whether it is of substantive or evidentiary significance. A full discussion of the whole issue of mistake of fact can be found in Chapter 4.

Chapter 4

The New Offences

During the debates on Bill C-127 the Honourable Flora Mac-
Donald made the following statement:

> This legislation makes a clear statement. It calls a spade a spade. It says that
> sexual assault is primarily an act of violence, not of passion; an assault with
> sex as the weapon.[1]

One gains a very clear impression from reading the debates that
there was considerable consensus on this aspect of the reform, but
an examination of what was actually done leads to substantial
doubt as to whether a spade has unequivocally been called a
spade. While the new offences emphasize violence, they tend to do
so as a means of classifying assaults as more or less serious, and
the violence in question is *other* than the sexual touching itself. It
is still conceptually possible, therefore, to separate the question of
consent from that of the violence used, so that the old need to
distinguish consensual from non-consensual sexual activity
remains. It seems inevitable that this will keep attention focused
on the "sexual" aspect of the attack. In addition, attention is
expressly drawn to this aspect of the matter, since the very definition of the basic crime includes the word "sexual."

This seems to suggest, at least superficially, that a sexual
assault is an assault with a sexual motivation, thus contradicting
what purports to be the basic thrust of the reform. The literature
reveals that it is impossible to classify all sexual assaulters in one
category. Some use aggression as a means to an end (that is,
sexual activity); with others violence is an end in itself.[2] Gutt-
macher and Weihofen found one group of rapists who act out of a

---

1 Parl. Debs. H.C., Vol. 124, No. 395, at 20041, 4 Aug. 1982.
2 See P. Gebhard, J. Gagnon, W.B. Pomeroy and C. Christensen, *Sex Offenders*
  (1965), p. 196.

deep-seated hatred of women,[3] and another comprising aggres-
sive anti-social individuals who are not primarily sex offenders at
all.[4] More recent commentators have stated as follows.

> Descriptively, the act of rape involves both an aggressive and a sexual com-
> ponent. In any particular sexual assault the part played by these impulses
> can be quite different. The primary aim may be hostile and destructive so that
> the sexual behaviour is in the service of an aggressive impulse. In other
> instances the sexual impulse is the dominating motive. . . . In a third pattern
> the two impulses are less differentiated, and the relationship between them
> can best be described as sexual sadism.[5]

Nevertheless, it may well be that "sexual assault" is in fact the
perfect term, indicating a combination of elements without a
commitment to any universal classification or pattern. Parliament has indicated, in creating the new offences, that this type of
behaviour is a form of assault, but that it is an especially serious
and offensive form of assault where a sexual component is present.
This is certainly vague enough to encompass all types, where
force is either a means or an end in itself.

What follows is an analysis of the various elements of sexual
assault, beginning with the *actus reus*, the elements other than
those relating to the state of mind of the accused.

1. THE ACTUS REUS OF SEXUAL ASSAULT

This can be broken down into three obvious components:
(1)   an application of force;
(2)   without consent;
(3)   of a sexual nature.[6]

(a) *The Application of Force*

This element coincides entirely with the offence of assault set
out in section 244(1).

---

3 *Psychiatry and the Law* (1952), p. 116.

4 *Ibid.* Gebhard, *et al.*, note 2 above, refer to this type as the amoral delinquent.

5 M.L. Cohen, R. Garofalo, R.B. Boucher and T. Seghorn, "The Psychology of
Rapists," in D. Chappell, R. Geis and G. Geis, eds., *Forcible Rape* (1977), at
297-8.

6 It is no longer necessary for the accused to have been over 14 years old. The
present s. 147 only applies to incest and s. 146 offences.

A person commits an assault when

    (a) without the consent of another person, he applies force intentionally to that other person, directly or indirectly;

    (b) he attempts or threatens, by an act or gesture, to apply force to another person, if he has, or causes that other person to believe upon reasonable grounds that he has, present ability to affect his purpose; or

    (c) while openly wearing or carrying a weapon or an imitation thereof, he accosts or impedes another person or begs.

Since sexual assault is an assault with an extra sexual element, all the jurisprudence on the crime of assault becomes directly relevant. It seems clear that, unless or until a distinctive jurisprudence emerges around the new crime of sexual assault, counsel will rely heavily on the authorities relating to assault and indecent assault.

Our present crime of assault is, in essence, a codification of the English common law. Thus we have adopted the common practice of using the term "assault" to cover both assault and battery.[7] The type of assault in section 244(1)(a) above is in strict terminology a battery, since the accused must have applied "force." The question will arise as to whether any touching, no matter how slight, can be termed the application of force. This is of far more significance with respect to sexual assault than assault *per se*. A slight touching might well be regarded as trivial in a non-sexual context, hardly noticed or only mildly annoying. When the touching is of a sexual nature, for example a pat on the bottom or a hand placed on the thigh, or is accompanied by words which make clear its purpose, the parameter of the new law will be tested in a revealing way. The judicial and prosecutorial response to this issue will indicate whether this offence will be utilized in the context of what amounts to low-grade sexual harassment.

The case law indicates that the judiciary could go in either direction. In the context of plain assault, the courts have flirted with the idea that an element of hostility is required; perhaps, although this is not expressed, because of reluctance to apply a criminal sanction where the assault seems technical only. The occasional judge has stressed the need for hostility or an act of violence. In *R. v. McGibney*[8] the accused was acquitted of assault after he had (the judge assumed) grabbed another man by the collar, addressed him in a loud voice and gesticulated violently. The court felt that the touching was of no significance as there

---

7 J.C. Smith and B. Hogan, *Criminal Law*, 4th ed. (1978), p. 350.

8 [1944] 3 W.W.R. 195 (Sask. C.A.).

was no violent intent. A more recent authoritative, but somewhat obscure, decision of the Quebec Court of Appeal points in the same direction. In *R. v. Lachapelle*,[9] the court seemed to approve the trial judge's view that an assault must be an act of violence.[10]

While the word "force" may suggest something more than a touching,[11] the overwhelming balance of authority points in the other direction, stressing that any unconsented-to touching is an assault. One recent indecent assault case will illustrate the point. In *R. v. Burden*,[12] the complainant was sitting in what was otherwise an empty bus when the accused sat down beside her and put his hand on her thigh for a few seconds. The County Court judge found that there was no assault and no circumstances of indecency, and the Crown appealed the former finding. The British Columbia Court of Appeal held that the trial judge was wrong and that placing a hand on another's thigh is indeed the application of force.[13] In so finding the court delved deeply into the authorities, quoting from Hawkins, *Pleas of the Crown*.[14]

> Battery seemeth to be when any injury whatsoever, be it ever so small, is actually done to a person of a man in any angry or avengeful or rude or insolent manner. . . . For the law cannot draw the line between different degrees of violence, and therefore, totally prohibits the first, and lowest stages of it, every man's person being sacred and no other having the right to meddle with it in any, the slightest manner.[15]

This seems to put the matter in a nutshell, even if today we might be inclined to state the issue in a somewhat different way.

---

9 (1969), 6 C.R.N.S. 190 (Que. C.A.).

10 However, it is not entirely clear whether the decision was based on the absence of assault or the implication of the presence of consent. "I am of the opinion that the Crown had to prove something here other than the passivity displayed by the girl in this case." *Per* Montgomery J., *ibid.*, at 193. William J. Rankin, in an annotation following the report of the case suggests, in disagreement, that it is clear that "there may be an assault in the absence of a violent physical attack" (at 197).

11 The Oxford English Dictionary (1961), stresses violence in most of its definitions of "force", but it also refers to the expenditure of energy, the exertion of one's strength. See also Black's Law Dictionary, 5th ed. (1979), "power dynamically considered," and *Swales v. Cox*, [1981] 1 All E.R. 1115, "the use of any energy," such as pushing open a door that is ajar.

12 (1981), 25 C.R. (3d) 283 (B.C. C.A.).

13 *Ibid.*, at 286.

14 (1716-21), p. 110, as quoted in Taschereau's *Criminal Code of the Dominion of Canada* (1893).

15 See also, in support of the proposition that any touching can be an assault, *Ex parte Kane* (1915), 26 C.C.C. 156 (N.B. S.C.); *Stewart v. Stonehouse* (1926), 20

The question here is whether individuals have the right to absolute control over their bodies, so that the criminal law protects their right not to be touched in any way, without their consent, or whether some harm other than the technical interference with that integrity should be caused before it is appropriate to use the criminal law.

Prosecutors and judges will not be helped in their task by any apparent philosophy behind the new provisions. Emphasis on the *violence* of sexual assault is not of assistance here since it is not clear whether the idea was to punish sexual touching on a scale of severity depending on the *accompanying* violence, or whether any sexual touching is now to be regarded as a form of violence in itself. To put the issue in a somewhat different way, it is not clear whether the interests being protected here are confined to freedom from physical harm alone or whether they include privacy and freedom of sexual choice.[16] It may be that this is a false issue, however, and that the new offences should be regarded as protecting individuals from violence in a number of senses. Depending on the circumstances in each individual case, sexual assault can be seen as an interference with one's physical, emotional and psychological integrity, as well as one's sense of dignity and autonomy. It may not be desirable to force the concept into any one particular mold.

In the context of a slight sexual touching, the harm involved may be non-physical in nature, but this is not a sufficient reason to depart from the well-established line of authority on the nature of assault. It is submitted that a departure would be unfortunate for several reasons.

The old cases on assault enunciate a clear value which ought to be embodied in the case law interpreting the new offences. It is suggested that Hawkins in his *Pleas of the Crown* gave very good advice. Since we cannot distinguish between degrees of violence, we should enunciate a rule that "every man's [sic] person is

---

Sask. L.R. 459 (C.A.); R. v. Jones (1963), 41 C.R. 359 (N.S. C.A.); *R. v. Beamish* (1966), 45 C.R. 264 (N.S. C.A.); *Bolduc v. R.*, [1967] S.C.R. 677 at 683 *per* Spence J.: "It is, of course, trite law that the force applied may be of very slight degree, in fact, may be mere touching"; *Fagan v. Metro. Police Commr.*, [1968] 3 All E.R. 442 at 445 *per* James J.: "Assault may be committed by the laying of a hand on another"; *Re Stillo and R.* (1980), 56 C.C.C. (2d) 178 (Ont. H.C.).

16 For an argument that rape laws are designed to protect the societal interest in women's privacy and freedom of choice, see R.D. Wiener, "Shifting the Communication Burden: A Meaningful Consent Standard in Rape" (1983), 6 Harv. Women's L.J. 143 at 159 *et seq.*

sacred." Case law stressing that every person has a right to be free from unwanted sexual touching would show the commitment of legislators and judges to the dignity and integrity of every individual.

A different approach could cause difficulty with respect to sexual assaults against children where consent is irrelevant.[17] If it is not yet fully understood or whole-heartedly accepted that any sexual touching is criminally offensive in itself, unless accompanied by a legally-significant consent, then it might be possible for courts to acquit where "consensual" sexual activity has taken place on the basis that the assault element had not been proved.[18] This would, of course, tend to negate the requirement that consent is irrelevant in these cases. It is important that the courts continue to enunciate a clear rule that *any* sexual touching of a child is of a criminal nature.

A final point that must be added is that any direct or indirect touching is prohibited. This may be of little significance with respect to sexual assault, since it would appear that most touchings will be directly inflicted. Thus the victim of the assault will in most cases be touched by a part of the accused's body or by an object used by the accused.[19]

(i) *Attempted or threatened force.* An assault is committed where the accused threatens to apply force and had the ability to carry out his or her threats, as in *R. v. Horncastle,*[20] where the accused pointed a firearm at his wife. The court held that it was unnecessary to show any intent to carry out the threat or prove any degree of alarm. In other words, threatening has been rendered criminal, so long as the threats have the potential to be put into effect.[21] It has been traditionally held that mere words are not

---

17 See, *e.g.*, s. 146 and s. 246.1(2).

18 This is precisely what one trial judge did in *R. v. Beamish,* note 15 above. The complainant, a 13 year-old girl had been lying on the ground with her clothes in disarray, and the accused lay down on top of her but was apparently unable to have intercourse. The magistrate stated that "the tacit acquiescence and the total absence of any hostile act support a finding that there was no assault." The Crown's appeal was successful.

19 It is difficult to think of an example of an indirect sexual assault. For plain assaults see J.C. Smith and B. Hogan, *Criminal Law,* 4th ed. (1978), p. 286. Nevertheless it is helpful that the possibility is clearly set out.

20 (1972), 4 N.B.R. (2d) 821 (C.A.).

21 But see *R. v. Judge* (1957), 118 C.C.C. 410 (Ont. C.A.) in which the accused was convicted of an assault in threatening a person inside a locked car. *Cf.* Smith

enough, there must be a threatening act or gesture.[22] There is an assault if the accused has caused the threatened person to believe upon reasonable grounds that he has present ability to effect his purpose. Thus the pointing of an unloaded gun would be an assault.[23] It might be possible to argue that "reasonable grounds" could vary depending on the sex, age and physical attributes of the threatened person.

(ii) *Begging with a weapon.* This last form of assault is insignificant in practice and particularly so in the context of sexual assault. However, it seems at least theoretically possible that such an assault could have a sexual element.

(b) *Without Consent*

For the purposes of any form of assault section 244(3) makes the following provision:

> ... [N]o consent is obtained where the complainant submits or does not resist by reason of
> (a) the application of force to the complainant or to a person other than the complainant;
> (b) threats or fear of the application of force to the complainant or to a person other than the complainant;
> (c) fraud; or
> (d) the exercise of authority.

There seems to be nothing in this section to indicate that this is an exclusive list of the situations in which no consent is obtained. It is therefore possible to argue that there was no consent even though none of the listed factors was present.[24] It is conceivable that an argument could be made that no consent was present because, for example, of threats other than the application of force or of mistake not caused by fraud. Thus Parliament has not really confronted a fundamental issue. Two ways of analysing consent are available. Attention can be focused on consent as a subjective issue in relation to the individual complainant. Using this

---

and Hogan, note 19 above, who state, at p. 282, that this is not an assault.

22 *R. v. Bryne* (1968), 3 C.R.N.S. 190 (B.C. C.A.). This seems inevitable because of the wording of our provision. For criticism, see Smith and Hogan, *ibid.*, p. 283.

23 If the threatened person does not have the belief, then there may be an attempted assault, if there is such a crime.

24 Although this argument may be weakened by the removal of a subsection from an earlier version of s. 244. Section 244(4)(a) of Bill C-53 stated that "it is a question of fact whether the complainant consented or not...."

approach, the relevant question would be "was this person's will overborne in all the circumstances?" Alternatively, it is possible to concentrate on the behaviour of the accused. This would require the identification of certain types of conduct which carry a particular danger of putting unbearable pressure on another individual. The former approach is a possibility since we must not forget that the *mens rea* barrier remains to weed out innocent accused (the test there being subjective from the perspective of the accused). The message of the criminal law would be: refrain from behaviour which you know will put pressure on another person to fulfil your will instead of his or her own. This approach has been suggested by Jocelyne Scutt, an eminent writer in this field.[25]

> There appears therefore, to be some confusion of legal and factual issues. The legal issue is that not every submission involves a consent. ... The factual issue is then: did this particular female in this particular instance consent, not merely submit. This is a question for the jury to consider in light of the surrounding circumstances of the purported non-consent, and such issues as age and physical strength, general disposition may be relevant.[26]

Gerald Dworkin has also commented that "coercion remains a descriptive and explanatory category with no logical ties to responsibility or the absence of it."[27] One might tend to advocate this approach if one believed that *any* pressure imposed by another to engage in sexual activity should attract the criminal sanction, based on the deprivation of freedom to make a choice uninfluenced by external pressures.[28] This approach was used by the English Court of Appeal in *R. v. Olugboja*.[29] The complainant, a teenage girl, along with her friend, had been taken from a discotheque to the home of the two accused. She was raped in the car by one accused and arrived crying and frightened. The other accused had intercourse with her, without using force. She did not struggle and in fact removed her own pants. The court felt that intimidation other than force or threats of force could negative consent and found that it was open to the jury to decide as a matter of fact that there was no consent. The appeal was dismissed.[30]

---

25 "The Standard of Consent in Rape" (1976), N.Z.L.R. 462.

26 *Ibid.*, at 466.

27 "Compulsion and Moral Concepts" (1968), 78 Ethics 227 at 232.

28 See C. Boyle, "Married Women: Beyond the Pale of the Law of Rape" (1981), Windsor Yearbook of Access to Justice 192 at 208.

29 [1981] 3 W.L.R. 585; petition for leave to appeal to the House of Lords dismissed, [1981] 1 W.L.R. 1382.

30 Laskin J.A., as he then was, seems to have suggested a *form* of subjective test

In contrast, there is what seems to be the traditional approach of listing certain unacceptable pressures, basically force and fraud. This approach conveys the message that individuals ought to have a certain level of fortitude. The new subsection certainly suggests a continuation of this approach, but does not clearly preclude the possibility of argument.

The difficulty arises because of a failure to confront the very difficult philosophical question of the distinction between submission and consent.[31] As Leslie Sebba and Sorel Cahan have pointed out, there is a problem of an appropriate standard.[32]

> In what circumstances should a sexual act be regarded as an offence? This is essentially an ideological problem, involving questions of the relative social status of the male and the female, the conduct norms applying in different situations, the meaning of various forms of coercion, etc.[33]

It seems to be an enormous task to begin to assess the culpability involved where a man, for example, takes advantage of his superior social and economic status and the relative docility and desire to please of a particular woman, or where sexual intercourse occurs because of fear of, not force, but negative social repercussions. Many of us are reluctant to grapple with these moral issues in our everyday lives, and Parliament has, in a sense, side-stepped the issue by continuing (with some significant additions) the old approach that was used with rape, that of listing factors which vitiate consent. It may well be that, because of the lack of sophistication of the criminal law, and its need to focus on factors that are relatively clear-cut in a factual sense, this is the better approach. Thus future reform may concentrate on refining

---

at one point. In dissent in *R. v. Maurantonio*, [1968] 1 O.R. 145 at 150 (C.A.), he quotes *Papadimitropoulos v. R.* (1957), 98 C.L.R. 249 at 261, "'... once the consent is comprehending and actual the inducing causes cannot destroy its reality.'" With respect, this seems to be the worst of both worlds. The law has always tended to focus on the "inducing causes." A shift to consideration of the actuality of consent in a vacuum would seem to leave us no way of distinguishing consent and submission.

31 Although it is recognised that there is a distinction: *R. v. Firkins* (1977), 39 C.R.N.S. 178 (B.C. C.A.), leave to appeal to S.C.C. refused 37 C.C.C. (2d) 227 n. However, a rape charge could be laid under the old s. 143(a) *or* (b)(i) where threats of bodily harm were made. *Quaere* since s. 143(b)(i) explicitly stated that "consent" could be extorted by threats or fear of bodily harm.

32 "Sex Offences: The Genuine and Doubted Victim" in I. Drapkin and E. Viano, eds., *Victimology: A New Focus*, Vol. 5 (1973), at 29.

33 *Ibid.*

the list[34] rather than radical change. There has been some incremental change in the factors which vitiate consent, but no radical transformation of the structure of the offence. A diagram comparing the change in vitiating factors may express this more effectively.

RAPE	SEXUAL ASSAULT
	application of force (including to another person)
threats or fear of bodily harm	threats or fear of the application of force (including to another person)
personation of husband false or fraudulent representation as to nature and quality of act	fraud
	exercise of authority

A further fundamental issue has been side-stepped in these reforms. It relates to the separation of force and consent. There has been considerable criticism in the past that, even though force was present, consent could still be in issue and thus the complainant's assertion that she had been raped had to be backed up by signs of struggle.[35] It appeared that the complainant had a duty to resist all forms of pressure not listed in the Code (or at least if she failed to do so she was unprotected by the law) and physically resist where force was brought to bear. The use or threat of force were not necessarily enough by themselves to lead to the conclusion of non-consent.

It would have been possible for Parliament simply to make forcible sexual touching an offence, but this has not been done, or at least not explicitly. Under the new provisions force and consent

---

34 Depending of course on prevailing notions of what ought to be criminalized. As P. Atiyah states in *The Rise and Fall of Freedom of Contract* (1979), at p. 436, "the idea, that a man's will is 'overborne' by certain types of pressure and not by others is, both in logic indefensible, and in practice impossible of application. The reality is that some forms of pressure are in conformity with the ... moral ideas of the community, and others are not."

35 See, generally, Scutt, note 25 above, and Note, "The Resistance Standard in Rape Legislation" (1966), 18 Stan. L.R. 680.

are, at least technically, separate issues, so it remains possible, if mind-boggling, for a finding to be made that a woman consented to sexual touching even though force was used or threatened. The placement alongside assault emphasises this possibility, if any-thing, since section 244(1) indicates expressly that it is legally possible to consent to the use of force.[36]

It may be that this possibility is remote, since section 244(3) uses the phrase "submits or does not resist." This is a clear ac-knowledgement of the fact that consent may be absent, even though there have been no overt signs of resistance. Where force is present or threatened it will be easy for the finder of fact to decide that the complainant submitted rather than consented. However, while it is settled that failure to resist does not, *in law*, indicate the presence of consent, in the mind of the finder of fact there may be a doubt as to whether it *in fact* indicates submission rather than consent. Since this may have been at the root of the problem all along, one can only hope that this new wording will have some effect.

A last point about consent in general is that it is irrelevant where the victim is under the age of fourteen and the offender is more than three years older.[37] In this situation the element of consent is missing entirely from the *actus reus* of the various sexual assault offences. Where the victim is under fourteen, the prosecution could proceed using one of these offences, without the necessity of proving absence of consent, or, where intercourse has taken place, proceed under section 146(1). The advantage of proceeding under section 146(1) is that it is in essence an absolute liability offence, as discussed in Chapter 5. It may however be preferable to use sexual assault for the foreseeable future to avoid the possibility of constitutional challenge.[38]

At this point it may be useful to discuss individually the list of factors in section 244(3) which vitiate consent.

(i) *The application of force to the complainant or to a person other than the complainant.* The express new element here is the

---

36 This is what makes it legally possible, for example, to engage in a boxing match. It is debatable whether there is even any public interest limitation on the scope of consent.

37 Section 246.1(2) [en. S.C. 1980-81-82, c. 125, s. 19].

38 Section 146(1) is gender specific and thus may offend ss. 28 and 15 of the Charter, while the absolute liability may conflict with the principles of fundamental justice in s. 7.

addition of a third party. An illustration can be found in the situation where a couple is accosted and the male is beaten up so as to induce submission on the part of the female.

One complicating factor in this provision is that the wording "application of force" is the same as in the definition of assault itself. It would seem that the sexual touching *is* the application of force if there is no consent and there is no consent if force is applied. While this appears unnecessarily complex, the key may be in the words "by reason of." There must be some causative link between the submission and the application of force. This force vitiates consent to a touching that in all other respects is a "sexual" assault. It would appear therefore that there are two "forces," the assault "force" and the consent "force." This is necessary, otherwise every touching would be an assault, since the touching in itself, being force, would negative the consent to it.

Emphasis on the causative link might also obviate difficulties arising over the need to construe the word "force" in the same way in both places. Even if the consent "force" is construed to mean any touching, it will still be possible to decide that the complainant did not submit "by reason of" it. However, this separation of the two forces and use of the causative link certainly allows distinctions to be made between the use of force and consent, as discussed above. The distinctions will be invidious when they turn on decisions relating to the degree of force used. Thus the finder of fact could decide that "not enough" force was used so that the complainant did not "submit or fail to resist" "by reason of" that force. The question then becomes one of consent. This is the back door through which the old duty to resist may enter. The objective of the redefinition of rape in terms of assault would be undermined. The leading work on rape in Canada stated in 1977:

> The presence of physical coercion rather than the absence of consent, should be the central feature of the offense of rape. . . . For women, the presence of physical coercion defines the nature of the act.[39]

It remains to be seen whether the new offences will focus attention on force rather than consent. It is submitted that the use or threat

---

39 M.G.L. Clark and D. Lewis, *Rape: The Price of Coercive Sexuality* (1977), p. 166. For a jurisdiction where this approach is taken, see *Wilson v. State*, 655 P. 2d 1246 at 1257 (1982, Wyoming), in which it was held that if facts to compel submission are proved, then lack of a consent is also proved, since "consent is swallowed up by acts of force."

of force should preclude the possibility of finding consent, and that the back door should be kept firmly closed on any negative assessment of the complainant's fortitude. It would be a perverse interpretation of section 244(3) that held that a complainant consented to a sexual touching accompanied by the use or threat of force.

A final note under this section is that the force does not have to be applied by the accused.

(ii) *Threats or fear of the application of force to the complainant or to a person other than the complainant.* Such threats would in most cases be an assault in themselves, but would also permit the Crown to prefer the more serious charge of sexual assault.

One fascinating part of this provision is the reference to "fear." Here is the one place in the list of vitiating factors where attention suddenly shifts, as in *Olugboja*,[40] to the subjective feelings of the victim rather than the behaviour of the accused. By utilizing this provision, a person can be convicted of sexual assault where he simply (with *mens rea*) took advantage of another's fear. This may be a recognition of the fact that a situation may be "instinct with coercion" so that threats are unnecessary— what I think of as the "four big men" argument. In *People v. Flores*[41] it was stated:

> If one were met in a lonely place by four big men and told to hold up his hands or do anything else, he would be doing the reasonable thing if he obeyed, even if they did not say what they would do to him if he refused.[42]

However, the old rape provision also had a reference to fear, so we can assume that no significant change was meant here. An example of a case where this factor could be used is provided by *R. v. Plummer*,[43] where the accused was charged with raping a girl after she had already been raped by another man. He simply found her naked and crying on the bed and had sexual relations with her. No threats were made but she submitted out of fear of bodily harm.[44]

---

40 [1981] 3 W.L.R. 585 (C.A.); petition for leave to appeal to House of Lords dismissed, [1981] 1 W.L.R. 1382.

41 145 P. 2d 318 (1944).

42 *Ibid.*, at 320 *Cf. R. v. Hallett* (1841), 9 Car. P. 748 where the victim was raped by eight men who attacked her. She did not resist after the initial attack so they were convicted of assault only.

43 (1975), 31 C.R.N.S. 220 (Ont. C.A.).

44 The Ontario Court of Appeal sent the case back for retrial as the trial judge

In one American case,[45] evidence that the accused had previously committed violent acts toward the victim or others was admitted as being relevant to establish fear. If admitted in Canada, this type of evidence may be particularly helpful in marital or quasi-marital situations.

(iii) *Fraud.* The extent to which the criminal law should recognise fraud as vitiating consent has always been a difficult theoretical issue, although it emerges rarely in the case law. The new scheme of sexual assault offences contains a significant change from the old provisions in that there is a simple reference to "fraud." Section 244(3)(c) states that sexual assault is committed where the victim submits or does not resist by reason of fraud.

The old offence of rape referred to situations in which consent was obtained by personation of the victim's husband,[46] or by false and fraudulent representations as to the nature and quality of the act.[47] In contrast, the old definition of assault had contained the wording "without the consent of another person, or with consent where it is obtained by fraud."[48] It appears that Parliament dropped the rape version and adopted the old assault approach across the board.[49]

This will not help clarify an otherwise obscure area of law if it is approached in a purely theoretical fashion by the judiciary. However, if it is now recognised that the decks have been cleared for a policy decision as to what is culpable in the context of fraud, then the law may be improved tremendously. A range of alternatives is available in this regard. They always were available under the old wording, but the change may force or encourage judges to consider the possibilities anew.

(1) Fraud could be construed to mean deceit as to the very nature

---

had not dealt adequately with the issue of intent.

45 *State v. Pancake*, 296 S.E. 2d 37 (1982, West Virginia App.).

46 Section 143(b)(ii) [repealed S.C. 1980-81-82, c. 125, s. 6].

47 Section 143 (b)(iii) [repealed S.C. 1980-81-82, c. 125, s. 6]. See the same wording in the old s. 149(2) [repealed S.C. 1980-81-82, c. 125, s. 8].

48 Section 244 [am. S.C. 1980-81-82, c. 125, s. 19].

49 It is interesting that reform stressing the violent quality of sexual attacks should also broaden forms of non-violent assault. This was going much further than was proposed by the Law Reform Commission, *Report on Sexual Offences*, No. 10 (1978), p. 15. "Consent obtained by misrepresentation as to the character of the act or the identity of the accused is not consent. . . ."

of sexual contact in itself, thus limiting the protection offered by this provision to the child (or equivalent) who has no understanding of sexual activity. In other words, only the ignorant (or perhaps innocent would be the preferred word) would be seen as deserving protection.

(2) Fraud could cover deceit as to significance, for example, the moral implications of the act. This would cover more victims, including those who know what sex is but are deceived into putting the act in question into some other category, for example, medical treatment.[50]

(3) Fraud could extend to deceit as to the individual involved, for example, Y pretending to be X, as in personation of a husband.

(4) Fraud could even go so far as to cover deceit as to an individual's qualities. This is a very large category, which perhaps ought to be broken down further. It could extend from deceit as to the quality of being a spouse (for example, after a fake marriage), through representations as to wealth or status, to the innocent deceits of some sexual encounters.

It is obvious that this area is rife with the possibilities of victim-judging and yet a line has to be drawn somewhere between the innocent child and the person beguiled by an entirely false display of interest in say poetry or cross-country skiing.

In the past, the wording of the rape and indecent assault provisions allowed a distinction to be drawn between fraud as to the nature of the act itself and fraud as to collateral matters. Thus in *R. v. Harms*[51] the accused was convicted of rape where he had represented to the victim that sexual intercourse was a form of medical treatment. In *Bolduc v. R.*[52] a conviction was quashed where a doctor had represented a friend to be a doctor also, so that he was permitted to observe a vaginal examination. This was not fraud as to the nature and quality of the act.

Bolduc was a classic instance of a classification merely giving the appearance of justification for a decision, since the judge was free to make the initial choice of description, which was not explained or justified in any way.[53] The case law is innocent of any discussion of the amount of protection which the judiciary

50 See J.A. Scutt, "Fraud and Consent in Rape: Comprehension of the Nature and Character of the Act and Its Moral Implications" (1976), 18 Cr. L. Q. 312, for a discussion of whether the old rape law extended to this category.
51 [1944] 1 W.W.R. 12 (Sask. C.A.).
52 [1967] S.C.R. 677.
53 See, *e.g., R. v. Maurantonio*, [1968] 1 O.R. 145 (C.A.) (appeal quashed and

thinks *ought* to be extended to the victims of fraudulent statements. It is submitted that this issue should be addressed at the first appropriate opportunity. It is an issue which relates to the fundamental human question of the ethics of sexual interaction. Of course in an ideal world we would be totally honest with each other, but what types of fraud ought to attract criminal penalties? There is very little guidance available.

It would appear that personation of a husband has now been swallowed up in the general fraud provision. This might, at first glance, appear to be of technical interest only, since such cases are rare.[54] However, it may have been that the personation provision had a narrowing rather than a broadening effect. Thus its repeal and inclusion in fraud would mean that the husband qualification would no longer be operative. Thus personation of a lover or cohabitee would come under the rubric of fraud.

Furthermore, once it is accepted that fraud covers some quality in the individual, such as identity, then the courts will ultimately have to confront the issue of what other qualities are relevant. There is some slight but prestigious authority for the proposition that falsely holding oneself out to be a doctor would be covered.[55] It will be open to the courts to go much further and decide that *any* fraudulent representation, which has a causative connection ("by reason of") with the submission or absence of resistance, means that there is no consent. This may cause consternation at what was foreseen in *R. v. Clarence*,[56] in which a husband's conviction for assault in infecting his wife with gonorrhoea was quashed. Fears were expressed that if fraud encompassed more than misrepresentation as to identity or the nature and quality of the act, then the familiar floodgates would open.

---

leave to appeal to S.C.C. refused 2 C.R.N.S. 375n.). A number of women underwent vaginal examinations by a man falsely holding himself out as a doctor. The majority said this was fraud as to the nature and quality of the act, but Laskin J.A. dissented.

54   See, *e.g., R. v. Thorne* (1952), 15 C.R. 129 (N.B. C.A.). A husband and wife were travelling from Halifax to Ottawa by train. The accused got in the lower berth and tried to have intercourse with the woman. She woke up and thought it was her husband until he spoke, when she screamed and he ran away.

55   Laskin J.A. stated in *R. v. Maurantonio*, note 53 above, that this type of deceit would be fraud for the purposes of assault but not for indecent assault, because of the old difference in wording. This was in dissent, the majority holding that it did go to the nature and quality of the examination in question.

56   (1888), 22 Q.B.D. 23.

> [E]very man . . . who knowingly gives a piece of bad money to a prostitute to procure her consent to intercourse, or who seduces a woman by representing himself to be what he is not [would be] guilty of assault, and, it seems to me, therefore, of rape.[57]

Even if this very broad approach were adopted, it might still force decisions as to culpability into the issue of whether there was a causative link between the fraud and the submission.

It is unfortunate that no legislative guidance has been provided. There may be a significant difference between, for example, misrepresenting oneself to be free from herpes, in order to induce another person to have sexual relations, and misrepresenting one's wealth or status, but no such distinctions are hinted at in section 244. *Any* fraudulent statement may therefore lead to the conclusion that the sexual activity was non-consensual.[58]

(iv) *The exercise of authority.* This is a new factor, so little guidance is available. The obvious issues are when one person can be said to be in a position of authority over another, and when that authority can be said to have been exercised.

With respect to authority, one possible analogy may be found in the rule relating to statements made under certain circumstances to persons in authority, the "confession" rule. However, there does not appear to be any clear test in that context, as the cases focus on the power to influence the prosecution[59] and are thus of little assistance here. Nor does there appear to be any settled rule as to whether the authority must exist in reality or simply in the mind of the person being influenced.[60]

One would expect the definition of authority to depend on the rationale for the rule itself but that is of limited assistance. The meaning of the word in this context, as with fraud, discussed in the previous section, will depend on the judiciary's view of the

---

57 *Ibid., per* Wills J., at 28.

58 A lesser difficulty is that the language of submission or failure to resist does not seem to fit very well with the language of fraud. It does not seem natural to say that someone submits to sexual activity by reason of fraud. However, since this is a stylistic problem across the board, whatever the meaning of fraud, I do not think that any argument could be based on it as to the scope of the concept.

59 See P.M. Williams, *Canadian Criminal Evidence* (1974), pp. 246-7.

60 *Ibid.* It would seem in this context that the position ought to be that a person who knowingly exploits another's mistaken impression that he possesses power over her is in the same position as the person who actually has the power.

scope of the morally reprehensible conduct which ought to attract the attention of the criminal law. The issue is this: when is the exploitation of power so bad as to be punishable? Case law and dictionary definitions will not be conclusive with respect to this normative issue. Nevertheless, the Oxford English Dictionary indicates that authority means, *inter alia*, the power or right to enforce obedience; the power to influence the conduct or actions of others; personal or practical influence. The possibility therefore exists that an extremely broad definition of authority will be adopted by the courts.

The term "exercise of authority" is used in section 154, dealing with the seduction of female passengers on vessels.

> Every male person who, being the owner or master of, or employed on board a vessel, engaged in the carriage of passengers for hire, seduces, or by threats or by the exercise of his authority, has illicit sexual intercourse on board the vessel with a female passenger is guilty of an indictable offence and is liable to imprisonment for two years.

This section might give us some guidance, but the range of potential offenders is very broad, including the owner or master of a vessel, or anyone employed on it. Since there are alternative ways of committing the offence, perhaps it was only intended to suggest that the owner or master is in a position of authority. The distinction between threats and the exercise of authority should be noted. This clearly indicates that the former are not necessary to establish the latter, a point which goes to the meaning of "exercise."

In any event it is safe to conclude that a ship's owner or master is in a position of authority. By analogy and on their own merits there seem to be other clear cases. Employers (including persons put in positions of authority by them), teachers, police officers, immigration officers, judges, all have power to enforce obedience and *a fortiori* the power to influence the conduct or actions of others. Husbands who insist on being the head of the household might well be in trouble here, if judged according to their view of reality. It may be easier for them to be found guilty of sexual assault than a stranger. This provision may well cover the not-unknown case of the professor who engages in sexual activity with a student. Doctor/nurse romances may become somewhat risky.

There is no doubt that this subsection should catch the most blatant cases of the exploitation of power but, in less obvious cases, it is going to be difficult to make the factual distinction between consent and submission. If a professor says to the graduate student he is supervising "Will you go to bed with me," and she says, "Yes," what are we to make of that? Is this again an invitation to judgment of the fortitude or moral standards of the victim? This is relevant again to the act of exercising authority since the professor could argue that, while he was indeed in a position of authority, he did not exercise it in any way. If someone simply has authority, knows it is influential, but neither makes a reference to it nor overtly uses it in any way, has that authority been exercised? Thus, it is not yet clear what the *actus reus* of this form of assault is. Conservative legal advice would be to refrain from sexual contact with anyone within one's power.

(v) *Implied consent.* It is trite law that consent can be either express or implied.[61] Difficulties may arise with respect to relatively minor touchings of a sexual nature. The defence may argue that such touching was impliedly consensual. Jurisprudence will have to develop on this issue.

There has been little case law in the past, possibly because indecent assault prosecutions were brought with respect to situations where it seemed unlikely that the touching could have been consensual (for example, where the stranger on a bus put his hand on the complainant's thigh, as in *R. v. Burden*[62]). While consent was a major issue with regard to rape, it was not central with respect to indecent assault, which was more analogous to assault.[63]

With a heightened awareness of the right to sexual autonomy, to which the law reform may well have contributed, and the increasing knowledge of sexual harassment, it is possible that sexual assault charges may be brought with respect to sexual touching by acquaintances and colleagues at work.[64] The paradigm of the "pat on the bottom," will have to be dealt with if

---

61 See, *e.g., Abraham v. R.* (1974), 24 C.R.N.S. 390 (Que. C.A.).

62 (1981), 25 C.R. (3d) 283 (B.C. C.A.).

63 Thus if a stranger punches one on the nose, a legal debate does not normally develop around consent. Sexual intercourse can be ambiguous, this rendering consent the crucial issue.

64 One can only speculate about what happened to these in the era of indecent assault. The literature on sexual harassment, however, reveals a reluctance to report such assaults. See, generally, C.B. Backhouse and L. Cohen, *The Secret Oppression: Sexual Harassment of Working Women* (1978) and *Sexual Harassment on the Job* (1981).

charges begin to be laid.[65] Unlike rape, which involved more complex interaction, a pat on the bottom is over in a second. There is no natural place to evince consent or the absence of it.[66]

It will be very interesting if the courts do develop the notion of implied consent. That development will tell us a great deal about "societal" views on what is supposed to be acceptable sexual behaviour. This will be very treacherous ground. A narrow doctrine may have to develop, based possibly on each particular situation, but there is surely no room for a general rule that we all consent to some level of sexual touching, no matter how prevalent it has been in the past. It is vital that consent either be expressed or implied from facts that are present in a particular context rather than any assumptions about what is acceptable.

(c) *Sexual*

This is of course the element that distinguishes assault from sexual assault. It is totally undefined in the Code,[67] yet is nonetheless of considerable significance because of the difference in maximum sentences between the assault and sexual assault offences.

The judiciary may sidestep the issue of the meaning of the term (as indeed Parliament has done) by using the approach taken in the past to the meaning of "indecent" which essentially boiled down to assertions that an assault is indecent if it is inde-

---

65 It is probably unlikely that the new offence of sexual assault will be used to tackle sexual harassment, even though it can be proceeded with summarily. If the charge is *not* used at this lower end of the spectrum, then the familiar issue of unenforced criminal law will have to be confronted.

66 It was held in *Nicholson v. State*, 656 P. 2d 1209 (1982, Alaska App.) that touching a sleeping woman on the breast was coercive even though she was momentarily stunned when she woke up and thus did not at once object.

67 In U.S. jurisdictions where similar reforms have taken place, various attempts have been made to make the offence more specific. The Florida definition is as follows: "'Sexual battery' means oral, anal or vaginal penetration by, or union with, the sexual organ of another or the anal or vaginal penetration of another by any other object; however, sexual battery shall not include acts done for bona fide medical purposes." F.S. §794.011(f). The Alaskan statute is even more specific: "'sexual contact' means (a) the intentional touching, directly or through clothing, by the defendant of the victim's genitals, anus, or female breasts; or (b) the defendant's intentionally causing the victim to touch, directly or through clothing, the defendant's or victim's genitals, anus or female breasts." A.S. 11.81.900(b)(51). For an application, see *Nicholson v. State*, note 66 above.

cent. A case which is frequently cited is *R. v. Louie Chong*.[68] "It is in each case a question of fact whether the thing which was done, in the circumstances in which it was done, was done indecently."[69] On the indecent side of the line was *R. v. Quinton*,[70] in which the accused had taken a child into the men's washroom and tried to pull down her pants. On the "decent" side of the line was *R. v. Bain*,[71] in which a man taking a photograph out of doors had pulled out the waistband of a child's swimsuit, apparently in order to adjust it.

An assault not in itself indecent may be so when coupled with intent,[72] although, as we shall see later,[73] an indecent intent was not a necessary element of indecent assault.

Our knowledge, therefore, of the meaning of indecency, is scanty in the extreme, and raises serious concerns about the uniformity of the law in its application both in the courts and in prosecutors' offices.[74] The vagueness of the term "sexual" also raises concerns about legality in that it could be argued that it does not give a clear warning in advance as to what is criminal conduct. This argument could take the form that the offence of sexual assault is unconstitutional for vagueness in that it offends section 7 of the Canadian Charter of Rights and Freedoms.[75] This section grants a right not to be deprived of life, liberty and security of the person except in accordance with the principles of fundamental justice. It might well be held that fundamental justice requires more specific notice of what behaviour the state proposes to punish as criminal. Another relevant section of the Charter is section 9, containing the right not to be arbitrarily detained or imprisoned.[76]

---

68 (1914), 32 O.L.R. 66 (C.A.).

69 *Per* Middleton J. *ibid.*, at 67.

70 [1947] S.C.R. 234.

71 (1970), 8 C.R.N.S. 99 (N.S. C.A.). The court was not satisfied that the accused had looked down the swimsuit.

72 *R. v. McKeachnie* (1975), 26 C.C.C. (2d) 317 (Ont. C.A.).

73 See the text accompanying notes 146-57, below.

74 With respect to the problem of vagueness see H. Packer, *The Limits of the Criminal Sanction* (1968), p. 316.

75 Constitution Act, 1982, as enacted by the Canada Act, 1982 (U.K.), c. 11.

76 For U.S. cases holding similar offences to be constitutional, see *State v. Olsen*, 335 N.W. 2d 433 (1983, C.A. Wisconsin) (sexual assault); *State v. Reed*, 276 S.E. 2d 313 (1981, West Virginia App.) (sexual gratification or sexual desire both plain and unambiguous on their face); *People v. Gross*, 670 P. 2d 799 (1983, Colorado) (sexual assault); *Reynolds v. State*, 664 P. 2d 621 (1983, Alaska App.) (sexual assault).

Although guidelines would be desirable, it will be difficult for the judiciary to determine what Parliament meant, if anything, by the word "sexual." The Shorter Oxford English Dictionary defines the word as relating "to the physical intercourse between the sexes or the gratification of sexual appetites." It would, however, be deeply ironic if reform, heralded as de-emphasizing the sexual nature of rape and stressing its violent quality, had the effect of focusing attention on sexuality, thus permitting some resurrection of the idea that sexual gratification is the motive behind such assaults.[77] The Canadian Law Reform Commission[78] suggested a definition of "sexual conduct" which may be helpful here: "Any touching of another with one's sexual organs... that is offensive to the sexual dignity of that person."[79] Apart from its narrowness in concentrating on touching with one's sexual organs, this is helpful in that it concentrates on effect rather than the motive of the accused. People engage in sexual assault for a wide variety of reasons, some for gratification of the sexual urge, some through a desire to humiliate and degrade, some through a desire of revenge against a sex that is perceived as having the power to deny access to sexual services.[80]

There is no doubt, and Parliament has confirmed this fact, that we distinguish in some significant way between sexual and other forms of violence. The difficulty is, of course, in pinning down the distinction. It is submitted that once it is accepted that many if not all sexual attacks are not for what is normally thought of as sexual gratification at all, some other distinguishing feature must be determined. It may be helpful to think in terms of particular offence to bodily dignity and integrity because of a *resemblance* to what is thought of as sexual. In other words, a touching might be considered sexual if it is the type of touching which in a non-assault situation might be related to sex. A violent act which bears some resemblance to those acts which society thinks of as providing sexual gratification is offensive to human dignity

---

77 Concern was expressed by the Hon. Bill Janis in the debates on the second reading of Bill C-53 about undue emphasis on the sexual nature of the offence because of the adjective sexual. Parl. Debs. H.C., Vol. XIII, 17 Dec. 1981, at 14192.

78 *Working Paper on Sexual Offences*, No. 22 (1978).

79 *Ibid.*, p. 49.

80 For a sense of the research, see W.L. Marshall, "The Classification of Sexual Aggressives and Their Associated Demographic, Social, Developmental and Psychological Features" in S.N. Verdun-Jones and A.A. Keltner, eds., *Sexual Aggression and the Law* (1983).

because it is important for one to be free to decide with whom one is going to be intimate.

The advantage of the resemblance approach is that it avoids the trap of debating whether, to give an example, the accused touched the complainant's breasts because that gave him sexual gratification or because he wanted to humiliate her by reminding her of a subordinate, female, objectified status. Whatever his reasons, he has done something which we have a right to retain in the sphere of private, consensual sexual activity.

Whatever the meaning of "sexual," it seems very likely that the courts will apply an objective test (as with indecency) and not focus on the subjective view of either the accused or the complainant. It also seems likely that most cases will be unproblematic, involving the touching of genitals or breasts, kissing, any touching accompanied by words relating to sex. But unclear cases will arise especially at the least serious end of the spectrum. Prosecutors may prefer to use a charge of assault, or accept a guilty plea to assault, rather than take a borderline case to court.

2. THE MENS REA OF SEXUAL ASSAULT

The mental element or *mens rea* of sexual assault can be broken down into two obvious elements and one contentious one. They will be discussed in the same order as their equivalent elements in the preceding sections on the *actus reus*.

(a) *The Intentional Application of Force*

Section 244(1) states explicitly that the accused must apply force "intentionally." The other forms of assault do not contain any *mens rea* words, but the normal presumption applies that *mens rea* is required.[81] It is trite law to say that, in the absence of any indication to the contrary, the *mens rea* of the first element of assault is the intentional or reckless doing of the prohibited act, for example, the intention to cause the apprehension of the application of force, or recklessness whether such apprehension be caused.[82] The word "intentionally" may be an indication to the contrary, showing that the form of assault involving the applica-

---

81 See *R. v. Rees*, [1956] S.C.R. 640; *Beaver v. R.*, [1957] S.C.R. 531.
82 See J.C. Smith and B. Hogan, *Criminal Law*, 4th ed. (1978) p. 353, citing *R. v. Venna*, [1976] Q.B. 421 (C.A.).

tion of force cannot be committed recklessly.[83] Thus, if A throws something out of a window, not intending to hit anyone, but having thought of the possibility, A would not be guilty of assault. This aspect of the *mens rea* is not an issue in practical terms.

(b) *Mistaken Belief in Consent*

It is clear that the accused had the requisite *mens rea* where he knew the victim was not consenting, or was reckless as to that fact.[84] One of the most contentious issues with respect to reform of this area of law was whether the accused should also be guilty where he honestly but unreasonably believed the victim was consenting. In other words, should there be a form of negligent sexual assault? Still another way of stating the issue is whether the question should be "did this man believe she was consenting?"—a subjective test—or "would any reasonable person have thought she was consenting?"—an objective test.

Section 244(4) addresses this issue, but sits rather uncomfortably on the fence. A mistaken belief in consent, if rarely raised, is the most significant *mens rea* defence and it is discussed in some detail here. Some background is necessary before addressing the new legislative provision. The major feature of the background is the Supreme Court of Canada decision in *Pappajohn v. R.*[85] It is vital to put *Pappajohn* in the context of the evolving Canadian position in the objective/subjective debate on *mens rea* and fault in criminal law generally.

It is only relatively recent that, in Canada, those who support a subjective test of any mental element have begun to gain the upper hand. Early English cases, such as the much-cited case of *R. v. Tolson*,[86] indicated in *dicta* that a mistake of fact must be honest and reasonable.[87] The subjective view that the belief need

---

83 This is the position taken by Professor Colvin in his instructive and carefully reasoned article, "Recklessness and Criminal Negligence" (1982), 32 U. of T.L.J. 345. He speculates, at 349, that the reason was "the variable draftsmanship of an era before attention was focused on the concept of recklessness." But see *R. v. Lafontaine* (1979), 9 C.R. (3d) 263 (Que. S.C.). For an example of the narrowing effect of a similar *mens rea* word "wilfully", see *R. v. Buzzanga* (1979), 25 O.R. (2d) 705 (C.A.).

84 For a simple example of recklessness *vis-à-vis* consent, see *R. v. P.* (1976), 32 C.C.C. (2d) 400 (Ont. H.C.).

85 [1980] 2 S.C.R. 120.

86 (1889), 23 Q.B.D. 168.

87 *Tolson* was a bigamy case, and the rule can still be found in statutory form in Canada. See s. 254(2)(a).

only be honest was taken in *Wilson v. Inyang*[88] in 1951. This view proved to be highly influential in Canada and was adopted in the leading Supreme Court of Canada cases of *Rees*,[89] *Beaver*[90] and, most recently, in *Pappajohn*[91] itself.

Nevertheless, the subjectivists cannot afford to be complacent. The vast majority of criminal and quasi-criminal offences in Canada are strict liability offences[92] governed by *R. v. Sault Ste-Marie*[93] and are therefore crimes of negligence with the onus of disproving fault on the accused. There are express crimes of negligence in the Code itself (for example, the careless use or storage of a firearm in section 84(2)), as well as in provincial statutes, careless driving in its various forms being the classic example.[94] Also to be noted is the lower courts' well-documented insistence[95] on applying an objective test to the concept of criminal negligence in spite of the views of the Supreme Court of Canada in *O'Grady v. Sparling*[96] and *LeBlanc v. R.*[97]

Further, objective tests are well-established in the context of defences in the Code, as it is a commonplace that people who defend themselves[98] and people who are provoked,[99] are judged against the standard of the reasonable person.[100]

The pinnacle of the objective approach in Canada can also be

---

88 [1951] 2 K.B. 799.

89 Note 81 above.

90 *Ibid.*

91 Note 85 above.

92 See the Law Reform Commission, Working Paper No. 2, *The Meaning of Guilt, Strict Liability*, p. 10.

93 [1978] 2 S.C.R. 1299.

94 See, *e.g.*, the Motor Vehicle Act, R.S.N.S. 1967, c. 191, s. 90 [am. 1970-71, c. 51].

95 See E. Colvin, "Recklessness and Criminal Negligence" (1982), 32 U. of T.L.J. 345 at 349-56. See also D. Stuart, *Canadian Criminal Law* (1982), pp. 176-179.

96 [1960] S.C.R. 804.

97 [1977] 1 S.C.R. 339. Note, however, that Dickson J., in dissent, stated, at 366, that "the *mens rea* of criminal negligence is determined by an objective standard." The self-confessed proponent of "subjective orthodoxy" and master of rigorous conceptual thought has not been totally negative about culpability based on negligence, even with respect to serious crimes.

98 See ss. 34 and 35.

99 Section 215.

100 The suggestion is not being made that issues of justification should *necessarily* be approached in the same way as issues relating to the elements of an offence. See, generally, on this point, G. Fletcher, *Rethinking Criminal Law* (1978), especially at pp. 575-9. The point is simply that anyone who supports a subjective approach with respect to sexual assault has to be prepared to discard or defend objective tests in other areas.

found in the Code, since responsibility for murder, our most serious crime, can be grounded in an objective test according to section 212(c). If one were therefore to represent the dividing line between *mens rea* crimes and crimes of negligence,[101] it would look something like this:

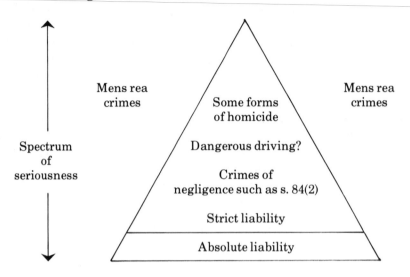

It can be seen at once that offences utilising an objective test go right up through the spectrum of seriousness to the very top. The issue that was confronted (although it did not have to be) in *Pappajohn* was, with respect to the factor of consent, whether to place rape inside or outside the pyramid of objective liability. The court decided on a subjective test, with an acknowledgement of the evidentiary relevance of the reasonableness of the belief. It was influenced by the House of Lords decision in *D.P.P. v. Morgan*,[102] which opted for a subjective test in rape trials, but there is no doubt that there was a *choice of analogies* within the Canadian criminal justice system. The failure to discuss and

---

101 I put it this way simply for convenience of exposition. I recognise the argument that negligence is a form of *mens rea*.

102 [1976] A.C. 182. It is profoundly interesting, on a political as well as a theoretical level, that the House of Lords has since departed from a pure subjective approach in *R. v. Laurence*, [1981] 1 All E.R. 974 (reckless driving), and *R. v. Caldwell*, [1981] 1 All E.R. 961 (criminal damage).

justify that choice has been satisfyingly criticised[103] as well as defended.[104] Suffice it to say here that, although the position is now codified, the new provision muddies the waters in the ongoing debate about culpability. Section 244(4) states as follows:

> Where an accused alleges that he believed that the complainant consented to the conduct that is the subject matter of the charge, a judge, if satisfied that there is sufficient evidence and that, if believed by the jury, the evidence would constitute a defence shall instruct the jury, when reviewing all the evidence relating to the determination of the honesty of the accused's belief, to consider the presence or absence of reasonable grounds for that belief.

As some commentators have suggested, this may be a codification of the *Pappajohn* approach,[105] and probably will be criticised as such.[106] The other view is that the provision is open to either interpretation, and indeed the subsection is silent as to the impact of a finding that the belief was not based on reasonable grounds. It is difficult for lawyers already familiar with *Pappajohn* to know how juries will construe such a direction, although judges sitting alone may well tend to read the provision through *Pappajohn* spectacles.

It is doubtful whether the underlying culpability issue was really confronted prior to this legislative reform. Vague terminology has been utilised with something for both camps, but which will probably be construed ultimately as continuing the subjective test. The debate may die down for a while,[107] but it is important to examine critically the choice (albeit a rather confusing one) made

---

103 T. Pickard, "Harsh Words on Pappajohn" (1980), 30 U. of T.L.J. 415.

104 D. Stuart, *Canadian Criminal Law* (1982), pp. 237-47. But even if one agrees with the result, surely we are entitled to know why, *e.g.*, Dickson J. thinks it is justifiable to punish negligent killing but not negligent rape.

105 See, *e.g.*, G. Parker, "The 'New' Sexual Offences" (1983), 31 C.R. (3d) 317 at 320-1. "The most difficult new provision is s. 244(4), which is meant to codify the rule in *Pappajohn*.... Or is it meant to change that rule? ... [There] seems to be no change in the law, but it is possible that the drafters thought they were changing the law."

106 For example, the Toronto Area Caucus of Women and the Law indicated in its Joint Statement on Bill C-53 that "at a minimum, the jury must be instructed that the defence of 'honest belief' must be based on honest *and* reasonable grounds, and that a mere 'honest belief' is not sufficient defence."

107 Although Svend Robinson has introduced a Private Member's Bill, which would add the following words to s. 244(4), "and where the accused establishes this belief was based upon reasonable grounds, he shall be found not guilty." Bill C-685, s. 1. Not only would this introduce an objective test, it would also reverse the onus of proof.

by Parliament. What follows is an attempt to state what the issue is, the range of possible responses, and an opinion on the policy issue involved.

The issue is a normative one of what is sufficiently culpable to be made criminal in the context of sexual assault.[108] It is submitted that there are no value-free responses to this question. It is certainly not the case that proponents of the subjective approach occupy a self-justifying value-free ground, while proponents of some other basis of culpability have the onus of justifying their position. Subjectivists are asserting that people with *mens rea* in the subjective sense deserve to be punished, and others do not, so evidently they are asserting a theory of culpability. It is not one with a long tradition to support it (and even if it were, it would still require justification on its own merits) and it is certainly not pervasive in our criminal system. Hence it does not derive much, if any, strength from the value of consistency.[109] It seems important to state this initially as, in spite of Fletcher's valiant attempt to put subjectivists on the defensive, they stubbornly refuse to accept that position.[110]

One must therefore insist that we all have the intellectual obligation to explain why we think X is criminally culpable[111] and Y is not.[112] This will be particularly difficult for those who accept

---

108 Professor Stuart seems to suggest that there is the subjective *mens rea* approach, and that there are alternative normative approaches. Surely all questions relating to criminal responsibility are normative in nature. In any event this is how I mean the term.

109 One is surprised however by the *claim* that a subjectivist approach holds out hope for consistency. See E. Colvin, "Recklessness and Criminal Negligence" (1982), 32 U. of T.L.J. 345 at 369. Would it not hold out more hope for the orderly development of the criminal law if we acknowledged reality, *i.e.*, that sometimes we use an objective test and sometimes a subjective test and that the real issue is how to classify the elements of each offence. This would be feasible unless one rejects all punishment based on negligence.

110 G. Fletcher in "The Theory of Criminal Negligence: A Comparative Analysis" (1971), 119 U. Of Pa. L.R. 401 at 423, asserts that his analysis forces "the case against punishing negligence into a defensive posture." *Cf.* Stuart, *Canadian Criminal Law* (1982), p. 187, "arguments in favour of the objective standard are persuasive but not overwhelming."

111 Of course one may think behaviour culpable but not "bad enough" to be deserving of any criminal sanction.

112 Stuart indeed, note 110 above, pp. 184-7, states the arguments that convince him to favour the subjective approach, and has accepted a degree of objective liability. See "The Need to Codify Clear, Realistic and Honest Measures of *Mens Rea*" (1973), 15 C.L.Q. 160.

strict liability and negligence offences and who are prepared to defend the mistake of law barricades,[113] and who try to support the subjective position in sexual assault cases in isolation.

There is a considerable and complex range of responses to the culpability issue. It is only possible to characterise them superficially here, but hopefully a sense of the on-going debate can be conveyed. The spectrum of positions could range, at least in theory, from absolute liability[114] through support for a uniform totally objective approach[115] (which would mean here that any mistake would have to be reasonable) to the argument that punishment for negligence is never justified.[116] Most commentators, however, take up a position on the spectrum somewhere between objective and subjective fault.

A number of outstanding arguments have been made that negligence (in the sense of making an unreasonable mistake in this context) can in some circumstances be viewed as culpable in itself, and that it is justifiable to punish such negligence so long as the external standard of reasonableness is individualized to take into account the individual's capacity to take care. The major offensive against the subjective approach was launched by Hart in his well-known essay "Negligence, *Mens Rea* and Criminal Responsibility."[117] He argued that to say that someone acted negligently is not simply a description, meaning that his mind was a blank (and thus free of any culpable element) but it is to make a judgmental statement that he failed to comply with a

---

113 See Fletcher, note 110 above, at 420-3.

114 As in s. 146(1) which creates absolute liability with respect to the age factor in the offence of sexual intercourse with a female under 14. This possibility is not canvassed here as it seems an extreme position to suggest punishment for sexual assault in the absence of fault.

115 Perhaps the closest to this position can be found in O.W. Holmes, *The Common Law* (1881), pp. 51 *et seq.*, though many people will defend the use of an objective test sometimes, as in the Code. The presumption of intent would have the same effect as a uniform objective test. See also H. Wechsler and J. Michael, "A Rationale of the Law of Homicide" (1937), 37 Col. L. Rev. 701, where deterrence is discussed as a justification for the punishment of negligent homicide.

116 A number of leading academics have argued in favour of the subjective approach. See J. Hall, "Negligent Behaviour should be Excluded from Penal Liability" (1963), 63 Col. L. Rev 632; J.W.C. Turner, "The Mental Element of Crimes at Common Law" in D. Seaborne Davies, *et al.*, eds., *The Modern Approach to Criminal Law* (1945), at 195; Glanville Williams, *Criminal Law: The General Part*, 2nd ed. (1961), pp. 122-4.

117 *Punishment and Responsibility, Essays in the Philosophy of Law* (1968).

particular standard of conduct. He suggested that the objective/ subjective terminology is not helpful and that rather we should think in terms of an "invariant" standard of care or "individualized conditions of responsibility."

> (i) Did the accused fail to take those precautions which any reasonable man with normal capacities would in the circumstances have taken?
> (ii) Could the accused, given his mental and physical capacities, have taken those precautions?[118]

In arguing against the idea that an individual is only culpable if the necessary thought came into his or her mind, Hart asks the important question of why we would assume that persons can control their actions once they have thought, but not assume likewise that they can, and should, control their thoughts.

> Only a theory of mental operations like attending to, or thinking about or examining a situation are somehow, "there or not there," and so utterly outside our control, can lead to a theory that we are never responsible, if like the signalman who forgets to pull the signal, we fail to think or remember. And this theory of the uncontrollable character of mental operations would, of course, be fatal to responsibility for even the most cold-blooded deliberate action. . . . For just as the signalman might say "My mind was a blank" or "I just forgot" . . . so the cold-blooded murderer might say "I just decided to kill; I couldn't help deciding."[119]

A rapist cannot say: "I took it into my head to rape her; I couldn't help it," since our response is "But you *ought* to have helped it." The question therefore becomes why he should be able to say: "It never occurred to me that she was not consenting; I can't control my thoughts." Should we not respond likewise "But you *ought* to have thought about it?"

This is similar to the approach taken by Professor Toni Pickard in her influential article on mistake of fact in rape cases.[120] She likewise argues for an "objective" but individualised approach, on the basis that it is easy to take care (that is, think about consent) in the sexual context, and the risk of harm if one does not do so is very great.

In contrast to this type of approach is that of Professor Colvin who argues that "recklessness" is a sufficiently elastic concept to encompass awareness of an objectively defined risk and

---

118 *Ibid.*, p. 154.
119 *Ibid.*, p. 151.
120 "Culpable Mistakes and Rape: Relating Mens Rea to the Crime" (1980), 30 U. of T.L.J. 75.

unutilised experience as well as consciousness of risk. This, combined with some loosening of the contemporaneity of *actus reus* and *mens rea* doctrine, would provide a broad enough concept to cover all or most cases covered by an objective approach.

Another influential writer in this field is George Fletcher, who argues for a limited culpability based on negligence (where one has failed to respond to circumstances that normally trigger one's sensibilities) in his article entitled "The Theory of Criminal Negligence: A Comparative Analysis."[121] In the context of rape he has suggested that consent is a justificatory factor, which only operates if the accused was free of fault,[122] that is, the definition of rape is sexual penetration "with consent functioning as a ground for regarding the sexual act as a shared expression of love rather than an invasion of bodily integrity."[123]

A number of interesting ideas can be extracted from the literature, although it is not clear that Fletcher's theory is particularly helpful since the issue surely still boils down to what is regarded as "fault" and when punishment is justified. Probably everyone would agree that a man who negligently commits sexual assault is at fault, but whether he is "bad enough" to be punished is the issue. This does not seem to be resolvable philosophically (although analysis can help to clear away irrational and inconsistent arguments and unwarranted assumptions) but rather is an issue for any society to resolve at any particular time.[124] Thus the decision is essentially the same as the decision, for example, to punish sexual touching submitted to because of the exercise of authority. The decision would no more threaten the internal struc-

---

121 (1971), 119 U. of Pa. L. Rev. 401. He is superb at separating conceptional from policy issues, as he indicates is his aim.
122 *Rethinking Criminal Law* (1978). An analogy could be drawn to the Supreme Court decision in *R. v. Kundeus*, [1976] 2 S.C.R. 272, in which it was arguably decided that a mistake of fact argument will not work, if, on the facts as the accused believed them to be, he would have been guilty of some other criminal offence. An even closer analogy is to self-defence, which cannot be argued if the accused has made an unreasonable mistake.
123 *Rethinking Criminal Law, ibid.*, p. 705. Stuart reads this to mean that sex with prostitutes would be rape. What would be so surprising about that? However, Fletcher does seem to suggest that only consent motivated by love would be consent. This appeals to me, but I think that the criminal law would be going too far to make sex in loveless marriages criminal.
124 Such resolution no doubt reflecting the interests of whatever group is dominant at that particular time, whether the exercise is one of simple self-protection or tactical flexibility.

ture of our criminal justice system than the decision to punish the careless storage of firearms or dangerous driving. We will still have a conceptual framework within which to organise our law of crimes.

Secondly, there seems to be considerable agreement that an accused person should not be judged beyond his or her capacities. This is central to the issues of fairness and justification for punishment. It seems fair to punish for what the accused could have done but did not, and this may have some deterrent and educational effect. One has to recognise, however, the serious line-drawing problem with respect to the characteristics of the accused that ought to be taken into account.[125]

Thirdly, there is some tendency to suggest that the subjective versus objective argument is a semantic one that makes little difference in practice.[126] There may be some truth in this, although an objective approach would have made a difference in *R. v. Cogan; R. v. Leak.*[127] It would also have made a difference at the trial stage in *R. v. Sansregret.*[128] The accused had broken into the victim's home, taken a butcher's knife from the kitchen and entered her bedroom, where she was calling the police. He forced

---

125 A discussion of this issue is not appropriate here. It is, however, a question that will have to be addressed (perhaps in the context of a decision whether and to what extent to follow *R. v. Camplin*, [1978] A.C. 705 (H.L.)) across the board, wherever objective tests are used.

126 The issue is "practically unimportant," according to Dickson J. in *Pappajohn v. R.*, [1980] 2 S.C.R. 120 at 156. See also J. Scutt "The Australian Aftermath of *D.P.P. v. Morgan*" (1977), 25 Chitty's L.J. 289 at 296. She suggests, in effect, that the jury may share the same "unreasonable" viewpoint of the accused so, until misconceptions of female roles and sexuality are altered, an objective test would make little difference.

127 [1976] Q.B. 217 (C.A.). A husband whose wife was afraid of him, for very good reason, invited a friend to have intercourse with her. He did so, the wife sobbing all the time. A jury found that he believed, unreasonably, that she was consenting, and a conviction was therefore quashed.

128 (1983), 34 C.R. 162 (Man Co. Ct.); reversed 37 C.R. (3d) 45 (Man. C.A.). The reasoning of the majority of the Court of Appeal is obscure and verges on the rejection of the findings of fact at the trial. Matas J.A. said there was no "air of reality" to the mistake defence in the circumstances and seemed to reject the applicability of the defence where the accused terrorized the victim prior to her pretence of consent. Huband J.A. found recklessness with respect to the genuineness of the consent, even though the trial judge had found a genuine belief in consent. Philp J.A., dissenting, held that, on the basis of the trial judge's findings of fact, *Pappajohn* required an acquittal. In spite of the eventual conviction of the accused, the facts of the case illustrate a real difficulty arising out of the reasoning in *Pappajohn*.

her to strip and tied her hands. She was absolutely terrified, as the judge later held. The accused hit her on the mouth, stabbed the walls and threatened to cut her cat in two. They then had intercourse. The judge found that he was motivated by jealousy stemming from his previous relationship with the complainant, but that he honestly believed she consented to intercourse, even though no "rational person . . . could possibly have believed that the complainant's responses were genuine and were induced by anything other than fear."[129] The accused was acquitted, the judge stating that he "saw what he wanted to see, heard what he wanted to hear, believed what he wanted to believe."[130]

These cases are significant, since one type of rapist has been discovered to be the type of person who imagines the victim to be a willing participant. Cohen, *et al.*, describe the rapist who uses violence to excite himself and projects the sadistic quality of the sexual experience onto the victim. Her struggling is seen as her own excitement: "'Women like to get roughed up, they enjoy a good fight.' This belief is maintained even when the victim is literally fighting for her life."[131] It may also happen that the rapist forces the victim to express desire for sexual activity, as in *Sansregret* itself. The *Pappajohn* case holds open the door to the acquittal of such persons.

There is no way of knowing how a substantive rule of this kind has an impact on reporting rates or police activity and prosecutorial discretion. It is particularly difficult to assess the impact in sexual assault cases since the decision-maker may or may not share the assaulter's view of the significance of certain types of behaviour such as sobbing, hitch-hiking, saying no and drinking late at night.[132] I suppose the safest thing to assume is that very little is known about the possible repercussions of choosing a subjective test (or any formulation thereof) over an objective test

---

129 34 C.R. at 167.
130 It may have been crucial that the complainant testified as to his honest belief, even though she had not consented, the judge accepting, at 167, that she "simply acquiesced in the accused's demands, and that only to a degree that was necessary to prevent a recurrence of the earlier rage of violence."
131 "The Psychology of Rapists" in D. Chappell, R. Geis, and G. Geis, eds., *Forcible Rape* (1977), pp. 307-8.
132 For a discussion of the communication gap between the sexes and a proposal that promotes the interest in improving effective inter-gender communication, see R.D. Wiener, "Shifting the Communication Burden: A Meaningful Consent Standard in Rape" (1983), 6 Harv. Women's L.J. 143.

(or any formulation thereof), so that assertions that the issue is of no practical significance are not helpful.

Lastly, the question seems to involve classification rather than culpability once one accepts that negligence constitutes fault in some sense. One way of dealing with this issue would have been to construct a hierarchy of offences based on the nature of the fault of the accused. There may be considerable consensus that negligent sexual assault is not as serious as intentional sexual assault, and much of the support for the subjectivist position might disappear if there were an offence of negligent sexual assault, resembling careless driving or negligent killing.

In conclusion, it is submitted that sexual activity may be regarded as an activity, somewhat like driving, with significant benefits if engaged in carefully, but carrying risks of very considerable harm if engaged in carelessly. The risks of misunderstandings are considerable and well-known, just as the risks of driving are, so it does not seem to be outrageous for the law to say "If you wish to engage in this activity, take care that you do not cause harm." In other words, there ought to be a duty to think, insofar as one has the capacity to do so. It remains to be seen what the judiciary will make of the new formula in section 244(4).

This new legislative attempt to tackle the issue of mistaken consent raises several problems of interpretation. First, an evidentiary issue may arise over the meaning of the words "if believed by the jury" since the judge must be satisfied that the evidence of belief would be accepted by the jury. The usual approach to proof in criminal law is, of course, to give the accused the benefit of any reasonable doubt. Thus, prior to the passage of this legislation, if a jury had a reasonable doubt about an accused's belief, then he was entitled to be acquitted. In other words, the jury did not have to believe in his belief, but simply not be sure that they disbelieved in it. The new wording hints, although it does not exactly say so, that a claim of a mistaken belief will only be a defence "if believed by the jury." Thus if the jurors thought "this might well be true, but we are not sure," the accused should still be convicted. It seems unlikely that such a significant change in the normal standard of proof would be made by implication. Yet one must assume that these words carry some meaning and that the intention of Parliament was to say something more than that the judge had to be satisfied that the evidence could constitute a defence, the normal threshold test.[133]

---

133 The wording seems to come from *Pappajohn*, note 126 above, since Dickson J.

A second "belief" problem: the subsection refers to the claim that the accused "believed" the complainant consented. Does this mean that the mistake of fact defence will only be possible where the accused held a positive belief in consent, as opposed to the case of total absence of thought about the matter? This may well be rare[134] but it does seem conceivable that an individual might be so intent on his own goal that the viewpoint of the other individual involved would not arise for consideration at all. This is particularly feasible in cases of relatively minor sexual assaults, since people may well act on the basis of unconscious assumptions.

A number of commentators have suggested that the non-thinking actor can be classified as reckless. Glanville Williams makes the assertion that "[s]imple ignorance is not enough to displace recklessness."[135] Likewise Mewett suggests that failure to direct one's mind to the issue of consent can be classed as recklessness.[136] Neither seems to explain, in any satisfying way, the justification for this position.

It is clear that the accused can fall into one of four categories:

(1) He believed she was consenting; he is governed by section 244(4).
(2) He never thought about the matter at all; this seems a practical possibility with simple assaults but increasingly less likely as the victim becomes less of a passive participant in the event.
(3) He believed she was not consenting; he is guilty as he has the purest form of *mens rea* possible.
(4) He thought she might not be consenting but proceeded anyway; he is guilty since he was reckless, on conventional principles.

---

speaks in terms of the unlikelihood of the jury believing that an unreasonable mistake was made. Naturally, judges in *Pappajohn* were not writing as legislative draftsmen.

134 As suggested by Pickard, "Culpable Mistakes and Rape: Relating Mens Rea to the Crime" (1980), 30 U. of T.L.J. 75 at 77.

135 *Criminal Law: The General Part*, 2nd ed. (1961), p. 152. This becomes "simple ignorance need not negative recklessness, because a person who acts without information on a subject can in appropriate circumstances be held to be reckless," in *Textbook of Criminal Law* (1978), p. 75. For comment on what seems like a surprising view, see Pickard, note 134 above, at 96-7, and Stuart, *Canadian Criminal Law* (1982), 232-3.

136 "The Reckless Rape" (1975-76), 18 Crim. L. Q. 418; see also E. Colvin, "Recklessness and Criminal Negligence" (1982), 32 U. of T.L.J. 345 at 368.

It does not seem possible to classify category 2 simply by the application of a theoretical framework, although perhaps subjectivists, *pace* Glanville Wiliams, would classify 2 along with 1. The question seems, rather, is 2 more like 1 than 3 and 4 from the perspective of relative seriousness? It is suggested that 2 seems more analogous to 4. The accused in case 4 is indifferent to the viewpoint of the particular victim. In case 2 he is indifferent to the viewpoints of others in general. This seems qualitatively different from case 1 where the accused at least came to some conclusion on the matter which justified his action as far as he was concerned. Since all sexual acts are either consensual or non-consensual, a person who engaged in such activity without considering that quality could be said to be reckless. However, it is difficult to suggest that he was consciously taking a risk that never entered his head, so one would have to acknowledge a broadening of the conventional legal meaning of the term reckless.

The principle *inclusio unius exclusio alterius* suggests that the reference to belief in section 244(4) would exclude ignorance from the ambit of the defence. However, the subsection does not purport to be a statement of the defence, simply a procedural provision. In addition, statutory references to any *mens rea* argument have not historically meant that all other normal *mens rea* arguments are excluded by implication. Hence there does not seem to be any obvious solution to the ignorance issue.[137] From a tactical defence perspective, it would seem safer to argue a belief in consent, unless section 244(4) is construed to attach more costs than benefits to this line of defence. At that point there might be some advantage to arguing ignorance as negating *mens rea* and thus to escape any restrictions imposed by the subsection.

(c) *Intoxication*

It seems convenient here to deal with the issue of intoxication,[138] which is often referred to as a defence, but is more properly

---

137 One writer has suggested that we abandon frustrating attempts to think of consent, whether absence of consent was manifest, and how the accused perceived the behaviour of the victim, and substitute a test of whether the victim overtly consented. This would have the effect of criminalizing failure to ensure consent and would, among other things, do away with any problem of the ignorant rapist. See R.D. Wiener, "Shifting the Communication Burden: A Meaningful Consent Standard in Rape" (1983), 6 Harv. Women's L.J. 143.
138 I mean by intoxication, unless otherwise stated, the voluntary use of alcohol or drugs. Non-self-induced or involuntary intoxication is not subjected to the

an argument that the Crown has not proved the *mens rea* of the crime in question. The most likely way in which the argument would arise here is that the accused was not aware of the absence of consent because he was under the influence of alcohol or a drug at the relevant time.

Could such an argument be made with respect to sexual assault? The short answer appears to be no. The slightly longer answer is that the Supreme Court of Canada in *Leary v. R.*[139] decided that intoxication was not a defence to the charge of rape. The offence of sexual assault has, in essence, the same basic structure, so it seems certain that *Leary* will be applied to sexual assault.[140] Further, the analogy to assault is now even clearer with the change from rape to sexual assault, and intoxication has never been accepted as a defence to assault.[141] It seems fruitless to debate the matter further at this stage of our legal development, although two points should be made.

First, if the courts do apply *Leary* and *Pappajohn*, as seems likely, the contrast between the decisions will continue to be extreme. The only justification for the application of *Leary* would be that intoxication is culpable in itself. A judiciary committed to the orderly development of doctrine in the public interest would feel the responsibility of explaining how intoxication can be distinguished from the negligent formulation of belief in consent as a reason for denying a particular avenue of defence for the accused. The oddity in the law becomes more evident when one considers that alcohol may provide the reason why an unreasonable belief in consent was developed in many cases. The drunken unreasonable person would have no defence while the sober

---

same process of limitation on pragmatic grounds as is the voluntary consumption of alcohol or drugs. Thus the courts have been prepared to consider this in the normal way, but whether in relation to the *actus reus* or *mens rea* is not at all clear. See, *e.g., R. v. King*, [1962] S.C.R. 746, *R. v. Saxon*, [1975] 4 W.W.R. 346 (Alta. C.A.). It seems that the courts use an objective test of whether the accused ought to have known of the possible effects of the substance in question.

139 [1978] 1 S.C.R. 29.

140 The doctrinal objection to this is set out in Mr. Justice Dickson's dissenting judgment in *Leary*, already recognised as a classic. See also A.D. Gold, "An Untrimmed Beard: The Law of Intoxication as a Defence to a Criminal Charge" (1977), 19 C.L.Q. 34; S.M. Beck and G.E. Parker, "Th ˈntoxicated Offender—A Problem of Responsibility" (1966), 44 Can. Bar Rev. 563; P.J. Connelly, "Drunkenness and Mistake of Fact: *Pappajohn v. The Queen; Swietlinski v. The Queen*" (1981), 24 C.L.Q. 49.

141 *R. v. George*, [1960] S.C.R. 871.

unreasonable person would. Of course, it may be possible for a defence counsel to argue mistake of fact while denying that mistake had anything to do with the intoxication of his or her client.

Secondly, it seems certain too that the decision in *Swietlinski v. R.*,[142] will be applied in the context of sexual assault, since all forms of it are included in the list of constructive murder offences in section 213. Thus, if the victim dies in circumstances which satisfy the provisions of section 213, intoxication will be a defence, even though a specific intent (in its traditional guise of a purposeful element) is not present.

Although the refusal to recognise intoxication as a defence (except to "specific intent" crimes) is controversial, there may indeed be a justification. Research suggests that, even while intoxicated, men are still able to tell that a woman is not consenting. Professor Marshall of the Psychology Department of Queens University has described his findings as indicating that, while normal males show greater sexual arousal to forced sex when intoxicated than when sober, rapists and intoxicated males recognise the inappropriateness of their arousal and can prevent themselves, if they wish, from becoming aroused.[143]

An interesting point is that the intoxication of the *victim* is relevant to the exercise of prosecutorial discretion. Clark and Lewis, in their Toronto study,[144] found a one hundred percent correlation between the classification that a report of rape was "unfounded" and the police perception that the victim was drunk.[145] So if the victim and the accused have both been drinking, either separately or together, the accused will not have a defence, but he may well never become an accused in the first place.

(d) A "Sexual" Intent?

The basic issue here is whether the *mens rea* of sexual assault differs in any way from that of assault. Is there an extra mental element to mirror the extra sexual element in the *actus reus*?

---

142 [1980] 2 S.C.R. 956.
143 "The Classification of Sexual Aggressives and Their Associated Demograpic, Social, Developmental and Psychological Features" in S.N. Verdun-Jones and A.A. Keltner, eds., *Sexual Aggression* (1983), p. 9.
144 Reported in *Rape: The Price of Coercive Sexuality* (1977).
145 *Ibid.*, pp. 87-9. See the table at p. 88.

With respect to indecent assault, Laskin J.A., as he then was, suggested that an extra mental element does exist:

> There is a double mental element involved in this offence; there is the intentional factor of assault as such and the additional factor to establish indecency.[146]

However, the overwhelming weight of authority points in the other direction, indicating that an "indecent" intent was unnecessary, although it might render a common assault indecent. *R. v. Resener*[147] indicates that the *mens rea* of indecent assault was the intent to do an act which could be objectively described as indecent. Likewise the Nova Scotia Supreme Court (Appeal Division) has delivered the following *dicta* in *R. v. Rhynard*.[148]

> The authorities defining indecent assault do not suggest that an intention to do an indecent act is an essential ingredient of the crime. . . . It is the circumstances under which the assault is committed that make it indecent.[149]

The matter was discussed in some detail by the Supreme Court of Canada in *Swietlinski v. R.*,[150] which seems likely to influence the issue considerably.

> The law has been settled that an indecent assault is an assault that is committed in circumstances of indecency. . . . What acts are indecent and what circumstances will have that character are questions of fact that will have to be decided in each case, but the determination of those questions will depend upon an objective view of the facts and circumstances . . . and not upon the mental state of the accused.[151]

The courts, when confronted with the issue of intent in the context of sexual assault, may simply follow the well-established indecent assault approach, or take the opportunity to make a fresh start and examine the question from a normative perspective. Interestingly enough, this may present the opportunity to develop an analysis which could provide some assistance with the perennial problem of the mental element in the offence of dangerous driving.

---

146 In dissent in *R. v. Maurantonio*, [1968] 1 O.R. 145 at 149 (C.A.).
147 (1968), 4 C.R.N.S. 64 (B.C. C.A.).
148 (1980), 41 N.S.R. (2d) 104 (C.A.).
149 *Ibid.*, at 109.
150 [1980] 2 S.C.R. 956.
151 *Ibid.*, at 968, *per* McIntyre J., speaking for the court. The authority of these *dicta* may well be weakened by the actual decision in the case, that murder committed in the course of an indecent assault is a specific intent crime, in spite of the fact that the accused was charged under s. 213(d).

It is submitted here that it would be unfortunate if the issue were categorised as one of whether sexual assault is a crime of specific intent. There is clearly no purposive element required and the classification is not a useful one anyway, serving merely to present an apparent rationale for more pragmatic classifications. The real issue here relates to all crimes where the Crown has to prove that the accused did something which has a particular quality. Here the Crown must prove assault with a sexual quality. With respect to dangerous driving, there must be driving with the quality of dangerousness. The question then becomes—does the Crown have to establish any mental element with respect to that quality? Putting the question in this way does not, of course, provide an answer, but it sets the normative issue clearly and in isolation.

Are there any factors which would point in one direction rather than the other? One is the extent of the maximum penalties involved, which are much greater in the case of sexual assaults than other assaults. This seems to be a pointer in both directions. On the one hand our system of criminal law does tend to use *mens rea* concepts to distinguish more and less serious criminal behaviour. The spectrum of driving offences is a good illustration of that.[152] The fact that the less serious, provincial offences usually lack *mens rea* also supports this idea. So there may well be some resistance to the idea that an accused can be convicted of the more serious crime B when he or she simply had the *mens rea* of the less serious crime A.[153] On the other hand, this is far from being an infallible guide to the range of criminal and quasi-criminal offences since, for example, the most serious crime of all, murder, can be committed negligently[154] and the requisite mental element can be constructed from that of another crime.[155] Indeed, another thread which runs through our hierarchy of offences relates to the seriousness of the consequences. Thus the reckless (or drunk) driver who actually kills someone is guilty of a much more serious offence than one with the same state of mind who is lucky enough not to. In the same way, a greater theoretical penalty could be

---

152 Criminally negligent driving is the most serious offence and requires *mens rea*. Careless driving is the least serious offence and does not. Dangerous driving is somewhere in the middle.

153 However, it is conceivable that the Supreme Court of Canada will not share that resistance. See *R. v. Kundeus*, [1976] 2 S.C.R. 272.

154 Section 212(c).

155 Section 213.

justified by the greater harm caused by a sexual rather than a non-sexual interference.

Another line of reasoning which might be more fruitful relates to the justifications for punishment for negligence. If "a sexual intent" is not required in addition to a determination that the act was objectively sexual, then in essence the punishment is for negligence with respect to that element of the *actus reus*. The accused might say "It never occurred to me that what I was doing was sexual in nature," but this would be irrelevant as he ought to have known, the act appearing sexual in nature to any reasonable person. It might be helpful therefore to consider the issue in terms of punishment for negligence, as discussed in the section on mistaken belief in consent.[156] The distinctive factor here, however, is that the accused will be guilty of assault in any case, so the issue is one that relates to labelling and sentencing rather than the threshold question of whether punishment is justifiable at all. The argument in favour of conviction for sexual assault, in the absence of any sexual intent, therefore seems much weaker than the argument for punishment in the case of an unreasonable mistake of fact. It is submitted, therefore, that in the absence of any compelling public interest to the contrary, an intent to touch in a sexual manner should be required, as suggested by Laskin J.A. in *R. v. Maurantonio*.[157]

3. SEXUAL ASSAULT WITH A WEAPON, ETC.

The heading does not indicate the full range of this form of sexual assault. In full, section 246.2 reads as follows:

> Everyone who, in committing a sexual assault,
> (a) carries, uses or threatens to use a weapon or an imitation thereof,
> (b) threatens to cause bodily harm to a person other than the complainant,
> (c) causes bodily harm to the complainant, or
> (d) is a party to the offence with any other person,
> is guilty of an indictable offence and is liable to imprisonment for fourteen years.

This is the in-between level of sexual assault on the spectrum of seriousness, and clearly the intent was to punish more severely

---

156 See the text accompanying notes 84-136.
157 See note 146 above.

where there is an element of violence, without the actual causing of anything more than bodily harm. Each form of the offence will be dealt with in turn.

(a) *Section 246.2(a) — "carries, uses or threatens to use a weapon or an imitation thereof"*

This provision is extremely broad because of the definition of weapon in section 2 of the Code, which states that it means:

(a) anything that is designed to be used as a weapon, or
(b) anything that a person uses or intends to use as a weapon, whether or not it is designed to be used as a weapon.

The section covers weapons *per se* such as guns and knives, but also any object carried by the accused where there is evidence of intent to use it to injure or frighten another person into submission. Section 246.2(a) does not specify that the submission of the complainant has to be linked to the presence or use of the weapon, so in theory it would be enough if the accused simply has a weapon, such as a knife, in his pocket. On the other hand, if the object in question were not designed to be used as a weapon, then it might be difficult to prove intent to use, without actual use of some kind. However, this is not beyond the realm of possibility if the object were such that its only purpose in its present state could be to injure or frighten.

(b) *Section 246.2(b) — "threatens to cause bodily harm to a person other than the complainant"*

This section is self-explanatory, and was designed to cover the situation where the complainant submits in circumstances of threat to another person. There is no requirement that the other person be present, that the accused have the present ability to carry out his threat (as in duress), or that there be a causal link between the threat and the submission. The complainant, for example, may submit because of fear for herself in the circumstances, or the other person, or both.

In a situation where bodily harm is actually caused to the other person, but the threat is not renewed (for example because that person escapes) and the complainant submits out of fear, it would appear that the accused is guilty of sexual assault only.[158]

---

158 The accused will of course be guilty of assault causing bodily harm *vis-à-vis* the other person under s. 245.1(b).

(c) *Section 246.2(c) — "causes bodily harm to the complainant"*

Bodily harm is a familiar term, defined in the Code as an interference with health or comfort which is more than merely transient or trifling in nature.[159] The definition simply seems to be a statutory formulation of the judicial definition.[160] The case law, however, is sparse, possibly because charges are not laid in borderline cases or because judges are of the view as was the House of Lords in *D.P.P. v. Smith*[161] that the expression bodily harm "needs no explanation."[162] It has been held in England that bodily harm includes an hysterical and nervous condition, but it remains to be seen what period of time is short enough to make an injury transient (a matter of minutes or hours?) or what type of injury is trifling (a bruise, soreness in the assaulted area?). If Canadian courts apply the ruling that a nervous condition is bodily harm then all sexual assaults apart from the most insignificant (which may well never be prosecuted anyway) would seem to fall into this area. This indeed may have been the intent of Parliament.

This provision suggests that a sexual touching in itself is not bodily harm, although surely it could be said that being subjected to a sexual assault of any kind is a hurt or injury that interferes with one's health or comfort in a non-transient non-trifling way. However, if this were the case then all sexual assaults would fall into this category.

It may be helpful to note that the bodily harm could be caused in two somewhat different ways. The bodily harm may occur in the attempt to secure the submission of the victim and evidence of this will thus perform the two functions of showing that no consent was obtained and classifying the type of assault. Alternatively, it may occur during the course of the assault itself, for example, where the vagina is bruised or torn or injuries are inflicted on a struggling victim.

(d) *Section 246.2(d) — "is a party to the offence with any other person"*

This is perhaps the most interesting form of the offence. The section was apparently designed to respond more seriously to

---

159 Section 245.1(2).
160 See *R. v. Maloney* (1976), 28 C.C.C. (2d) 323 (Ont. G.S.P.). See also *R. v. Miller*, [1954] 2 Q.B. 282.
161 [1961] A.C. 290.
162 *Ibid.*, at 334.

what have been termed gang-rapes, but now are simply sexual assaults where more than one party is involved.[163] Although the three-tier approach indicates, correctly, that a wide range of behaviour falls under the rubric of sexual assault, this spectrum is abandoned where more than one assault is involved. The seriousness or otherwise of the type of assault will have to be reflected at the stages of prosecutorial discretion or sentencing. Although one might feel that, for example, a man who grabs a woman in the street, urged on by his mates, is not normally in the same category as the classic gang-rapist, nevertheless the intent of Parliament is clear and certainly there is a logic to the equation of acting in concert with others to the carrying of a weapon.[164] Both constitute a more frightening, determined effort to impose one's will on another.

"Party" is described in sections 21 and 22 of the Code, including the familiar aiding or abetting and "common intent" provisions in section 21, and counselling and procuring in section 22. The law relating to parties generally is fully addressed elsewhere,[165] so one issue only, that of the spectator, will be addressed here. Is a person who watches a sexual assault taking place ever a party, and thus guilty of a section 246.2(d) offence?

It is obvious that a person who observes a minor sexual touching suddenly occur could not be said to be aiding and abetting by inaction, as the incident may be over before any opportunity for action arises. The issue would arise in cases which resemble the old rape situations, as where a group of men take a woman to or detain her in a deserted place and assault her. Some may actively engage in the sexual assault while others may assist in various ways ranging from holding the victim down, keeping a look out or shouting encouragement. Some may simply observe. Are they all guilty?

The Supreme Court of Canada has discussed this matter in the case of *Dunlop v. R.*[166] The majority of those addressing the

---

163 For some of the literature on gang rape, see W.H. Blanchard, "The Group Process in Gang Rape" (1959), 49 J. of Soc. Psych. 259; G. Geis and D. Chappell, "Forcible Rape by Multiple Offenders" (1971), 11 Abstracts in Crim. and Pen. 431; G. Geis, "Group Sexual Assaults" (1971), 5 Human Sexuality 100.
164 Although this might not justify the situation where the other party is not present but has helped in some other way.
165 See D. Stuart, *Canadian Criminal Law* (1982), pp. 489-507.
166 [1979] 2 S.C.R. 881.

issue held that "[m]ere presence at the scene of a crime is not sufficient to ground culpability."[167] There was no evidence of the "something more" which was needed.

A case on the other side of the line is *R. v. Black*,[168] in which the accused persons had laughed and shouted at the victim of a lengthy series of assaults. The court found that their presence ensured against the escape of the victim so was more than "mere" presence. This distinction may be used to distinguish *Dunlop* since silent physical presence may, depending on the circumstances, provide assistance to others. Failure to do or say anything to stop the assault, or to leave the scene, may be categorised as an omission,[169] but presence itself can be seen as the result of an act, except in rare cases where an individual is simply minding his own business and an assault takes place before his eyes.

A qualification to the rule in *Dunlop* was introduced (although not expressly) by the Ontario Court of Appeal in *R. v. Popen*,[170] a case of manslaughter. Martin J.A., speaking for the court, indicated:

> In some circumstances, a person who is present at the commission by another of an unlawful act, which he has a duty to prevent, may by mere inactivity encourage the unlawful act.[171]

The court felt that section 197 was broad enough to require a parent to provide protection for a child, but that there was also a common-law duty to do so. This latter ground opens the door to the development of a more general duty to prevent harm to another.[172]

---

167 *Per* Dickson J., at 891. Laskin C.J.C., Spence and Estey J.J., concurred. It is curious that the Supreme Court of Canada thinks that there is a duty to give one's name to the police in certain circumstances, as in *Moore v. R.*, [1979] 1 S.C.R. 195, but not a duty to alert the police to the fact that a serious crime is being committed, even in cases where this would pose no risk to the individual involved.

168 (1970), 10 C.R.N.S. 17 (B.C. C.A.).

169 And thus would raise traditional concerns about the punishment of omissions. For a comment on *Black*, see R.G. Murray, (1970) 10 C.R.N.S. 37.

170 (1981), 60 C.C.C. (2d) 232.

171 *Ibid.*, at 238. He cites J.C. Smith and B. Hogan, *Criminal Law*, 4th ed. (1978), pp. 118-19, who give examples of a husband standing by and watching his wife drown their children or a licensee of a public house watching his customers drink after hours.

172 This is the central difficulty in the law relating to criminal negligence. If as indicated by s. 202, we are criminally negligent in omitting to do something it is our duty to do, and duty means a duty imposed by law and law includes judge-made law, what guidelines do we have in predicting when a moral duty

So it would appear that, unless or until the Supreme Court of Canada rejects this qualification, passive acquiescence will make certain individuals parties where they are in a position of responsibility toward the victim. Examples would be the responsibility of a parent toward a child being assaulted by another person (for example the other parent), that of a spouse under section 197(1)(b), that of a person to another "under his charge" under section 197(1)(c), and quite possibly that of a police officer to all members of the public. For example, section 452(2) of the Halifax Charter states that members of the police force have a duty to prevent crimes and preserve the peace within the city.[173]

The extent of our obligations towards each other in this respect is an issue which would, if there is any dissatisfaction with the law, be more appropriately dealt with in legislative reform than piece-meal by the judiciary, the necessary consequence of the latter raising legitimate concerns about the legality of the *ex post facto* creation of duties and the certainty of the law.

One possible legislative model can be found in section 402(4), which relates to cruelty to animals and states:

> [E]vidence that an accused was present at the fighting or baiting of animals or birds is, in the absence of any evidence to the contrary, proof that he encouraged, aided or assisted at such fighting or baiting.[174]

4. AGGRAVATED SEXUAL ASSAULT

Section 246.3 contains the most serious form of sexual assault, with a maximum sentence of imprisonment for life. Subsection (1) states:

> Everyone commits an aggravated sexual assault who, in committing a sexual assault, wounds, maims, disfigures or endangers the life of the complainant.

---

becomes a legal duty? How do we go about answering the question "do we have a legal duty to assist a victim of a crime or to go for help?" If we have a duty, what is its scope? This is an area untouched in Canadian jurisprudence as yet, but it is clear at least that judges have the power to create legal duties, so that this difficult issue cannot be answered by a simple conjuring-up of the word "omission."

173 S.N.S. 1963, c. 52.
174 Suggested by B. Dickens, "Sexual Aggression and the Law: Implications for the Future" in S.N. Verdun-Jones and A.A. Keltner, eds., *Sexual Aggression and the Law* (1983), at 59.

The "wound, maim, disfigure, endanger" formulation is taken from section 228 (causing bodily harm with intent) so some assistance with the meaning of these terms can be gleaned from existing case law. "Wound" has been consistently construed to mean any breaking of the skin[175] and includes bodily harm.[176] The meaning of "maim" has been discussed in the British Columbia Court of Appeal and the Alberta Supreme Court Trial Division. In *R. v. Innes*,[177] Robertson J.A. discussed the common-law history of the concept and concluded that to maim means to injure a man rendering him less able in fighting.[178] A similar interpretation had been given in *R. v. Schultz*.[179] Smith C.J.A., delivering the judgment of the court, referred to several definitions, all stressing disablement for fighting and concluded that a man was maimed when he had his leg broken. The meaning of the word only seems significant where the injury does not involve a breaking of the skin, and it is clear from *Schultz* that broken limbs qualify. The meaning of "disfigure" was also discussed by Robertson J.A. in *R. v. Innes* using the same authorities. He indicated that it means more than a temporary marring of a person's appearance: a black eye, for example, is not a disfigurement. Examples are cutting off an ear or the nose or causing a permanent scar by throwing acid.[180]

In sum, therefore, if the accused breaks the skin of the victim, causes her some injury that disables her from fighting or inflicts some permanent damage to her appearance then the appropriate verdict is one of aggravated assault. It is clear that the intent of

---

175 *R. v. Hostetter* (1902), 7 C.C.C. 221 (N.W.T. S.C.); *R. v. Taylor and Young* (1923), 56 N.S.R. 382 (C.A.). See also *R. v. Innes* (1972), 7 C.C.C. (2d) 544 (B.C. C.A.).

176 *R. v. MacPhee* (1978), 29 N.S.R. (2d) 492 (S.C.).

177 See note 175 above.

178 Robertson J.A. was dissenting in the result, the majority having found on the facts at least an intent to disfigure. However, there was no express disagreement about the substantive meaning of "maim." The authorities utilized by Robertson J.A. were Blackstone's *Commentaries on the Laws of England* (1857), Vol. IV; Hawkins' *Pleas of the Crown*, c. XV, Archbold's *Criminal Pleading*, 36 ed. (1966), para 2654. See the same sources for the meaning of disfigure. See also *R. v. Robertson* (1946), 86 C.C.C. 353 (Ont. C.A.), in which it was held that a woman who had been stripped, tied up, beaten, and suffered first-degree burns from a red-hot poker, had not been maimed or disfigured.

179 (1962), 38 C.R. 76 (Alta. C.A.).

180 Note 175 above, at 551.

Parliament is to punish severely the most violent forms of sexual assault. However, there will still clearly be considerable room for the exercise of sentencing discretion since a wide range of injury is involved.

Chapter 5

Offences Against Children and Other Vulnerable People

Remaining in Part IV of the Code (Sexual Offences, Public Morals and Disorderly Conduct), although with some changes, are certain offences against children and others which can be considered assaultive in nature. The sections provide varying degrees of extra protection for people who are regarded as requiring protection from exposure to sexual activity or from certain types of pressure to engage in sexual activity.

Offences involving children are sometimes referred to as statutory rape, although that is not a term of legal art in Canada. There are various ways of thinking about the rationale of such offences. One view is that children under a certain age are simply not capable of giving consent to sexual activity in any meaningful way, so that such sexual activity is by definition non-consensual, and is therefore, to use the new terminology, assaultive. Another perspective is that it is wrong to expose children to sexual activity and that therefore consent is irrelevant. A further perspective, particularly given the structure of our present offences, is that these offences are simply designed to prevent female children from engaging in sexual activity. In other words, they are restrictions on sexual autonomy under the guise of protection.[1] What follows is an examination of each of these offences as well as a discussion of the relevant, that is, assaultive, aspects of incest.

---

1 The statement in *R. v. Tyrrell*, [1894] 1 Q.B. 710 at 721 that this type of law is "for the purpose of protecting young women and girls against themselves", was adopted by the Alberta Court of Appeal in *R. v. Wiberg* (1955), 22 C.R. 321.

1. SEXUAL INTERCOURSE WITH A FEMALE UNDER FOURTEEN

Section 146(1) states as follows:

Every male person who has sexual intercourse with a female person who
(a) is not his wife, and
(b) is under the age of fourteen years,
whether or not he believes that she is fourteen years of age or more, is guilty of
an indictable offence and is liable to imprisonment for life.

It will be noticed at once that only female children are protected by this provision, while only males can commit the offence. This will no doubt be challenged as unconstitutional.[2] There are no qualifications of the "chaste character" variety,[3] and the maximum punishment is incredibly severe, possibly because of the fact that the prohibition covers behaviour ranging from sexual experimentation between two young people to rape of an infant by an adult male.

Apart from the requirements as to the sex of the individuals involved, there are four elements in the *actus reus*. First there is the requirement of sexual intercourse, which is defined in section 3(6), to mean that "sexual intercourse is complete upon penetration to even the slightest degree, notwithstanding that seed is not emitted." Other sexual touchings fall under the rubric of sexual assault (and formerly would have been dealt with as indecent assault, a charge of rape not being possible).[4]

---

2 However, in *R. v. Rae*, [1976] W.W.D. 88 (B.C. S.C.) it was held that such offences were not discriminatory on the basis of sex, contrary to the Bill of Rights, but merely embodied a differentiation on the basis of biological composition. Gender-based distinctions have been upheld as constitutional in the U.S. if the statute bears a fair and substantial connection to legitimate state ends. In *Michael M. v. Superior Ct. of Sorama County.*, 101 S. Ct. 1200 (1981), the Supreme Court held that California statutory rape legislation was constitutional as one of the purposes of the law was to prevent teenage pregnancies. For a discussion, see N.T. Christakos, "Comment: Gender-Based Statutory Rape Legislation and the Equal Protection Clause..." (1981), 19 Am. C.L.R. 99. See also R. Eidson, "The Constitutionality of Statutory Rape Laws" (1980), 27 U.C.L.A.L.R. 757, in which the writer argues that gender-based classifications perpetuate stereotypical images of female passivity and male aggression.

3 Although this factor may affect sentencing. See *R. v. Kirby* (1976), 24 Nfld. & P.E.I.R. 260 (Nfld. Prov. Ct.).

4 Indecent assault was an included offence. See *R. v. Doel* (1981), 15 Alta. L.R. (2d) 62 (C.A.). The courts seem to go as far as possible, however, in extending the definition of intercourse. Thus, it was held in *R. v. Johns* (1956), 25 C.R. 153

Secondly, the offence is not committed where the child is the wife of the accused. This odd provision seems to suggest that the legislators were thinking more of the control of female sexuality (which of course would have been unnecessary where the parties were married) than of the protection of girls from premature exposure to sexual activity. Although provincial Marriage Acts provide formalities for people above certain ages, usually sixteen years,[5] the capacity to marry is a federal matter, and Parliament has never legislated to change the common-law age of capacity. It is therefore possible, though only remotely so in a factual as well as a legal sense, that this requirement could provide a defence, or more accurately, that the Crown would be unable to prove the absence of marriage.

Thirdly, the victim must be *under* the age of fourteen years.[6] Section 585 deals with proof of age generally, and indicates, *inter alia*, that an inference can be drawn from appearance, in the absence of other evidence. However, *R. v. Gosselin*[7] did not permit such an inference with respect to the age of a complainant, and other cases have been strict as well. Thus *R. v. Denton*,[8] albeit a decision under the Juvenile Delinquents Act,[9] indicated that the person's own testimony is not enough to establish her age where age is an element of the offence. Likewise, it has been held in *R. v. Hauberg*[10] that a complainant's evidence of her own age was not evidence to go to the jury.

Fourthly, section 147 adds that the accused must be over the age of fourteen years, a provision which applied to rape, and which also still applies to the offences of incest and sexual intercourse with a female between fourteen and sixteen. The background to this was that there was a presumption at common law that a boy under fourteen was incapable of sexual intercourse.[11] This provision is revealing more perhaps for what it

---

(B.C. Co. Ct.) that penetration of the labia suffices, even without penetration of the vagina.

5 See, *e.g.*, the Solemnization of Marriage Act, R.S.N.S. 1967, c. 287.

6 The day of the fourteenth birthday used to be included. In *R. v. Balaberda*, [1972] 1 W.W.R. 556 (Man. C.A.), the accused was convicted of having intercourse with a girl on her fourteenth birthday, applying s. 3(1) of the Code, mysteriously repealed S.C. 1980-81-82, c. 125, s. 2.

7 (1927), 31 O.W.N. 473 (C.A.).

8 (1950), 10 C.R. 218 (B.C. S.C.).

9 S.C. 1929, c. 46 as re-en. 1947, c. 37, s. 1.

10 (1915), 8 Sask. L.R. 239 (S.C.).

11 See, *e.g.*, *R. v. Groombridge* (1836), 173 E.R. 256, and *R. v. Waite*, [1892] 2 Q.B.

does not say than for what it does, since it leaves open the possibility that a young boy of fourteen or slightly over can be convicted, even though there may be no significant difference in age between the victim and the accused to supply a coercive factor. This point will be returned to in the discussion of proposals for reform below.

Although section 146(1) makes no mention of absence of consent as an element of the offence, section 140 in addition spells this out expressly, indicating that with respect to a "person under the age of fourteen years, the fact that the person consented to the commission of the offence is not a defence to the charge."

With respect to the *mens rea* elements, there must of course be a deliberate act of sexual intercourse, but any further requirements are more problematic. It is conceivable that an accused could have mistakenly believed that the girl in question was his wife. Leaving aside cases of mistaken identity, the most likely scenario would appear to involve mistake as to legal status rather than mistake of fact. For example, a person whose religion endorsed the practice, might have polygamously married a girl under fourteen and brought her to Canada, and had intercourse with her, genuinely believing that she was his wife. In such a case, the court would have a number of alternatives. The mistake could be labelled as one of law, with section 19 utilised to deny a defence, the judge perhaps noting the absence of any colour or claim of right language in the section. The mistake could simply be labelled as one of fact, a popular device for avoiding injustice caused by the unsatisfactory nature of the distinction in this context, without getting into difficulties caused by the need to decide which mistakes of law should be treated as mistakes of fact and which should not.[12] Lastly, the court could blaze a trail in Canada and create a category of mistakes as to civil rights, status or an element of the *actus reus,* as opposed to mistakes about or ignorance of the prohibition itself, which can be classified as

---

600. It has been held that the onus is on the accused to put himself within the exception. *R. v. Schneider,* [1927] 1 W.W.R. 306 (Sask. C.A.). A boy over 14 can be convicted as a party even though the actual perpetrator was under 14. *R. v. Cardinal* (1982), 23 Alta. L.R. (2d) 113 (C.A.), leave to appeal to the S.C.C. granted 3 C.C.C. (3d) 376. The holding is that s. 147 is no longer a declaration of incapacity but an immunity. Such a boy can be convicted of assault. *R. v. Hartlen* (1898), 40 N.S.R. 317 (C.A.).

12 See *R. v. Prue; R. v. Baril,* [1979] 2 S.C.R. 547. See also *R. v. Woolridge* (1979), 49 C.C.C. (2d) 300 (Sask. Prov. Ct.) with respect to belief in divorce in a bigamy case.

sufficiently similar to mistakes of fact to be treated in the same way. From the perspective of the conceptual purity and consistency of the law, it is submitted that the last analysis should be adopted, but the categorisation as a mistake of fact would of course produce the same result in a pragmatic sense.

Normally, there would be a further *mens rea* element, knowledge or recklessness *vis-à-vis* the age of the victim, but this has been expressly excluded by statute. Given that it would be difficult to have intercourse accidentally, and the above dilemma with respect to a mistaken belief in marriage may well never arise, then, in practical terms, this is an offence of absolute liability. It hardly needs saying that this is highly unusual, particularly given the severe nature of the maximum punishment. On this substantive level the law conveys a sense of total commitment to the protection of young girls. Legislators were evidently disinclined to imagine themselves in the shoes of the accused, who is here denied the normal mistake of fact argument, no matter how reasonable the mistake.

This unusual imposition of absolute liability raises a constitutional issue. In *Baptiste v. R.*,[13] the argument was made that it offended section 2(e) and (f) of the Canadian Bill of Rights, the fair hearing and presumption of innocence provisions. The court rejected the argument that the accused would not have a fair hearing in accordance with the principles of fundamental justice if denied the *mens rea* argument, as these principles went to the conduct of the hearing alone. With respect to the presumption of innocence, the argument for the accused was that this provision went even farther than the normal reverse onus clauses, and therefore was even more offensive. The court contented itself with applying the reasoning in *R. v. Appleby*[14] that the accused was being proven guilty "according to law," the law in question having removed from the Crown the normal responsibility, with respect to true criminal offences, of proving *mens rea*. The matter will now have to be re-examined in the light of the Charter, and has indeed been raised in the Ontario Court of Appeal in *R. v. Stevens*.[15] The facts were that the accused had intercourse with a girl who was nearly fourteen, reasonably believing her to be at least fifteen. He was sixteen at the time. His counsel argued that

---

13 (1981), 25 C.R. (3d) 252; affirmed (1982), 29 C.R. (3d) 286 (B.C. C.A.).
14 [1972] S.C.R. 303.
15 (1983), 3 C.C.C. (3d) 198.

the provision infringed the right given by section 7 of the Charter not to be deprived of life, liberty, and security of the person "except in accordance with the principles of fundamental justice." The argument and the appeal were unsuccessful. The court, speaking through Houlden J.A., merely stated its rejection and noted that several democratic countries had similar provisions. Indeed, probably the most significant thing about the decision was that the court was prepared "to assume, without deciding, that section 7 of the Charter permits judicial review of the substantive content of legislation."[16] The issue is important in that it relates to whether the principles of fundamental justice have a substantive as well as a procedural content.

A case which unequivocally states that they do, although unrelated to the topic of sexual assault, is *Ref. Re S. 94(2) of the Motor Vehicle Act*[17] in which the Lieutenant-Governor had referred to the British Columbia Court of Appeal the question whether the above section—which provides that a person who drives while prohibited commits an absolute liability offence and is subject to a mandatory penalty of seven days imprisonment— was consistent with the principles of fundamental justice. The Court of Appeal held that it could review the substantive content of offences and that this section was inconsistent with such principles. The reasoning behind this decision was not revealed, the court concentrating instead on the *Sault Ste. Marie*[18] view of the general offensiveness of punishing the normally innocent and thus apparently equating offensiveness with constitutional offensiveness. However, the court was careful to state that not all absolute liability offences would automatically be unconstitutional.

It will be necessary for the Supreme Court of Canada to decide whether "fundamental justice" covers substance as well as procedure. However, even if the answer is no, the court will still be invited to consider whether the imposition of absolute liability is procedural in any event, since it relates to the burden of proof on the Crown,[19] and is thus possibly unconstitutional. If the answer

---

16 *Ibid.*, at 200.
17 (1983), 33 C.R. (3d) 22 (B.C. C.A.). Another pro-substantive case is *R. v. Rolbin* (1982), 1 C.R.R. 186 (Que. S.P.) (affirmed (1982), 2 C.R.R. 166 (Que. C.S.)) while procedure only cases are *R. v. Holman* (1982), 28 C.R. (3d) 378 (affirmed 34 C.R. (3d) 380 (B.C. S.C.)) and (under the Bill of Rights) *Curr v. R.*, [1972] S.C.R. 889. See also Professor Stuart's note at 33 C.R. (3d) 22-3.
18 (1976), 13 O.R. (2d) 113; affirmed [1978] 2 S.C.R. 1299.
19 *R. v. Campagna* (1982), 70 C.C.C. (2d) 236 at 245.

is yes, then the distinction, if any, hinted at by the British Columbia Court of Appeal, between constitutional and unconstitutional absolute liability, will have to be drawn.

Some clue to that distinction might be found in the oral judgment of Paradis Prov. J. in *R. v. Campagna*,[20] also relating to driving while prohibited. The judge stressed the connection between absolute liability and slight penalties. An accused could always plead due diligence at the sentencing stage, but here there was a minimum jail sentence. Although the sentence for sexual intercourse with a girl under fourteen is not mandatory, the maximum is so very severe that it can be argued forcefully that the connection (between absolute liability and slight penalties) so crucial to the reasoning of Dickson J. in *Sault Ste. Marie* does not exist. Thus absolute liability offences with more than slight punishments may be unconstitutional.

Opinions are certainly divided on whether this type of provision is defensible. Smith and Hogan offer the most persuasive defence. They suggest that, on the face of it, such rules are illogical and unjust.

> Presumably no element is included in the definition of an actus reus unless it contributes to the heinousness of the offence. If the accused is blamelessly inadvertent with respect to any one element in the offence, and does not therefore appreciate the full heinousness of his conduct, is it then proper to hold him responsible for it?[21]

However, Smith and Hogan go on to say that this can cause difficulties where the law has had to make a somewhat artificial distinction with respect to circumstances of a "morally indifferent nature." Whether a girl was slightly over or slightly under the age of fourteen would not affect the morality of the accused's conduct. This is certainly an attractive argument, the law in effect saying that males have intercourse with girls, whom they must be aware are of some age, at their own risk, since they should not be doing so anyway, but the results of the law do seem unjust. The male who reasonably believes the girl to be over fourteen is guilty, while the male who believes her to be under that age (and indeed may wish to have intercourse with her for that very reason) is not guilty of this offence, if she happens to be above the requisite age in fact. The rule is irrelevant with respect to the most serious form of the offence, intercourse with very young children, where one can

---

20 *Ibid.*
21 J.C. Smith and B. Hogan, *Criminal Law*, 4th ed. (1978), p. 57.

suppose that a mistake of fact argument would not work anyway, and the inclusion of vastly different forms of behaviour and degrees of moral blameworthiness in one omnibus offence may confuse the issues of retribution and dete~~r~~ that, if the state's purpose is to punish peop have intercourse with girls they believed fourteen, then the principle of legality requ of what precisely the impugned conduct is. course the occasional acquittal based on th of an arbitrary line, but obviously this da very outer edge of the protected group.

Age 14

Under 16

S. R.

2. SEXUAL INTERCOURSE WITH A F] FOURTEEN AND SIXTEEN

This offence shares several elements with the offence of intercourse with a female under fourteen, but also provides considerable contrast. Section 146(2) states as follows:

> Every male person who has sexual intercourse with a female person who
> (a) is not his wife,
> (b) is of previously chaste character, and
> (c) is fourteen years of age or more and is under the age of sixteen years,
> whether or not he believes that she is sixteen years of age or more, is guilty of an indictable offence and is liable to imprisonment for five years.

It will be seen at once that this provision shares the gender differentiation between the parties, the absence of the marital relationship and the express removal of what would otherwise be a normal mistake of fact argument. Another common element is that arbitrary lines are drawn with respect to age, the difference being simply that an older age group is being targeted for protection here, with a significant corresponding reduction in the maximum punishment. It should also be noted that section 147 relating to males under fourteen years applies.

In contrast, an important new element is added, in that there is a requirement that the victim be of "previously chaste character." Since at first glance it would appear that it is impossible for a girl between fourteen and sixteen to have intercourse without it being "statutory rape," it seems that the law is saying that, once a girl is victimised in this way, she cannot be victimised again: it is legal to have intercourse with someone already exposed to sexual activity at an age which the law has determined to be too young. It would certainly appear that the law is openly withdrawing protection from young girls who have engaged in sexual intercourse. However, it is clear from an examination of associated provisions that the legislators had in mind some kind of half-way house between rape and "statutory" rape. Since the legislators were evidently not trying to punish all intercourse, whether consensual or not, the matter is not quite so simple as saying that a girl cannot be statutorily raped more than once. This is clear from section 146(3), which opens the door to a consent-type argument, stating:

> Where an accused is charged with an offence under subsection (2), the court may find the accused not guilty if it is of the opinion that the evidence does not show that, as between the accused and the female person, the accused is more to blame than the female person.

What does this provision mean? The cases are of very little assistance. They reveal, however, that judges have been anxious to use the provision for the benefit of the accused. The Ontario Court of Appeal in *Lopresti v. R.*[22] held that failure to stress this rule and refer the jury to cogent evidence would result in a reversal of conviction. Shortly thereafter, in *R. v. Royal*[23] the court held that the section was not permissive, in spite of the word "may." It upheld the direction to the jury that "unless they found beyond a reasonable doubt that the accused was more to blame, ... they *must* acquit him." In the more recent case of *R. v. Quesnel*,[24] there was evidence that the girl engaged in intercourse for pleasure and that "it just sort of happened." A new trial was ordered for the reason, *inter alia*, that the judge had merely read the section to the jury and not related the evidence to the elements of the offence. The implication from this is that, where a girl is a willing partner, even though she did not initiate the sexual activity, the accused will not be more to blame. This comes extremely close to making the provision otiose, since the combination of the chaste character and the comparison of blame provisions mean that only chaste unwilling girls are protected. The subsection is deceptive because of its structure and the company it keeps with section 146(1). It appears to give girls between fourteen and sixteen some special protection but the difference, if any, between it and the old rape offence, is minimal. In fact, these girls may have even less

---

22 (1965), 49 C.R. 277.
23 [1970] 1 O.R. 425 (C.A.).
24 (1979), 51 C.C.C. (2d) 270 (Ont. C.A.).

protection than young women between eighteen and twenty-one under the scope of seduction.

Parliament may have recognised that section 146(2) comes very close to merely proscribing non-consensual intercourse, since a significant limitation is contained in section 140. It states that consent is not a defence to a section 146 charge, but only where the victim is under fourteen, thus confining its effect to section 146(1). While section 146(2) does not contain absence of consent as an element, and thus the Crown does not have to prove it, section 146(3) may well bring the issue in by a side door.

What does "chaste character" mean? Again there are few cases, but the cases on the seduction offences, which also employ this concept, provide some assistance. It seems settled that one can be chaste without being a virgin,[25] the courts having accepted the doctrine of rehabilitation. In *Magdall v. R.*,[26] the Supreme Court of Canada held that, where the complainant had intercourse with the accused three months after their previous act of intercourse, it was open to the jury to find that she was of chaste character: there was no minimum time for rehabilitation.[27] On the other hand, it may be possible to be unchaste while still a virgin, according to a recent case which held that, in order to establish the unchaste character of a girl of fifteen, explicit evidence was required of wantonness, lewdness, looseness or promiscuity. This could be construed to suggest far more than loss of virginity but the court indicated that a lack of chastity may be indicated "by what is sometimes termed looseness, even though there has been no loss of virginity."[28] It has been held by the Nova Scotia Supreme Court (Appeal Division) that a chaste character is a matter of personal virtue and not of reputation.[29]

The chaste character and comparison of blame provisions were always an uneasy compromise and provide significant ammunition for those who argued that our sexual offences law only offered protection to those women and girls who conformed to traditional ideals of the virtuous female while other women

---

25 *R. v. Comeau* (1912), 46 N.S.R. 450 (C.A.); *R. v. Hauberg* (1915), 8 Sask. L.R. 239 (C.A.); *Magdall v. R.*, [1920] 3 W.W.R. 454, affirmed 61 S.C.R. 88.

26 *Ibid.*

27 The case may have turned on its odd facts as the previous intercourse was outside the seduction limitation period, so in effect the accused was pleading his own wrong as a defence.

28 *R. v. Trecartin* (1980), 32 N.B.R. (2d) 621 at 623-624 (Q.B.).

29 In *Comeau*, note 25 above.

were "open territory." Moreover, the chaste/unchaste distinction is overt and substantive, not hidden in enforcement practices. It may well be removed when a general overhaul of these offences takes place. In the meantime, it would appear unlikely that any prosecutor would knowingly subject a complainant to the questioning about her chastity that such a charge would involve. The encouragement of such questioning now stands in stark contrast to the present strict limitations on it in the context of sexual assault.[30]

3. BILL C-53 PROPOSALS: SECTION 146—SEXUAL ASSAULT WITH A FEMALE UNDER FOURTEEN OR BETWEEN FOURTEEN AND SIXTEEN

It is submitted that section 146 is problematic and in need of reform. The section has a narrow focus on sexual intercourse. Males are left entirely unprotected from premature exposure to sexual activity, and thus there is the distinct possibility of a constitutional challenge. There is the imposition of absolute liability, the distinction between the chaste and the unchaste and the comparison of blame provision. The provisions of Bill C-53 (other parts of which ultimately became law as Bill C-127) which fell by the wayside in Parliament are perhaps the best guide to possible reform. If the Bill had passed, the offences discussed above (as well as a number of others)[31] would have been replaced by offences utilising the concept of "sexual misconduct," but otherwise would have been substantially the same. There would have been an offence of sexual misconduct with a person under fourteen, with a maximum punishment of ten years. This broadens the scope of the offence, making it gender-neutral and providing a more realistic maximum punishment. However, provisions would have remained excluding spouses and making the offence one of absolute liability. The only really novel change would have been that the accused could only be convicted if more

---

30 That contrast was drawn as early as 1917 in *R. v. Pieco*, [1917] 1 W.W.R. 892 (Alta. C.A.), in which it was held that the accused must be allowed to lead evidence of another man who had intercourse with the complainant. A distinction was drawn between this type of case and rape, where the court felt (in advance of its time) that chastity was irrelevant.
31 *E.g.*, s. 166, parent or guardian procuring defilement; s. 167, householder permitting defilement; and s. 168, corrupting children.

than three years older than the victim, thus excluding those of a similar age engaging in sexual experimentation, including the girls themselves, who otherwise would have been guilty of an offence if the boy were under sixteen.[32] The law in that event would have contained an outright prohibition of sexual activity between young people, rather than providing protection for the especially vulnerable. It may be questionable, however, whether the criminal law is the appropriate mechanism for discouraging the young from sexual activity with each other.

Sexual misconduct with a person between fourteen and sixteen would also have been a broader, gender-neutral version of its predecessor, with the important exception that a mistaken belief that the complainant was over sixteen would have been a defence, albeit one to be established by the accused.[33] A further defence would have been a modernised version of the present "more to blame" provision. Section 167(2)(d) would have created a defence if the accused established that "he is less responsible than the complainant for the sexual misconduct that took place." This appears to constitute a continued invitation to "blame the victim" and, in any event, requires the finder of fact to make a very difficult determination of degrees of responsibility for sexual activity, including consensual sexual activity. It seems to make clear that the offence was not really designed to protect fourteen to sixteen year olds from premature exposure to sexual activity since the need for protection would surely persist whether the misconduct is acquiesced in or aggressively and energetically sought. The underlying message would have been that people three years older than children between the ages of fourteen and sixteen ought not to engage in sexual misconduct with them, but they do not have to try very hard not to. The offence taken as a whole thus would give very mixed messages as to who *ought* to take responsibility for abstinence from sexual activity. This issue is addressed more clearly in the sections drafted by the Law Reform Commission, which will be referred to shortly.

Apart from this the most significant change proposed was the move to sexual misconduct rather than intercourse. It is a concept that attracts the rather obvious comment that it contemplates by implication a form of behaviour capable of being labelled sexual conduct, and thus not subject to criminal sanction. It is a

---

32 For an equivalent provision with respect to sexual assault, see s. 246.1(2).

33 A similar approach was taken with respect to the other defences.

departure from the recommendations of the Law Reform Commission,[34] which utilised the concept of sexual interference. The proposals of the Commission are reproduced in full as it is submitted that they merit reconsideration. A number of offences were suggested:

4. Sexual Interference with Persons Under Fourteen Years of Age.

Every one who, for a sexual purpose, directly or indirectly touches a person under the age of fourteen years, with or without the consent of that person, is guilty of an indictable offence and liable to imprisonment for five years.

5. Sexual Interference Due to Dependency

(1) Every one who, for a sexual purpose, directly or indirectly touches a person fourteen years of age or older but under eighteen years of age, whose consent was obtained by the exercise of authority or the exploitation of dependency is guilty of an indictable offence and liable to imprisonment for five years.

6. Due Diligence—Spouses

(1) An accused is not guilty of an offence under sections 4 or 5 if, after the exercise of reasonable diligence, proof of which lies upon him, he believed at the time of the offence the person to be older than the age specified in those sections.

(2) Sections 4 and 5 do not apply to conduct between spouses.

It is submitted that these proposals are preferable to those contained in Bill C-53. It is clear that any touching, if for an improper, that is, sexual purpose, is included. Admittedly, there is a definitional problem with respect to "sexual," but this will persist so long as we wish to protect children from certain kinds of touching and not others. The offences are no longer absolute liability, although a compromise has been chosen with respect to the age factor. The idea that culpability lies in making an unreasonable mistake with respect to age seems preferable to the present approach, and thus these provisions may be more often utilised. The provision dealing with older children leaves their sexual autonomy intact but directly addresses those with the potential to exploit them, that is, those in authority or those on whom the young person in question is dependent. The only questionable provision is that respecting marital immunity. If consent is irrelevant with regard to children under fourteen, why should it make any difference that there had already been consent to

---

34 *Report on Sexual Offences* (1978).

marriage? In addition, marriage to young persons of the relevant age may be the paradigm of the exploitation of dependency, and there seems no reason why it should be tolerated in that context in contrast to others.

4. INCEST

The definition of incest is contained in section 150(1).

> Every one commits incest who, knowing that another person is by blood relationship his or her parent, child, brother, sister, grandparent or grandchild, as the case may be, has sexual intercourse with that person.

The Law Reform Commission has recommended abolition of this crime, in light of its proposal of a new offence of sexual interference due to dependency,[35] but it was present in a simplified form in the Bill C-53 proposals. It is possible, therefore, that, of all the offences relating to children, this is the most likely to be retained. At present it covers consensual intercourse between adults as well (which might well be removed), but that is outside the scope of this book, which only covers sexual activity capable of being labelled assaultive, as where the victim has not given a true consent. The relevant form of the offence in that context would be sexual intercourse with a related child, the paradigm being intercourse with a dependent related child.

The elements of the offence are simple. There must be sexual intercourse, that is penetration as discussed with respect to section 146(1) above, and a blood relationship,[36] as far as the *actus reus* is concerned. The important practical element of the *mens rea* is knowledge of the blood relationship, the use of the word "knowing" probably excluding the reckless mode of committing the offence. This is of minimal practical significance, as only a tiny number of incest charges are actually brought, even where it is obvious that there is knowledge of the blood relationship.

It is debatable whether any form of incest can really be included under the rubric of sexual assault in its present legal form although perhaps it ought to be considered a form of assault. Other offences dealing with sexual intercourse with children discussed above arguably contemplate some form of coerciveness

---

35 *Ibid.*, pp. 25-30.
36 It has been suggested that this includes the illegitimate relationship, *R. v. Schmidt or Smith*, [1948] S.C.R. 333.

inherent in the youth of the victim and the sex of the parties,[37] and indeed the existence of a victim is envisaged (though much more clearly with section 146(1) than with 146(2)). The crime of incest is designed to punish the culpable conduct of both parties. Criminal sanction might or might not be appropriate with respect to adult incest, but is hardly appropriate in what is probably in the public mind the paradigm of incest, intercourse between a father and his female child. Subsection (3) makes it clear that the guilt of the "victim" is contemplated:

> Where a female person is *convicted* of an offence under this section and the court is satisfied that she committed the offence by reason only that she was under restraint, duress or fear of the person with whom she had the sexual intercourse, the court is not required to impose any punishment on her.[38]

What direction should reform take, if indeed any is desirable? It is clear that it is necessary to think through the question of the harm addressed by the law of incest and restrict or expand the offence accordingly. The Law Reform Commission did this and concluded that the harm was the exploitation of dependency, so that part of the present crime could safely by subsumed in a general offence of that sort. The thinking behind the provisions of Bill C-53 was obviously that the present crime was justified. One academic commentator, Diana Majury,[39] has proposed another direction for reform. She suggests that the specific crime be retained for its symbolic value in that it contains an explicit statement that incest is so seriously wrong as to be a crime, but that the law should be changed to focus on any form of sexual activity in the coercive context of a relationship between a dependent and a person with parental authority.[40] This position shares a lot of

---

37 Although, as we have seen, this argument breaks down where there is only a slight difference in age between the victim and the offender, a matter which would have been remedied by Bill C-53.

38 Italics added. This provision was surprisingly retained in Bill C-53, the only modification being that the onus of proof was placed on the accused. But see s. 147.

39 Whose 1980-81 Women and the Law class at the Faculty of Law, University of Windsor, conducted an in-depth study of the crime of incest. For a variety of perspectives see S. Wolfram, "Eugenics and the Punishment of Incest Act 1908", [1983] Crim. L.R. 308; and D.H.J. Hermann and M.A. Wilcox, "An Economic Analysis of Incest: Prohibition, Behaviour, and Punishment" (1982), 25 St. Louis U.L.J. 735.

40 "Incest," a paper presented at a conference entitled "The Changing Law of Sexual Assault" held at the Faculty of Law, Dalhousie University, in January, 1982.

common ground with that of the Law Reform Commission, but stresses the need for Parliament to make a strong statement about the special potential for exploitation and harm in the context of the family. It also has the merit of avoiding public concern if Parliament were to be perceived as "abolishing incest."

5. SEXUAL INTERCOURSE WITH STEP-DAUGHTER, ETC., OR FEMALE EMPLOYEE

This is the odd-man-out in the series of offences discussed in this section. It has elements similar to "statutory rape" and incest. It is in among the seduction offences, as if it really belonged with them. However it is a total prohibition of sexual intercourse with certain persons.

Section 153(1) states:

Every male person who
   (a) has illicit sexual intercourse with his step-daughter, foster daughter or female ward, or
   (b) has illicit sexual intercourse with a female person of previously chaste character and under the age of twenty-one years who
      (i) is in his employment,
      (ii) is in a common, but not necessarily similar, employment with him and is, in respect of her employment or work, under or in any way subject to his control or direction, or
      (iii) receives her wages or salary directly or indirectly from him,
is guilty of an indictable offence and is liable to imprisonment for two years.

(2) Where an accused is charged with an offence under paragraph (1)(b), the court may find the accused not guilty if it is of opinion that the evidence does not show that, as between the accused and the female person, the accused is more to blame than the female person.

Subsection (1)(a) seems like a functional extension of incest. The main difference is, of course, that the step-daughter,[41] foster daughter or female ward is not also guilty of the offence, so this is an unequivocal recognition of the potential for exploitation in a family situation.

An unanswered question relates to the significance of the adjective "illicit," which also appears in section 154 (seduction of female passengers), section 166 (parent or guardian procuring

---

41 It has been held that a step-daughter is the issue of a previous marriage of the wife, so that illegitimate children were excluded from the protection of this provision. *R. v. Groening* (1953), 16 C.R. 389 (Man. C.A.).

defilement) and section 167 (householder permitting defilement). The case law does not give any guidance on whether the addition of this word means that only a certain type of intercourse is prohibited. It may be otiose or it may have been intended to exclude marital sex from the ambit of the offence. The last possibility is the most likely, and support for that view can be found in *R. v. Karn*[42] which dealt with "unlawful" carnal knowledge. It was held to mean the same thing as "illicit," that is any carnal knowledge except that between husband and wife. The Ontario Court of Appeal in *R. v. Williams*[43] referred to the provision as prohibiting "wilful sexual intercourse,"[44] but this was said in the context of denying that consent was a defence to the charge and not in addressing the issue of what makes intercourse illicit. The most important cases would in any event be covered by section 146(1), with its total prohibition of intercourse with girls under fourteen.

Section 153(1)(b) constitutes an interesting recognition of the fact that there is a particular danger of the sexual exploitation of vulnerability in certain non-family settings. Chaste females under twenty-one are offered a measure of protection from males who have power over them at work. This is the closest that the Criminal Code comes to the acknowledgement of sexual harassment in the workplace as an offence. It would appear that intercourse is totally prohibited in this context, unless the accused is not "more to blame." The inclusion of the comparison of blame means that the male is not solely responsible for avoiding intercourse in this setting.

Bill C-53 proposed the repeal of these offences, but discussion will be deferred until all related offences have been covered.

6. SEDUCTION OF A FEMALE PERSON BETWEEN SIXTEEN AND EIGHTEEN

As was briefly mentioned in Part I, the Code still contains a number of offences involving seduction and this first one provides some protection for chaste young women too old to be included in the "statutory rape" section. Again the victim must be female and

---

42 (1909), 20 O.L.R. 91 (C.A.).
43 (1973), 1 O.R. (2d) 474. Leave to appeal to the S.C.C. dismissed 12 C.C.C. (2d) 453n.
44 *Ibid.*, at 476.

the accused male, and the chaste-unchaste distinction is utilised in section 151:

> Every male person who, being eighteen years of age or more, seduces a female person of previously chaste character who is sixteen years or more but less than eighteen years of age is guilty of an indictable offence and is liable to imprisonment for two years.

A limitation period of one year is imposed in section 141.

The only thing that is not self-evident about this provision is the meaning of seduction, a concept which is common to this and the next two offences to be discussed. There are very few cases, which is hardly surprising in view of the fact that victims in the past were unlikely to wish to publicise the event and seduction may be viewed as something of an anachronism at the present time. Seduction is a form of consensual intercourse but the terms are not synonymous.[45] The Saskatchewan Court of Appeal addressed the issue in the case of *R. v. Gasselle*,[46] drawing a distinction between seduction and illicit intercourse, seduction involving "the surrender of chastity as a result of persuasion, solicitation, promises, bribes or other means than force."[47] This is very wide, particularly in view of the fact that many people may regard an element of persuasion on the part of the male as normal and commonplace rather than culpable. There may technically, therefore, be very little difference between seduction and simply having sexual intercourse, the latter occurring only when the female initiates the sexual activity or where it occurs as a kind of spontaneous expression of mutual desire. This may not be of much practical importance if the seduction offences are all obsolete, but legitimate concern may be felt that this behaviour is even technically labelled as criminal. The fact that the law is unenforced because there is no longer a "fit" between it and societal standards is of course a matter of concern and a powerful argument for reform.

---

45 *R. v. Schemmer*, [1927] 3 W.W.R. 417 (Sask. Dist. Ct.), holding that evidence of force is inconsistent with seduction.

46 [1934] 3 W.W.R. 457.

47 *Ibid.*, at 460. See also *Gibson v. Rabey* (1916), 10 W.W.R. 199 (Alta. C.A.) which described seduction in a civil action as enticing or persuading the plaintiff to commit the act. The elements of the offence were also discussed briefly in *R. v. Haines* (1960), 127 C.C.C. 125 (B.C. C.A.).

7. SEDUCTION UNDER PROMISE OF MARRIAGE

Section 152 states:

Every male person, being twenty-one years of age or more, who, under promise of marriage, seduces an unmarried female person of previously chaste character who is less than twenty-one years of age is guilty of an indictable offence and is liable to imprisonment for two years.

The section 141 one year limitation period applies. It will be seen at once that the forms of seduction are narrowed here to one particular form of persuasion or bribery, the promise of marriage, which must have been, and may well remain, a very powerful inducement. Women between the ages of eighteen and twenty-one are either expected to have the inner fortitude to withstand other forms of seduction or are regarded as having the right to succumb to them, depending on how one views this whole structure of sexual offences. Marriage to the victim used to be a defence, as indeed it was to all the seduction offences, but this is no longer the case since the repeal of section 139(2) in the Criminal Law Amendment Act.[48] The result is that it is entirely irrelevant that the promise of marriage was sincere and indeed carried out. If a man over twenty-one wants to ensure that he is entirely law-abiding, he should abstain from intercourse with his betrothed if she is under twenty-one. Again the case law is extremely sparse, merely indicating that the promise must be an absolute rather than a conditional one,[49] and that there must be a causative link between the promise and the decision to "yield."[50]

8. SEDUCTION OF FEMALE PASSENGERS ON VESSELS

This is contained in section 153.

Every male person who, being the owner or master of, or employed on board a vessel, engaged in the carriage of passengers for hire, seduces, or by threats or by the exercise of his authority, has illicit sexual intercourse on board the vessel with a female passenger is guilty of an indictable offence and is liable to imprisonment for two years.

---

48 S.C. 1980-81-82, c. 125, s. 5.
49 *R. v. Comeau* (1912), 46 N.S.R. 450 (S.C.); *R. v. McIsaac*, [1933] O.W.N. 251 (H.C.).
50 *R. v. Walker* (1893), 1 Terr. L.R. 482 (N.W.T. C.A.).

This is a more complex crime. The *actus reus* can be committed with respect to a female passenger of any age, by any male owning or employed on a passenger vessel. It includes any form of seduction, but any act of sexual intercourse is illegal if procured by threats or the exercise of authority.[51] There is no limitation on the form of the threats, but presumably Parliament was concerned about exploitation of the passenger's vulnerable position. To the knowledge of this writer, there are no reported cases.

9. SEDUCTION: LAW REFORM

These seduction offences raise issues pertaining to reform that are of broader significance with respect to the whole range of offences protecting children and other vulnerable persons. There seems to be considerable agreement that seduction should be removed from the Criminal Code as was proposed in Bill C-53, and it may be safely assumed that this will happen sooner or later.[52] The fact that these sections are rarely if ever used is perhaps a conclusive justification for their removal, although this is not necessarily true in other contexts, where attention might instead be directed to the need for more energetic law enforcement. It is submitted, however, that careful attention should be paid by law reformers to the harm that these offences address. It may well be that, stripped of their somewhat old-fashioned language, and their sexist distinctions and assumptions, there is an element in these offences which ought to be retained.

When our whole scheme of offences is examined, it can be seen that we are dealing with different levels of coerciveness; in other words, different levels of fortitude in responding to pressure to engage in sexual activity is expected from women and girls. At one end of the spectrum comes the true statutory rape, since the law contains a blanket prohibition against intercourse with female children under fourteen. It is assumed that all such inter-

---

51 And thus it is a precursor of the new form of sexual assault in s. 244(3)(d).

52 The Hon. Ray Hnatyshyn has stated, *e.g.*, that these offences are "anachronisms that presently haunt the law in this area. I think now of present section 152 which makes it an offence to seduce a woman under promise of marriage and section 154 where it prohibits 'illicit intercourse' with the captain of a vessel", Parl. Debs. H.C., Vol. X, at 11306, 7 July 1981.

course is inherently coercive since a child of this age is incapable of giving a true consent. Some forms of incest might also be added to this category. At the other end of the spectrum come the new sexual assault offences, with a listing of criminal forms of pressure in section 244(3), including force, fraud and the exercise of authority. In simple terms, Parliament has stated that it is wrong to force any person to choose between engaging in sexual contact and, for example, being beaten. At the moment all persons are protected from this type of forced choice, while girls under fourteen are protected against any choice involving sexual intercourse. It seems inevitable that our legal system will continue with this structure, that is, a total ban on certain forms of coercion and a total ban on sexual activity with people under a certain age. Any debate in this context will probably focus on the appropriate age and the scope of the ban on sexual activity (for example, intercourse, sexual misconduct, sexual conduct).

That ought not to be the end of the matter, however. Our law up to this point has had an in-between category, occupied by the crime of intercourse with girls under sixteen, the feeble-minded (until recently), step-daughters, employees, and passengers on board ship, as well as incest and seduction. On the most abstract level, it is recognised that certain people are in a particularly vulnerable position, not necessarily because of their age, and laws are required that offer protection from the particular forms of pressure to which they are vulnerable, which may be extremely subtle. A good example may be the addition of "the exercise of authority" with respect to sexual assault. In that regard, Parliament obviously did not want to place a complete prohibition on sexual relations between employer and employee or between professor and student, for example, but wished instead to flag the special coercive potential inherent in such relationships. It is submitted, therefore, that these in-between offences, while they have a superficially anachronistic air about them, are solidly based on the principle of exploitation of vulnerability, and should not be repealed without careful thought having been given to whether any special groups remain who should be targeted for extra, if not total, protection from exposure to sexual activity.

The Law Reform Commission explicitly addressed this issue but, while recognising the need for protection from exploitation of vulnerability due to age (or age combined with dependence), it felt that the mentally-handicapped should not be given special protection except insofar as their handicap had been exploited. It was suggested that this should be a question of fact, as indicated in the following provision:

> Whether or not valid consent is given by a mentally handicapped person ... is a question of fact to be determined by the trier of fact.[53]

While this would be the ideal position, and indeed this writer has advocated such an approach in a broader context,[54] as has Jocelynne Scutt in her article "The Standard of Consent in Rape,"[55] it seems to be terribly difficult to apply in practice. People, including mentally handicapped people, engage in sexual activity for all kinds of reasons, because they feel like it, they want to please the other person, they want to have a baby, they are bored or want to hurt another individual, their social skills are not such as to let them say no graciously, they are frightened, confused or intimidated, or they are completely and physically under the control of someone else. In all except the last situation, a choice is made, and only the first is pure desire based on a liking for sex and possibly the other person involved. In all the others, it is difficult to distinguish consent and submission, and all of these reasons can in some sense be exploited by another. Historically distinctions have been made by focusing on the nature of the pressure brought to bear, for example, that the promise to marry is unacceptable pressure for young women between eighteen and twenty-one. Once that approach is abandoned, one is faced with perplexing philosophical questions about the nature of consent. For example, would a mentally handicapped person who was in need of affection be consenting to sexual activity? What about a person who did not have the fortitude to handle the disappointment or displeasure of others? If these factors do not vitiate consent, or rather indicate submission rather than consent, why are they different from factors such as force, and what is the test for making the distinction? Notwithstanding these concerns, this provision seems to be an improvement over a complete omission of any reference to mentally handicapped people, as in Bill C-53. At the very least it indicates that the traditional vitiating factors, the

---

53 *Report on Sexual Offences* (1978), p. 23.
54 "Married Women — Beyond the Pale of the Law of Rape" (1981), 1 Windsor Yearbook of Access to Justice 192 at 208. "Thus the *act* of *rape* should be a fact like any other to be decided on the basis of whether the victim was deprived of freedom to make a choice based simply on the experience of sex itself and the attraction of the male."
55 [1976] N.Z.L.J. 462.

main one being force, do not necessarily have to be present.

There are also difficulties with the proposal of the Law Reform Commission with respect to the exploitation of employees. It is increasingly recognised that female employees especially are vulnerable to coercive sexual touching and activity,[56] but the Commission seems somewhat complacent about the response of the legal system in stating that "individuals dismissed from employment because of refusal to submit to their employers' sexual importunities have more effective means of redress."[57] No replacement for the present narrow[58] provision is suggested. The Commission's proposals in this respect coincide with those of the Department of Justice in Bill C-53, although one should not forget the new "exercise of authority" provision in that context.

It is submitted that, when reform of the offences covered in this Chapter is again contemplated, careful thought should be given to the question of whether there are categories of especially vulnerable people who should be covered in separate offences. Apart from young people, those who should perhaps be given protection especially tailored to the particular source of their vulnerability are the mentally disabled, employees and those with a family-type relationship such as dependent children and spouses.

---

56 See generally, C.B. Backhouse, *The Secret Oppression: Sexual Harassment of Working Women* (1978), and the same author with L. Cohen, *Sexual Harassment on the Job* (1981).
57 Note 53 above, p. 25.
58 In that it deals with sexual intercourse with women under 21 years only.

Part III

Control of Decision-Making in the Criminal Justice Process

Chapter 6

Pre-Trial Decisions: An Overview

In this Part attention is focused on the evidentiary, procedural and sentencing aspects of the prosecution for sexual assault. The issues are discussed in the order that they tend to occur. This chapter contains a discussion of pre-trial matters such as the labelling of an event as a sexual assault by the victim, police and prosecutor, the decision to prosecute and the significance of plea bargaining in this context. Chapter 7 concentrates on the trial itself, the area in which the new law may have made the most profound changes. Issues such as the doctrine of recent complaint, the questioning of the complainant about her sexual history and corroboration are raised. Chapter 8 deals with sentencing.

The unifying theme of this Part is the assertion that one of the key functions of law reform is the exertion of control over the decision-makers at various levels of the criminal justice system.[1] This is not unique to the area of sexual assault, but is a particularly sensitive issue where there is justifiable concern that decisions at all stages of the process have, either consciously or unconsciously, favoured the interests of one sex over another. It can be seen from the discussion of the substantive law in Part II that a certain amount of control has been imposed on judicial decision-making on substantive issues, although enormous scope still remains for judicial law-making. Indeed the judiciary now has total control over the meaning of the basic concept of sexual assault. This is subject only to the cumbersome process of legislative law reform.

Is the picture any different with respect to control over prosecutorial discretion, or with respect to judicial decision-making on evidentiary, procedural or sentencing matters? These are certainly the issues which will help students of the criminal justice

---

1 J. BenDor, "Justice after Rape: Legal Reform in Michigan" in M.S. Walker and S.L. Brodsky, eds. *Sexual Assault* (1976).

system determine the extent and value of the changes made by the Criminal Law Amendment Act.

It is now trite to assert that it is useful to consider criminal law as a process rather than as a body of substantive law. The process is made up of a series of decision-making stages which receive more or less public scrutiny.

	1	2	3	
Victim's decisions	Police and prosecutorial decisions	Judicial decisions: trial	Judicial decisions: sentencing	Decisions by correctional officers

Obviously decisions made at all three of the stages which form the subject-matter of this Part (that is, police through to sentencing decisions) may affect a victim's decision to report the fact that a crime has been committed. Concern has been expressed by those interested in law reform about the type of decisions made at all three of these stages. It may be surmised, however, that the Criminal Law Amendment Act will have little inevitable impact on the pre-trial stage. Also, little if any change will be caused at the sentencing stage, although new maxima are introduced.[2] The Act focuses primarily on the trial stage, with most control of judicial discretion being exercised with respect to evidence. Once research reveals what is actually happening in the wake of the passage of the Act, criticism may well focus on the absence of any greater attempt to control prosecutorial and sentencing discretion. In essence, all that can be hoped is that there will be a kind of trickle-down effect of some beneficial impact of the new approach to sexual assault.

The very first stage in the process is the identification by the victim herself that she has been sexually assaulted. It might seem that this should be fairly obvious, but research has shown that the social definition of rape has not coincided with the legal definition of it,[3] and it would not be unreasonable to assume that victims

---

2 To complete the picture, it should be added that absolutely no attempt was made to reform the correctional stage. No new initiatives have been taken by Parliament with respect to the treatment or punishment of sexual offenders.

3 S.H. Klemmack and D.L. Klemmack, "The Social Definition of Rape" in M.J. Walker and S.L. Brodsky, eds., note 1 above.

might share societal perceptions of what has happened to them. Klemmack and Klemmack have carried out a study in which a group of respondents were presented with seven situations all falling within the legal definition of rape. A striking variation was found in the degrees to which each situation was identified as rape.[4] The most striking aspect was that even a violent sexual attack was not identified as rape by one hundred percent of the respondents. It was clear that the majority did not identify "social rapes" as rape. In other words, there was a considerable discrepancy between legal definitions and normative standards. There is nothing inherent in the legislation that will change this. If people have not in the past identified an unwanted sexual contact as an indecent assault there is no reason why they should do so now. However, increased public sensitivity about the right to sexual autonomy, to which the process of law reform may have contributed, may encourage victims and others to identify what has happened to them as a crime.

The next stage is, of course, the report that a crime has occurred. While no part of the legislation is directed at this *per se* it was no doubt hoped that the removal of the special evidentiary barriers to conviction and increased control over the use of evidence of past sexual conduct would encourage victims to come forward. It may also happen that the use of the term "sexual assault" rather than "rape" will contribute to this same goal. The former should not carry the same stigma, and helps to protect the privacy of the victim.

Lewis and Clark have helped to focus attention on the exercise of police discretion to label complaints as founded or unfounded. Their work suggests a certain amount of police scepticism in the past toward rape claims[5] and a greater willingness to "found" rape complaints where the victim is a young virgin or respectable married woman rather than a person who lives in an unorthodox situation, was drunk, or was raped while hitchhiking.[6] Research

---

4 *E.g.*, 92 percent reported that rape had occurred where a woman was attacked in a parking lot by a man who beat her up and had sexual relations. Only 18.8 percent thought that rape had occurred where a woman had been dating a man for three months: they were kissing and embracing in his apartment when she said she wanted to stop and he had sex with her after a struggle. *Ibid.*, at 142.

5 *Rape: The Price of Coercive Sexuality* (1977). See also N. Gagner and C. Schurr, *Sexual Assault: Confronting Rape in America* (1976), and L. Holmstrom and A. Burgess, *The Victim of Rape: Institutional Reactions* (1978).

6 Other research in the U.S. has shown officials to take less seriously complaints by women who are black. See, *e.g.*, Comment, "Police Discretion and the Judg-

comparing sexual assault to other crimes provides another perspective. Myers and Lafree conducted a comparative study from which they concluded that victim attributes do not affect the way in which complaints are processed any differently for sexual than for other crimes.[7] Rather, any crucial differences depended on characteristics of the accused, the context of the crime and evidence.[8] No doubt greater research is necessary to give us a full picture of what happens at this stage of the criminal justice process. The point that is relevant here is that the legislation did not address this issue. However police exercise their discretion, they may be seen to have nearly total control over the entry-point to the process.[9]

Similarly, once a charge is laid,[10] the prosecutor has a vast amount of control over the matter.[11] This control makes possible the controversial practice of plea bargaining. It is not possible to deal with that massive subject here,[12] but it is nevertheless rele-

---

ment that a Crime has been Committed—Rape in Philadelphia" (1968), 117 U. Pa. L. Rev. 277 at 302-7, and G.D. Lafree, "Variables Affecting Guilty Pleas and Convictions in Rape Cases: Toward a Social Theory of Rape Processing" (1980), 58 Soc. Forces 833.

7 "Sexual Assault and its Prosecution: A Comparison with Other Crimes" (1982), J. of Crim. Law and Criminology 1281.

8 To a great extent, this does not conflict with the findings of Lewis and Clark, since they stress the reluctance of police to proceed with complaints which they feel have no chance of proceeding to conviction. The difference in perspective arises from the fact that Lewis and Clark concentrate on rape and make no comparative assertions. They estimated that two-thirds of the cases labelled unfounded are classified in that way because of the influence of pragmatic considerations of what the likely outcome of a trial would be. Note 5 above, p. 58.

9 See B.A. Grosman, *The Prosecutor* (1969), pp. 23-7, and generally on police and prosecutorial discretion, K.C. Davis, "Discretionary Justice: A Preliminary Inquiry" (1969) and "Observation: An Approach to Legal Control of the Police" (1974), 52 Tex. L.R. 703; W.R. Lafave, "The Police and Non-enforcement of the Law," [1962] Wisc. L.R. 104 and 179; J. Goldstein, "Police Discretion Not to Invoke the Criminal Process: Low Visibility Decisions in the Administration of Justice" (1960), 69 Yale L.J. 543; B.M. Barker, "Police Discretion and the Principle of Legality" (1965-66), 8 Crim. L.Q. 400.

10 Grosman, *ibid.*, p. 20.

11 The prosecutor can decide whether to prosecute or not. See Grosman, *ibid.*, pp. 20-1. The prosecutor can reduce the charges, stay proceedings (ss. 508 and 732.1) or withdraw them altogether with the leave of the court.

12 See generally, G.A. Ferguson and D.W. Roberts, "Plea Bargaining, Directions for Canadian Reform" (1974), 52 Can. Bar Rev. 497; D.W. Perras, "Plea Negotiations" (1979), 22 Crim. L.Q. 58; S.N. Verdun-Jones and F.D. Cousineau, "Cleansing the Augean Stables: A Critical Analysis of Recent Trends in the Plea Bargaining Debate in Canada" (1979), 17 Osg. H.L.J. 227.

vant to ask whether the new offences will facilitate or discourage plea bargaining in this context, and whether that is a cause for congratulation or concern.

The hierarchy of assault and sexual assault offences would appear to invite plea bargaining. Even though, under the old law, in many cases it would have been possible to plead guilty to indecent assault or assault rather than rape, the perception of the range of offences may now subtly change. The list of assault and sexual assault offences may have a stronger appearance of quantitative rather than qualitative difference, and this could promote plea bargaining. It may not, for example, be so controversial to accept a plea to sexual assault causing bodily harm rather than proceeding with aggravated sexual assault charges. Where a minor sexual assault has occurred, a prosecutor may be tempted to accept a guilty plea to simple assault, particularly where there are interpretation problems with the meaning of the word "sexual." It should also be remembered that the prosecution has the option of proceeding summarily or by way of indictment on the lowest level, so this may be an element of the negotiations prior to some trials.

Plea bargaining carries with it the obvious dangers of overcharging and, in rare cases, the possibility of a total miscarriage of justice where the accused is not guilty but the case against him appears overwhelming. These are not new dangers, but the structure of the present law may exacerbate them. On the other hand, the interests of the victim are of considerable significance.[13] It may be in the public interest to secure a conviction to *some* type of assault rather than to require her to undergo the traumatic experience of testifying with the attendant risks, incidental to any trial, of failing to secure a conviction. No doubt it would be ideal if the advantages of plea bargaining could be enjoyed without the associated costs but, as things stand, there is bound to be difference of opinion on whether this aspect of the new offences is to be labelled as a positive factor or a cause for concern.

Again, the bottom line is that the reform did not touch the exercise of prosecutorial discretion. Apart from the structure of the offences, no new element has been added to the debate about control over this stage of the criminal justice process. This is not

---

13 This is so both because she ought to be protected from unnecessary distress in a civilized society and because practices discouraging reporting will leave other members of the public at risk.

necessarily a criticism, as Parliament may be justified in taking the view that the provinces should take the initiative in this matter.[14] To place the reform in perspective, it cannot be seen as a radical re-ordering of the way we are tackling the social problems of sexual assault. It is much more linked to manipulation of the substantive concepts, as well as some evidentiary matters which are the subject of Chapter 7.

---

14 "The basic question of who has the power to investigate and prosecute a crime which is clearly criminal in the constitutional sense is still unresolved in Canada. As the ultimate answer offers the key to the control of the criminal justice system, there is perhaps no more important undecided constitutional question in Canada." See L. Arbour and L.T. Taman, *Criminal Procedure, Cases, Text and Materials* (1980), p. 38 and generally pp. 37-59, including their note on *R. v. Hauser*, [1977] 6 W.W.R. 501 (reversed [1979] 1 S.C.R. 984), pp. 57-8. See also L.T. Taman, *"Hauser* and Control Over Criminal Prosecutions in Canada" (1980), 1 Supreme Court L.R. 401.

Chapter 7

Evidence and the Trial Process

Rape and some other associated sexual offences have always been regarded as requiring distinctive rules of evidence in order to ensure a fair trial. As suggested in Chapter 1, the primary value embodied in the rules of evidence was the protection of accused persons from the false accusations of complainants. The accused was therefore unique in the criminal process in that he enjoyed such extraordinary protections as those relating to corroboration and the privilege of questioning the complainant extensively about her sexual history.

The Criminal Law Amendment Act went a long way towards standardising the rules of evidence in the context of sexual offences. These changes, along with a brief discussion of the issue of trial publicity, are the subjects of this chapter.

1. THE SEXUAL HISTORY OF THE COMPLAINANT

The Criminal Law Amendment Act made some significant changes to the law relating to evidence of the complainant's sexual activity with persons other than the accused. Before proceeding to a discussion of the new section 246.6 of the Code, however, it may be helpful to the reader to be aware of the history of this area of law and of this latest attempt to protect the complainant from unnecessary embarrassment and to avoid the possibility of bias.[1]

Prior to April 1976, a complainant could be asked questions about prior sexual conduct, but could not be obliged by the accused

---

1 For some empirical findings on the effect on a jury, see K. Catton, "Evidence Regarding the Prior Sexual History of an Alleged Rape Victim—Its Effect on the Perceived Guilt of the Accused" (1975), 33 U. of T.L. Rev. 156, and S.H. Nelson, "An Experimental Study Concerning Jury Decisions in Rape Trials" (1978), 1 C.R. (3d) 265.

to answer.[2] Nor could the accused lead evidence to contradict her testimony.[3] Nevertheless, many complainants were unaware of their rights in this respect[4] and concern grew that they were being caused needless pain and embarrassment when subjected to extensive cross-examination about their life-style by defence counsel.[5]

This concern led to the old section 142 of the Code,[6] which was apparently intended to set some reasonable limits on questioning regarding the sexual history of the complainant, and thus hopefully increase the rape reporting rate.[7] Section 142 stated that no question could be asked as to the sexual conduct of the complainant unless:

(1) reasonable notice was given;

---

2 *Laliberté v. R.* (1877), 1 S.C.R. 117. For a fuller discussion of the case law, see C. Boyle, "Section 142 of the Criminal Code: A Trojan Horse?" (1981), 23 C.L.Q. 253 at 253-4.

3 See *R. v. Holmes* (1871), L.R. 1 C.C.R. 334; *R. v. Greatbanks* [1959] Crim. L.R. 450; *R. v. Bashir*, [1969] 3 All E.R. 692; *R. v. Basken* (1974), 28 C.R.N.S. 359 (Sask. C.A.); *Forsythe v. R.*, [1980] 2 S.C.R. 268.

4 Although Mr. Justice Haines suggested that judges had the power to protect complainants. See "The Character of the Rape Victim" (1975), 23 Chitty's L.J. 57.

5 See, *e.g.*, J.A. Scutt, "Admissibility of Sexual History Evidence and Allegations in Rape Cases" (1979), 53 A.L.J. 817, and C. Bohmer and A. Blumberg, "Twice Traumatized: The Rape Victim in the Courtroom" (1975), 58 Judicature 391. See also the remarks of Bray C.J. in *R. v. Gunn, Ex parte Stephenson*, [1977] 17 S.A.S.R. 165 at 167-8, quoted by the Federal/Provincial Task Force on Uniform Rules of Evidence (1982), p. 67.
   "I find it hard to believe that any reasonable person at the present time could assent to any of the following absurd propositions:
   1. That a willingness to have sexual intercourse outside marriage with someone is equivalent to a willingness to have sexual intercourse outside marriage with anyone;
   2. That the unchaste are also liable to be untruthful;
   3. That a woman who has had sexual intercourse outside marriage is a fallen woman and deserves any sexual fate that comes her way.
   Yet it is all too likely that a covert appeal, if not to the affirmative of these propositions, at least to the attitude that underlies them, has been made in the past by means of cross-examination as to credit."

6 Criminal Law Amendment Act, S.C. 1974-75-76, c. 93.

7 The Honourable Ron Basford, then Minister of Justice, on moving the Second Reading of Bill C-71, stated that the amendment was "aimed at minimizing the embarrassment the victim must undergo, thereby increasing the number of rapes that are reported and prosecuted." Parl. Debs. H.C., Vol. IX (1975), at 9204.

(2) with sufficient particulars of the evidence sought to be adduced; and

(3) the judge, after an *in camera* hearing, decided that exclusion would prevent the "just determination of an issue of fact in the proceedings, including the credibility" of the complainant.

The Supreme Court of Canada had the opportunity in *Forsythe v. R.*[8] to explain the meaning of this provision.[9] It was indicated in *dicta* that the complainant was a compellable witness at the *in camera* hearing and that her evidence, once given, could be contradicted in evidence led by the accused. Thus, it seemed that an amendment touted as an improvement in the position of the complainant had the opposite effect.[10]

Complainants were entirely dependent on protection by the judiciary who, for example, allowed questions "intended to establish that the complainant had sexual encounters with truck-drivers during her travels as a hitchhiker,"[11] and questions "intended to establish that the complainant was in the habit of attending at licenced premises with the intention of meeting males with the eventual purpose of sexual gratification."[12] However, a number of judges stressed that questioning should not be allowed to turn into a fishing expedition,[13] and in *R. v. O'Brien*,[14]

---

8 Note 3 above.

9 For a discussion of *Forsythe*, see generally C. Boyle, note 2 above.

10 Thus, as suggested by Steele D.C.J. of Newfoundland in *R. v. O'Brien* (1976), 36 C.R.N.S. 84 at 95, "to make the complainant a compellable witness would to a large extent defeat the purpose of the amendment." *Cf.* also *R. v. Lloyd* (1977), 37 C.C.C. (2d) 272 (N.S. C.A.) and *R. v. Turner* (1976), 35 C.R.N.S. 398 (N.W.T. S.C.) which held that s. 142 was in essence declaratory of existing procedure. This is also the view expressed in the *Report of the Federal/Provincial Task Force on Uniform Rules of Evidence* (1982), which contains a very full discussion of the old s. 142 and relevant case law, at pp. 65-77.

11 *R. v. MacIntyre* (1978), 42 C.C.C. (2d) 217 (Ont. Dist. Ct.).

12 *R. v. McKenna* (1976), 32 C.C.C. (2d) 210 (Ont. Prov. Ct.). In both the above cases no further particulars of the questioning were required.

13 See *Lizotte v. R.* (1980), 18 C.R. (3d) 364 (Que. C.A.). See also *R. v. Lawson* (1978), 39 C.C.C. (2d) 85 (B.C. C.A.) where the trial judge was upheld in refusing an *in camera* hearing where the particulars of the notice were inadequate. The questions proposed included: "Have you ever had sexual intercourse with any person other than the Accused prior to the alleged sexual intercourse. . . .? Have you ever performed an act of a sexual nature involving oral genital contact with another person, whether male or female. . . .? Have you ever participated in completed or incompleted anal intercourse?"

14 See note 10 above.

the court would not admit evidence of intercourse with two other men roughly a month and a year respectively before the incident in question.

Whether or not *Forsythe* subverted the intent behind the old section 142,[15] it has now been repealed, and Parliament has made a second attempt at embodying the value of protecting witnesses from harassment in some more foolproof way.

It will be seen that the new provisions relate to all sexual assault offences, and the admissibility requirements can be classified as establishing new tests of relevance and as procedural in nature. As well, other privacy protections are included.

(a) *The Tests of Relevance*

The evidence can be adduced if it falls into one of the three categories in section 246.6(1):

> In proceedings in respect of an offence under section 246.1, 246.2 or 246.3 [that is, all the sexual assault offences], no evidence shall be adduced by or on behalf of the accused concerning the sexual activity of the complainant with any person other than the accused unless
>
> (a) it is evidence that rebuts evidence of the complainant's sexual activity or absence thereof that was previously adduced by the prosecution;
>
> (b) it is evidence of specific instances of the complainant's sexual activity tending to establish the identity of the person who had sexual contact with the complainant on the occasion set out in the charge; or
>
> (c) it is evidence of sexual activity that took place on the same occasion as the sexual activity that forms the subject-matter of the charge, where that evidence relates to the consent that the accused alleges he believed was given by the complainant.

Rebuttal evidence, in section 246.6(1)(a), seems self-explanatory, though it is difficult to think of circumstances under which the Crown would perceive it as advantageous from a tactical perspective to lead evidence of the complainant's sex life. Perhaps the crucial phrase is the reference to the "absence" of sexual activity. If the Crown evidence suggests that the complainant was not a sexually-active person then the defence can rebut this. Obviously the Crown should exercise some caution in this respect.

Section 246.6(1)(b), the "identity" provision, is more complex, and its inclusion is testimony to the fact that this issue is not

---

15 Madam Justice Wilson, in commenting on the effect of *Forsythe*, stated in *R. v. Konkin* (1983), 34 C.R. (3d) 1 at 9 (S.C.C.) that in "effect, s. 142, instead of minimising the embarrassment to complainants, increased it."

susceptible to simplistic solutions. The tendency in this area has been, unfortunately, simply to assert or deny the relevance of the sexual activity of the complainant.[16] One can appreciate the reluctance of those concerned about the abuse of such evidence in the past to concede its relevance in any context, but the problems have arisen with respect to the introduction of the evidence to suggest consent or to undermine the credibility of the complainant. Its use for these purposes is unjustifiable since the tests of relevance, common sense and human experience, suggest that people exercise choice over each sexual partner.[17] Moreover, there is no evidence to suggest that sexual activity has any link with credibility. Indeed, acceptance of such an idea would surely be against the interests of the accused, who normally admits the sexual activity, but wishes to be believed on the issue of consent.

Nevertheless, it is possible to think of rare cases where the theory of the defence is not consent, but mistaken identity. An example would be where it is part of the Crown's case that the complainant contracted venereal disease from the accused, and the defence wishes to give evidence that the accused did not have the disease and that she contracted it from some other person.

It is important to note, however, that the identity provision is extremely narrow. The evidence must tend to establish the identity of the person who had sexual contact with the complainant *on the occasion set out in the charge,* so that evidence that simply points away from the accused, but towards anyone else in particular, or does not relate to that occasion, is inadmissible. In addition, it must be noted that only evidence of *specific instances* is admissible, so defence counsel must not be permitted to ask broad-ranging questions about the sexual life-style of the complainant. Unless the judiciary gives an unexpectedly broad interpretation to this provision (as indeed happened in *Forsythe*) it is

---

16 See, *e.g.,* S.A. Andrews, "Issues as to the Credibility of Witnesses," [1965] Crim. L.R. 461 at 466, where it is stated boldly that the evidence "may be highly relevant to the issue of consent." A joint statement on Bill C-53 issued by the Toronto Area Caucus of Women and the Law stated that the relevant section "must state clearly and simply that previous sexual history is irrelevant and inadmissible."

17 In a comment on *Forsythe* in C. Boyle, "Section 142 of the Criminal Code: A Trojan Horse?" (1981), 23 C.L.Q. 253, it was noted that, even in the case of a prostitute, the reasonable assumption would seem to be that choice is exercised in each case, even if that choice relates to the amount of money offered.

submitted that this is a principled and justifiable exception to the general rule of inadmissibility.

The same cannot be said of the last, most controversial subsection, the "same occasion" provision. Section 246.6(1)(c) relates to the defence of mistake of fact and its effect is that, where this is the theory of the defence, the accused can ask questions about sexual activity on the same occasion as the act that forms the subject-matter of the charge, in an attempt presumably to strengthen his argument that he thought the complainant was consenting. Boiled down to its essentials, therefore, the defence would go like this: "The complainant had just had sex with one, two or more persons so I thought she was consenting to have sex with me."

In one sense this is a narrow provision in that it relates to a very particular set of facts, and more importantly it is confined to the mistaken belief in consent issue. If the accused argues consent (as is usual) he will often be precluded from *also* arguing mistake of fact, applying the *ratio* in *Pappajohn*,[18] and he will not be able to use this provision. The accused will therefore normally be forced to put his eggs in the mistake of fact basket, thus conceding the absense of consent, a dangerous step in many cases, in order to ask the complainant questions under this subsection.[19]

Nevertheless, it is still difficult to discern the reasoning behind the provision. The defence would be based on the accused's belief that, because the complainant has sex with X, she was consenting to have sex with him. In other words, the subsection seems to endorse the view that it is non-culpable to think that sexually-active women are "fair game" for everyone, even if only on the same occasion.[20] Is it appropriate for Parliament to give that view of women the status of a rule of law rather than indicating that it is culpable in itself?

An issue arises as to whether the subsection could be used in the context of a "gang-rape." If the victim had been sexually

---

18 See section 7 of this chapter, "*Pappajohn*: Alternative Defences."

19 This may not be a practical limitation as, once the evidence is in, it may influence the finder of fact to find consent, even if this is not officially argued, but it still will pose a tactical dilemma for the defence.

20 To demonstrate how ridiculous this is, apply it to a married woman who had just had intercourse with her husband. Technically, an accused could introduce that sexual activity as the basis for his belief that she consented to have sex with him immediately afterwards. If this is discarded as outrageous what does that tell us about the view of other women that this provision envisions? It tells us that it is all right to think that, because a woman has had sex with one man, she immediately will consent to intercourse with another.

assaulted already and, still in fear, submitted to the accused, could he argue that he thought she had willingly had sex with the others so he mistakenly thought she was consenting to have sex with him? Looking at this from the perspective of the accused, it would seem that he should be able to do this. The only counter-argument would turn on the meaning of "sexual activity." Since the whole section relates to the sexual activity of the complainant, it would seem to be a distortion of the natural meaning of the term to label being sexually assaulted as *her* sexual activity. (Indeed, one might question whether it is sexual activity of any description.) If that view were adopted, however, it would mean that evidence that the complainant had been sexually assaulted by others on the same occasion would fall outside this section altogether and not be subject to the limitations within it.

One decision of the Supreme Court of Canada deserves discussion at this point, that in *R. v. Konkin*,[21] relating to the sexual activity of the complainant *subsequent* to the offence. At the Court of Appeal level[22] it was held that the trial judge had erred in not allowing evidence of the fact that the complainant had had sexual relations with several men in one evening on more than one occasion after the offence. The complainant indicated that her intention was to degrade men as she had been degraded. The trial judge had invited defence counsel to demonstrate the relevance of this evidence, stating:

> "I really have difficulty following your reasoning there. . . . What has her sexual conduct after the event got to do with her credibility? I mean, are you saying that people that have a lot of sex are dishonest?"[23]

On appeal to the Supreme Court of Canada, Laskin C.J.C., speaking for the majority, did not address the issue of post-offence sexual activity, but simply upheld the decision of the Alberta Court of Appeal on the ground that the trial judge excluded the evidence in principle and not after the exercise of his discretion. Madam Justice Wilson dissented on the ground that the trial judge *had* decided the evidence to be irrelevant on the facts of the case. He had invited defence counsel to demonstrate the relevance and counsel had not succeeded in doing so. No guidance as to the relevance of post-offence sexual conduct was provided by the court, the case being sent back for a new trial. All that can be

21 (1983), 34 C.R. (3d) 1.
22 [1981] 6 W.W.R. 632.
23 Note 21 above at 5.

extracted from the decision is that this type of evidence *could* relate to credibility[24] and that no reinforcement was given to the trial judge's concern to limit inquiry into "the traumatic effect of the rape."[25]

While the *Konkin* decision may well cause considerable concern about the commitment of the Supreme Court of Canada to the protection of the victim of sexual assault, the admissibility of such evidence will now be governed by section 246.6, which does not distinguish between pre- and post-offence sexual activity. Will post-offence sexual activity ever be admissible as evidence? It would appear that it could come under section 246.6(1)(a), although the Crown has the power to prevent this. It could not come within the terms of section 246.6(1)(b) unless it related to the identity of the person who engaged in the sexual contact in question. Section 246.6(1)(c) could never be applicable as it seems impossible to reason that the accused believed in consent on the basis of sexual activity that had not yet taken place.

In effect, therefore, the most significant change that has taken place is the removal of the suggestion in the old section 142 that sexual activity could relate to credibility. Now that this has been removed, it is hoped that a vague and broad decision like *Konkin* could never occur again.

(b) *Procedure*

Certain procedural protections are contained in subsections 246.6(2) and (3):

> (2) No evidence is admissible under paragraph (1)(c) unless
>   (a) reasonable notice in writing has been given to the prosecutor by or on behalf of the accused of his intention to adduce the evidence together with particulars of the evidence sought to be adduced; and
>   (b) a copy of the notice has been filed with the clerk of the court.
>
> (3) No evidence is admissible under subsection (1) unless the judge, magistrate or justice, after holding a hearing in which the jury and the members of the public are excluded and in which the complainant is not a compellable witness, is satisfied that the requirements of this section are met.

---

24 If it could sometimes, why not all the time?

25 The learned trial judge had a predecessor in *R. v. Barker* (1829), 172 E.R. 558, in which it was stated (at 558-9) that, with respect to criminal conversation, "the conduct of the wife before the alleged adultery is no doubt highly material ... but not her conduct afterwards, because that may have been caused by the conduct of the party himself."

Section 246.6(2) is similar to the old section 142(1)(a) and (b),[26] but with some significant changes.

This new provision speaks of the admissibility of evidence, in contrast to the old section which referred to questions. Thus it would seem that there has been a weakening of the requirement that notice and particulars be given, as the old section referred to "notice of . . . intention to ask such question together with particulars of the evidence to be adduced *by such question.*"[27] If there was indeed a requirement that notice and particulars of each question be given under the old provision, this has now been removed. One could speculate that Parliament was simply catching up with the actual practice of judges here, as there was no consistent demand that the accused satisfy the requirements of the subsection.[28] Nevertheless, at least one court had insisted on the full vigour of the protection granted,[29] so that this change could certainly be seen as a real diminution in the admittedly uneven protection of the complainant from surprise.

---

26 Which were held applicable to cases where rape was charged along with other offences. See *R. v. Calabrese (No. 1)* (1981), 63 C.C.C. (2d) 239 (Que. S.C.). Hugessen A.C.J. indicated, at 241, that in any event the proposed questioning was irrelevant. "It would be, in my view, equivalent to allowing a bank teller, who testifies to having been the victim of a hold-up, to be cross-examined as to his or her private life and sexual conduct. What can that possibly have to do with the facts of the offence to which he or she has testified?" *Cf. R. v. Deslaurier* (1977), 36 C.C.C. (2d) 327 (Ont. C.A.).

27 Section 142(1)(a) [repealed 1980-81-82, c. 125, s. 6] (italics added).

28 See, *e.g., R. v. MacIntyre* (1978), 42 C.C.C. (2d) 217 (Ont. Dist. Ct.). Here the particulars accepted by the court indicated that the evidence was "intended to establish that the complainant has had sexual encounters with truck drivers, during her travels as a hitchhiker." The decision to permit this questioning was partially based on her evidence that she sometimes told truckers she was 14 "'because then they don't . . . come on to me sexually because they are frightened of the law and it helps because a lot of them do come on and it's very horrible (at 219).'" See also *R. v. McKenna* (1976), 32 C.C.C. (2d) 210 (Ont. Prov. Ct.).

29 "The section requires notice of the specific questions proposed." *Per* Meredith J. in *R. v. Morris* (1977), 1 C.R. (3d) 284 at 287 (B.C. S.C.). This in order to avoid surprise. See also *Lizotte v. R.* (1980), 18 C.R. (3d) 364 (Que. C.A.), and *R. v. Blondheim* (1980), 54 C.C.C. (2d) 36 (Ont. C.A.). The particulars here were deficient, and thus the court was not required to hold the *in camera* hearing. The complainant was a resident of a centre for retarded adults and the accused was a counsellor there. The notice referred to her sexual conduct with a named resident, and other conduct, that had "given rise to the complainant's reputation as a sexually loose and promiscuous person" and her manipulation of "sexual favours resulting in conflict with other trainees."

The requirement of notice and particulars only relates to evidence admissible under section 246.6(1)(c), the "same occasion" exception. A hearing must still be held under 246.6(3) with respect to all evidence of sexual activity, but the Crown is not entitled to notice and particulars of evidence admitted under subsections (1)(a) and (1)(b). The omission of subsection (1)(a) is hardly significant as the Crown will presumably expect rebuttal evidence, but one wonders why a distinction has been made between subsections (1)(b) and (1)(c). Again, this is a reduction in the protection provided for the complainant by the old section 142, which required notice of all questioning relating to sexual conduct. It would begin to appear as if improvements in the tests of relevance have been "balanced" by reduction in the procedural protections.

The requirement of reasonable notice remains the same and is a question of fact for the trial judge, who may take into account the time sufficient "to allow the Crown to conduct whatever interview he might then have deemed necessary to be conducted with the complainant."[30] It is submitted that this should not be the only test, but that the reasonableness of the notice should depend on the nature of the evidence in each case. In some circumstances, the Crown may require time for investigative work other than an interview with the complainant. This highlights the desirability of full particulars in the notice and underscores the oddity of the failure to require notice vis-à-vis section 246.6(1)(b).

With respect to subsection (3), which applies to all types of evidence admitted under subsection (1), the most significant change is that the complainant is not a compellable witness at the mandatory in camera hearing, held to determine whether the requirements of the section are satisfied. This is a direct legislative reversal of the Forsythe decision. Its effect is that the accused has to persuade the court, without the assistance of the complainant, that the evidence is admissible, in that it satisfies one of the tests of relevance.

Subsection (3) is silent, however, on the question of whether the complainant can be required to give evidence of her sexual activity at the trial proper. This is a complex issue. The section itself does not expressly state that the complainant must answer such questions, so one might therefore assume that the position

30 R. v. McKenna, note 28 above, at 214. See also R. v. Lawson, (1978), 39 C.C.C. (2d) 85 (B.C. C.A.), which indicates that the usual time for the application would be after the examination-in-chief of the complainant, and before or during cross-examination.

remains as it was at common law, when the accused could not insist that the complainant respond.[31] Nevertheless, *Forsythe* indicated that the complainant *is* a compellable witness on this issue in spite of the absence of any express change in the common-law position in the old section 142. However, *Forsythe* was a decision on the *in camera* hearing only and its *ratio* has, in the clearest possible terms, been overturned by Parliament. Is it therefore of any value as the basis of an argument by analogy? Whether it is or not, it is predicted that section 246.6 will be construed as giving the accused the right to insist on answers on the same basis as *Forsythe*, that is, that Parliament has indicated that sometimes evidence of sexual activity is relevant. It was reasoned that, therefore, it would be unfair to the accused if he were not permitted to compel the complainant to answer. In other words, the courts may read more into the section than it actually says. It indicates exceptions to the general rule that evidence may *not* be adduced, but does not say that the complainant is under an obligation to provide any evidence that falls within the exceptions. The ironic result may be similar to that produced in *Forsythe*. Some evidence, perhaps a great deal, may be excluded, but what is admitted has been stamped by Parliament as having a more directly relevant quality.[32] Thus the complainant is denied the protections she had prior to legislative intervention, *with respect to precisely the same evidence.*[33]

One final point should be made. Case law suggests that the judge has to be satisfied on the balance of probabilities that the evidence satisfies the requirements of the section.[34] Like all standards of proof, this is a flexible standard, not susceptible to precise quantification. Whether it is satisfied must be influenced by the decision-maker's preparedness to be persuaded and, thus, the absence of the complainant's evidence may well influence the court. It will be very difficult to tell, therefore, whether the reversal

---

31 Although it would appear that the judge always had the discretion to insist that the complainant answer. *Laliberté v. R.* (1877), 1 S.C.R. 117. However, this case is sometimes cited for the view that she can never be required to answer, as in *Gross v. Brodrecht* (1897), 24 O.A.R. 687.

32 Since it relates to more than simply a "collateral" matter.

33 It may be that this problem was anticipated in England in the equivalent provisions there. Section 2(4) of the Sexual Offences (Amendment) Act 1976, states that "[n]othing in this section authorizes evidence to be adduced or a question to be asked which cannot be adduced or asked apart from this section." Section 2 provides an admissibility test of fairness to the accused.

34 *R. v. O'Brien* (1976), 36 C.R.N.S. 84 (Nfld. Dist. Ct.).

of *Forsythe* actually cuts down on the questioning of the complainant. If the judge feels that it would be fair to the accused to ask the questions then he or she can probably give permission and require the complainant to answer the questions at the trial proper. The result is that the judge still has the ultimate control over this type of questioning. However, it would seem an impossible task to forbid the judge to be influenced by a refusal to give evidence. Even if the section clearly said that a complainant is *never* compellable on this matter, it is not within the power of Parliament to forbid the judge to have a certain type of reasonable doubt. That would require a commitment of the particular judge to the ideals reflected in the legislation.

It is submitted therefore, that one will have to wait for an answer to the question whether the non-compellability of the complainant at the hearing stage is a significant or an illusory protection.

(c) *Other Protections*

Additional protections are to be found in subsections 246.6(4), (5) and (6):

> (4) The notice given under subsection (2) and the evidence taken, the information given or the representations made at a hearing referred to in subsection (3) shall not be published in any newspaper or broadcast.
> (5) Every one who, without lawful excuse the proof of which lies upon him, contravenes subsection (4) is guilty of an offence punishable on summary conviction.
> (6) In this section, "newspaper" has the same meaning as in section 261.

These provisions duplicate the equivalent parts of old section 142 although section 142(5), containing a definition of "complainant," has been removed to its proper home in section 2 of the Code.[35] Although we do not have the benefit of judicial interpretation as yet, it can be seen that these provisions raise two interesting issues, one relating to the meaning of newspaper in subsection (6), the other to the reverse onus clause in subsection (5).

The only place where I have seen particulars of the notice given under subsection (2) is in case reports and case comments.[36] Could these be newspapers? Applying the definition in section 261,[37] it would appear that any periodical published at intervals

---

35 It means the victim of the alleged offence.
36 Indeed I have just quoted some of them in footnotes. See, *e.g.*, note 13 above.
37 Section 261 contains a definition of newspaper:
  In sections 262 to 281, "newspaper" means any paper, magazine or

not exceeding thirty-one days would be covered, since it would certainly contain "reports of events," if not "public news." If this is so, it would appear that the newspaper net has been cast too widely,[38] even if the risk of prosecution is remote.

The values which ought to be protected by a provision of this nature do not conflict, in the sense that they can all be accommodated without difficulty. First of all, there is the privacy of the complainant. Certainly that privacy should not be invaded unless there is some more significant interest at stake. Other interests are those of potential complainants in public discussion and criticism of the judicial enforcement of the measures designed to protect them. (Sample issues relate to whether judges require particulars to be given in the notice, and if so, what kind of particulars.) There is also the public interest generally in knowing how the criminal justice system functions. Accused persons must also benefit from public knowledge of the working of the criminal justice system. Apart from this, there does not appear to be any interest of the accused involved. The interests of both the public and potential complainants can be protected by permitting publication without any identifying information. It may not always be feasible to conceal the identity of the complainant in such media as daily newspapers so that further protection of privacy is justified in that instance. However, concealment of identity is much more realistic, and the likelihood of the analysis being in the public interest is much higher, in case report series and academic journals.

It is possible that, if an academic publisher were prosecuted, legal education and/or research would be construed as a "lawful excuse." This is a notoriously vague phrase,[39] which has received

---

periodical containing public news, intelligence or reports of events, or any remarks or observations thereon, printed for sale and published periodically or in parts or numbers, at intervals not exceeding thirty-one days between the publication of any two such papers, parts or numbers, and any paper, magazine or periodical printed in order to be dispersed and made public, weekly or more often, or at intervals not exceeding thirty-one days, that contains advertisement, exclusively or principally.

38 In one sense it may be seen to have been cast very narrowly since publication in a book or any single publication has not been prohibited at all. This could prove useful to those who wish to publish studies of judicial decision-making in this context.

39 Glanville Williams seems to throw up his hands saying "whatever may be the meaning of 'without lawful excuse'. . . ." *Textbook of Criminal Law* (1978), p. 413. Stuart comments that the meaning "is most uncertain, referring sometimes to conduct where there is some express authorization by law and

very little judicial interpretation in Canada,[40] probably for the same reason that the term is used in the first place: discretion is perceived as desirable because of the view that unforeseen circumstances may occur. No exhaustive definition of the term is attempted in the leading cases of *R. v. St. Clair*,[41] *R. v. Cameron*,[42] *R. v. Kiverago*,[43] or *R. v. McFall*[44] (all focusing on obscenity), but *Kiverago* indicates that the goal of medical/scientific education or research would be an excuse for publishing obscene material. Since this situation is closely analogous to that of the publication of evidence in sexual assault cases in reports and academic journals, the courts are likely to apply the "lawful excuse" standard in both instances.[45] However, even if this is the case, the vagueness of the "lawful excuse" provision is surely contrary to the public interest and perhaps unconstitutional. Vagueness in itself may discourage publication which the judiciary, if given the chance, would find to be legal. It therefore is an interference with freedom of expression. This type of vague formulation in a sense also gives judges an offence-creating power which, in spirit, may offend section 8 of the Code prohibiting common-law offences. Surely it is the role of Parliament to consider when the publication of this material is in the public interest.

A further avenue for judicial "creativity" will open up if these provisions are challenged under section 11(d) of the Canadian Charter of Rights and Freedoms. Section 246.6(5) of the Code could be offensive constitutionally as infringing the right to be presumed innocent until proved guilty. This right has recently received considerable judicial[46] and academic[47] attention, and it

---

sometimes to anything that would result in an acquittal, including a lack of *mens rea*." (1983), 32 C.R. (3d) 324.

40   This in spite of the fact that it is a relatively popular formula. See Code ss. 78, 86, 115, 116, 159(2), 185(2)(a), 193(2)(b), 239, 262 and 401.

41   (1913), 28 O.L.R. 271 (C.A.).

42   [1966] 2 O.R. 777 (C.A.).

43   (1973), 11 C.C.C. (2d) 463 (Ont. C.A.).

44   (1975), 26 C.C.C. (2d) 181 (B.C. C.A.).

45   Particularly since it can be reinforced by s. 2(b) of the Canadian Charter of Rights and Freedoms, (en. by the Canada Act, 1982 (U.K.), c. 11, Sched. B), *i.e.*, "freedom of . . . expression, including freedom of the press. . . ." A s. 1 argument might well justify prohibition of publication of such matters in newspapers, but not be strong enough to save a ban on publication in academic journals, etc.

46   See, *e.g.*, *R. v. Oakes* (1983), 32 C.R. (3d) 193 (Ont. C.A.), and *R. v. Carroll* (1983), 32 C.R. (3d) 235 (P.E.I. C.A.).

47   See the definitive article by Wayne MacKay and Tom Cromwell, "*Oakes*: A Bold Initiative Impeded by Old Ghosts" (1983), 32 C.R. (3d) 221.

is not appropriate in this book to go into the subject in the depth it deserves. Some comments may be helpful, however.

The leading cases so far have focused on section 8 of the Narcotic Control Act,[48] and therefore provide little assistance in this context. *Oakes* suggests a "rational connection" test between the fact proved and the fact to be proved. This test would not be useful in the context of unlawful publication, since the Crown does not have to prove any initial fact with respect to the absence of a lawful excuse, but simply the elements of the crime. The accused then has the opportunity to raise an argument if possible in the circumstances.[49] Reverse onus clauses of this kind will therefore require their own analysis. This issue has been tackled in a number of Charter cases already, most notably *R. v. Holmes*,[50] an Ontario Court of Appeal decision relating to section 309(1), which states as follows:

> Every one who, without lawful excuse, the proof of which lies upon him, has in his possession any instrument suitable for house-breaking, vault-breaking or safe-breaking, under circumstances that give rise to a reasonable inference that the instrument has been used or is or was intended to be used for house-breaking [etc.], is guilty of an indictable offence and is liable to imprisonment for fourteen years.

The reasoning of *Holmes* is confusing, but seems mostly to reject the suggestion that the "reasonable inference" formula offends the Charter. That may be arguable but is not relevant here. What is relevant is that Lacourcière J.A., speaking for the court, indicated (in what may be *dicta*) that the "lawful excuse" reverse onus clause simply imposed an evidentiary onus on the accused and did not offend the Charter.[51] In reaching this conclusion the court seemed to be suggesting that an accused must be acquitted if there is a reasonable doubt as to any element of the offence but convicted if he or she fails to tip the balance in favour of an "extraneous" excuse. The only support for this novel idea, which seems to run contrary to well-established principles of

---

48 R.S.C. 1970, c. N-1. See *Oakes* and *Carroll*, note 46 above.

49 See MacKay and Cromwell, note 47, above, at 234-5. "The test will not assist challenges to reverse onus provisions that do not depend on the proof of basic facts. For example, the burden of proving lawful justification or excuse is placed on the accused in numerous situations. Some other method of analysis will have to be found to assist with such provisions."

50 (1983), 32 C.R. (3d) 322 (Ont. C.A.).

51 For a case in which a true reversal of an evidentiary onus was found unconstitutional by the Ontario Court of Appeal, see *R. v. Boyle* (1983), 35 C.R. (3d) 34.

Canadian criminal law,[52] is a quote from Glanville Williams,[53] making the unexceptional point that many statutes shift the persuasive burden onto the accused. No one would disagree with that, but it is the constitutionality of such a legislative practice that the Court of Appeal was addressing. In any event, not only did the court decide that the lawful excuse reversal does not offend the Charter, it did so in terms broad enough to allow the Crown to argue a non-legislative reversal with respect to all "extraneous" excuses, such as duress.[54] If the court is correct, then the reversal words themselves are otiose.[55]

It would appear that this issue is urgently in need of careful reconsideration. However, the trend in the case law is towards upholding the "lawful excuse" reverse onus clause. *Holmes* has been followed by the Manitoba Court of Appeal in *R. v. Kowalczuk*,[56] without comment. The implications of this approach are disturbingly radical.

2. SEXUAL REPUTATION

Section 246.7 of the Code states:

> In proceedings in respect of an offence under section 246.1, 246.2 or 246.3 [that is, all the sexual assault offences], evidence of sexual reputation, whether general or specific, is not admissible for the purpose of challenging or supporting the credibility of the complainant.

This prohibition extends to two types of evidence of sexual reputation,[57] general and specific, both of which are inadmissible with respect to credibility.

---

52 See the comment by Stuart at (1983), 32 C.R. (3d) 323-4. This approach seems to put all defences in the same boat as insanity, without the statutory authorisation to do so.

53 *Textbook of Criminal Law* (1978), p. 115.

54 The court in *Holmes* even labeled intoxication and automatism as "clearly extraneous excuses" (note 50 above at 332), although conventional theory classifies them as going to specific intent, a part of the *mens rea* and the *actus reus* respectively. The elements of the offence seem therefore only to be those set out in the statutory provision itself.

55 Some doubt seems to be expressed, as an alternative ground of rational connection is offered (*ibid.*, at 333). But it would seem that this must refer to the "reasonable inference" issue as no one could suggest a rational connection between proof of the possession of house-breaking tools and the existence of a lawful excuse.

56 [1983] 3 W.W.R. 694.

57 It does not cover evidence of a witness's reputation for truth or veracity. See

General evidence of sexual reputation has always been in a class by itself. The complainant could be cross-examined as to her unchastity and, where the complainant led evidence as to her chastity, the accused could adduce evidence to contradict her.[58] For example, it was stated in *R. v. Finnessey*:[59]

> The prosecutrix may be asked questions to shew that her general character of chastity is bad. She is bound to answer such questions and if she refuses to do so the fact may be shewn. . . . Such evidence is relevant to the issue since . . . it bears directly upon consent and the improbability of the connection complained of having taken place against the will of the prosecutrix.[60]

It is clear that such evidence did not go solely to credibility but also to consent. This was acknowledged not only in *Finnessey* but also by the Supreme Court of Canada in *Forsythe*.

> It was, also, open to an accused . . . to ask questions as to the complainant's general reputation for chastity, as a matter going to credibility *and consent*, but the accused was entitled to bring evidence to contradict a denial of unchastity, subject in some circumstances to the discretion of the trial judge to disallow such questions.[61]

One might wonder, therefore, since section 246.7 confines the prohibition to credibility, whether the evidence might not still be admitted with respect to any fact in issue. It is submitted that the evidence would have to satisfy the criteria of section 246.6. In other words, since general evidence of sexual reputation "concerns the sexual activity of the complainant with any person other than the accused,"[62] it will have to fall into one of the categories of section 246.6(1). The only possible home for it would

generally, the *Report of the Federal/Provincial Task Force on Uniform Rules of Evidence* (1982), Chapter 25. The Task Force recommends, at 25.2, that such evidence be inadmissible in all cases.

58 In the same class was evidence that the complainant was a prostitute, *R. v. Bashir*; *R. v. Manjur* (1970), 54 Cr. App. R. 1, and evidence that the complainant was promiscuous, *R. v. Krausz* (1973), 57 Cr. App. R. 466.

59 (1906), 11 O.L.R. 338 (C.A.).

60 *Ibid.*, at 341. See also *R. v. Clarke* (1817), 171 E.R. 633; *R. v. Barker* (1829), 172 E.R. 558; *R. v. Greatbanks*, [1959] Crim. L.R. 450; *R. v. Krausz* (1973), 57 Cr. App. R. 466; *R. v. Basken* (1974), 28 C.R.N.S. 359 (Sask. C.A.). *Forsythe*, [1980] 2 S.C.R. 268 at 274, indicated that this issue was not affected by the old section 142. See also *Halsbury's Laws of England*, 3rd ed., Vol. 10, p. 448, para. 826.

61 *Forsythe, ibid.* (italics added). See also *Phipson on Evidence*, 13th ed. (1982), pp. 13-53.

62 This would appear to be so even if one argues that the evidence is not of sexual activity, but of the reputation for sexual activity, which is not always the same thing, since it still "concerns" the sexual activity of the complainant.

appear to be section 246.6(1)(a) so, if the Crown leads evidence of
the reputation for chastity of the complainant, this would open
the door to general rebuttal evidence. That this is the proper interpretation is supported not only by the general tenor of the
provisions but also by the Ontario Court of Appeal in *R. v. Blondheim.*[63] In that case, the court applied the notice provisions to
evidence of general sexual reputation as well as more specific
evidence.

With respect to specific evidence of sexual reputation, the case
law had consistently stressed its inadmissibility. However, the
reference to specific evidence may have been *ex abundanti cautela*
or because of a need to eradicate all vestiges of the idea that any
evidence relating to sexual activity goes to credibility.[64] This is an
idea which had had a particularly negative upon the prosecution's case since the old section 142 had been construed as making
credibility a fact in issue.[65]

3. SEXUAL ACTIVITY WITH THE ACCUSED

The last type of evidence which the defence might wish to
adduce is that of sexual activity with the accused himself. This
matter is left untouched by the provisions discussed above. This
evidence has always been admissible as it was felt to be relevant
to consent.[66] The accused, therefore, can cross-examine the complainant on their past sexual relationship and can, of course, give
evidence about it himself.

This is an issue to which little attention has been devoted, but
it may become of more significance in the future, particularly
because of the removal of the marital immunity from sexual

---

63 (1980), 54 C.C.C. (2d) 36 (Ont. C.A.).

64 There may be judges and jurors who still believe that allegations of sexual
assault are especially liable to be false, in spite of the evidence to the contrary.
See M.T. MacCrimmon, "Consistent Statements of a Witness" (1978), 17
Osgoode Hall L.J. 283 at 309-12.

65 Hence, judges had "no power to tackle the antiquated common law myth that
the unchaste were also untruthful." *Report of the Federal/Provincial Task
Force on Uniform Rules of Evidence* (1982), p. 71.

66 See, *e.g., R. v. Martin* (1834), 172 E.R. 1364; *R. v. Cockcroft* (1870), 11 Cox, C.C.
410; *R. v. Holmes* (1871), L.R. 1 C.C.R. 334; *R. v. Riley* (1887), 16 Cox, C.C. 191;
R. v. Bradley, [1910] 4 Cr. App. R. 225; *R. v. Gardner*, 4 April 1973, referred to in
Susan Edwards, *Female Sexuality and the Law* (1981), p. 66. For a case on
post-offence sexual intercourse see *R. v. Aloisio* (1970), 90 W.N. (Pt. I) (N.S.W.)
111 (C.A.).

assault offences.[67] It raises interesting questions about the "fit" of the criminal law with actual behaviour, its enforcement and, hence, the practical limits of the criminal sanction.

The reason why it has not been a significant issue, in spite of the fact that many rapists are known to their victims[68] is probably because of a failure to report cases of rape by a person with whom an individual has had or is having a sexual relationship. The exercise of police and prosecutorial discretion may be influential factors as well.[69] It is conceivable, however, that if a number of husbands are prosecuted successfully for sexual assault, this may pave the way for prosecutions in situations involving non-marital sexual relationships. Parliament has now indicated, categorically, that it is possible to be raped by someone with whom one has been on the closest terms of sexual intimacy.

The issue of whether questions about sexual activity with the accused ought to be allowed is probably best left until it becomes apparent whether this practice will be abused. This could occur by means of a blanket refusal[70] by Crown attorneys to enforce the law or by questioning by defence counsel which is simply designed to harass the complainant rather than to illicit information which could reasonably be viewed as relevant to a fact is issue.

4. THE DOCTRINE OF RECENT COMPLAINT

The issue of recent complaint is now referred to very briefly if somewhat obscurely in the Code. Section 246.5 states:

> The rules relating to evidence of recent complaint in sexual assault cases are hereby abrogated.[71]

---

67 See s. 246.8.

68 See A. Medea and K. Thompson, "Against Rape: A Survival Manual for Women" (1974), p. 142. The research is discussed by L.M.G. Clark and D.J. Lewis, *Rape: The Price of Coercive Sexuality* (1977), pp. 71-6, who criticise the categorisation in other studies of people the victim has just met (*e.g.*, in a bar) as known to her. They conclude that it is impossible to draw definitive conclusions about victim-offender relationships, but that much rape does occur between persons known to each other.

69 In the Clark and Lewis sample, only 20 percent of the rapes where the victim knew the rapist were classified by the authorities as "founded." *Ibid.*, p. 71.

70 Rather than after the exercise of discretion influenced by normal factors such as the cogency of the evidence.

71 Its predecessor in Bill C-53 was more complex:

What does this provision mean? To abrogate means to annul, so the intent is clearly to do away with any special rules relating to sexual assault cases, which will then be governed by any general rules that exist.

The general common-law rule is that a witness's prior consistent statement is usually inadmissible.[72] The reasons for the exclusion seem to be that such evidence is superfluous, since there is no reason to doubt the evidence of the witness,[73] it would waste time, and could be easily fabricated.

One exception was traditionally recognised with respect to sexual offences[74] where prior consistent statements in the form of complaints were admitted, not as going to the truth of the matter,

---

246.4 (1) The rule that permits a previous consistent statement of a complainant to be admitted in evidence as a recent complaint is abrogated.

(2) In a proceeding for an offence in which a question is raised as to the consent of the complainant to the conduct of the accused; the complainant may give evidence of the making of a complaint concerning that conduct, but no evidence may be given of the particulars of the complaint unless the accused has questioned the credibility of the complainant on the basis of recent fabrication or previous inconsistent statement relating to that conduct.

(3) The judge in a proceeding referred to in subsection (2) is not required to give the jury any direction respecting the lack of a complaint concerning the conduct of the accused made within a reasonable time subsequent to the offence.

72 The rule is variously called the rule against narrative, self-confirmation or corroboration, or self-serving statements. See the *Report of the Federal/Provincial Task Force on Uniform Rules of Evidence* (1982), p. 295. See also *Cross on Evidence*, 5th ed. (1979), p. 236, and M.T. MacCrimmon, "Consistent Statements of a Witness" (1979), 17 Osg. Hall L.J. 285. The above sources, especially MacCrimmon, give a very full account of the recent complaint rule in this context, hence I propose to omit discussion of the details of the abrogated rule here.

73 Cross, *ibid.*, cites this as the most "convincing" reason.

74 The scope of the exception is somewhat controversial. It is agreed that it covers complaints of sexual offences, including those of males, but not whether it extends to all forms of violence. MacCrimmon, note 72 above, at 307, asserts that it does, citing *R. v. Hurst* (1966), 55 W.W.R. 358 (B.C. C.A.), but Cross says that the preponderance of evidence suggests otherwise, fn. 69 above, at 241. The Federal/Provincial Task Force sides with Cross, note 72 above, p. 302. It is unclear whether it applies to other sexual offences such as incest and seduction. It is submitted that, in principle, it should not apply, since the general rules relating to an allegation of fabrication would allow evidence of complaint where this was relevant, *i.e.*, in non-consensual cases. See the text accompanying fns. 80-4 below. However, see *R. v. Proteau* (1923), 33 B.C.R. 39 (C.A.), an incest case.

but to demonstrate consistency. The reason why it was felt necessary to demonstrate consistency arose from the fear of false accusations. In effect, the complaint does not enhance credibility but counters the very negative assumption that would otherwise be made that the witness was lying.[75] It is clear from the case law that a strong presumption existed that a woman who was raped would complain of that fact at the earliest opportunity[76] and, indeed, judges were required to direct the jury to draw an adverse inference from failure to so complain.[77]

It is now known that the danger of false accusations is no greater in sexual than in other cases,[78] and it is appreciated that rape victims may be reluctant to complain for various reasons including fear of the offender or of being accused of provoking the rape, treatment at the hands of the police, shame and a desire to protect her reputation.[79] Probably even the desire to protect the offender should be added, since it may take a victim a considerable length of time to decide to complain of being sexually assaulted by someone known to her. Hence the reform embodied in section 246.5.

This reform needs to be set in the context of the general law on consistent statements. Are there any other exceptions to the exclusion rule that would still be applicable in sexual assault, as in other, cases? It is of course possible, in any case, for the defence

75 This assumption pervades the literature. See, *e.g.*, Glanville Williams, "Corroboration—Sexual Cases," [1962] Crim. L.R. 662, who suggests lie detector tests for victims, since sex cases are prone to false charges; Ralph Slovenko, *Sexual Behaviour and the Law* (1965), p. 9, and M. Ploscowe, "Sex Offences: The American Legal Context" (1960), 25 Law and Contemp. Probs. 217 at 223: "far too many men have been railroaded on sex offence charges." The assertions of Williams and Ploscowe are innocent of any authority or evidence and Slovenko simply cites Ploscowe.

76 Lamer J., speaking for the Supreme Court of Canada in *Timm v. R.*, [1981] 2 S.C.R. 315 at 321, put it in a nutshell that the "exception was recognized as necessary to negate the adverse effect of the alleged victim's silence might have on her credibility. . . . That possible adverse effect is predicated upon the assumption that the true victim of a sexual offence will, under normal circumstances, complain at the first reasonable opportunity."

77 *Kilby v. R.* (1973), 129 C.L.R. 460 (Aust. H.C.); *R. v. Kistendey* (1975), 29 C.C.C. (2d) 382 (Ont. C.A.) *per* Dubin J.A.; *R. v. Boyce* (1974), 28 C.R.N.S. 336 (Ont. C.A.). Fauteux J., speaking for the Court in *Kribs v. R.*, [1960] S.C.R. 400 at 405, said that a complaint is "a virtually essential complement to [a complainant's] story."

78 The research is documented by MacCrimmon, note 72 above, at 309-13.

79 See T. Danow, "Jury Instruction in a Rape Trial: Recent Revisions and the Argument for Further Reform" (1976), 1 Crim. Just. J. 113 at 115.

to suggest that a witness is lying, to allege in effect that she has fabricated the evidence. The common law developed a doctrine of recent fabrication[80] in order to permit evidence of prior consistent statements, not to establish the truth of the complaint, but to demonstrate consistency and rebut the allegation of fabrication. Only certain types of impeachment of the witness's evidence are encompassed by this exception to the rule of inadmissibility. Otherwise any attack on credibility would allow in previous statements, thereby rendering ineffectual the general rule designed to exclude superfluous evidence and save the court's time. Examples of these types of impeachment include express or implied allegations of bias, interest and corruption, and failure to speak when it would have been natural to do so.[81]

The "failure to speak" argument[82] may raise the most concern that the abrogation of the recent complaint rule will have little impact. The doctrine was, in effect, a blanket assumption of an allegation of recent fabrication, so that the right to rebut by the introduction of prior consistent statements did not depend on the defence tactics adopted by the individual accused. The only change, therefore, may be that the approach will shift from a general one to one that depends on the conduct of any particular trial. It would appear that the accused will still be able to attack the evidence of the complainant by showing that she did not complain quickly. It could well be argued that this is such a subtle change that Parliament must have intended something much more substantial. The better view may be that courts should not permit to be done, on a case by case basis, what Parliament has rejected overall. What can be seen to have been abrogated here is the idea that any adverse inference can be drawn from failure to complain quickly in a sexual assault case. This interpretation can

---

80 The "recent" is otiose.

81 For a discussion see the *Report of the Federal/Provincial Task Force on Uniform Rules of Evidence* (1982), pp. 304-11, or MacCrimmon, note 72 above, at 296-304. An often-cited article is by R.N. Gooderson, "Previous Consistent Statement," [1968] Camb. L.J. 64. For a short history, including the roots of the rule in the requirement of a "hue and cry," see S.A. Schiff, *Evidence in the Litigation Process*, Vol. I, (1978), pp. 574-8.

82 For examples see *R. v. Neigel* (1918), 13 Alta. L.R. 137 (C.A.), and *R. v. Campbell* (1977), 17 C.R. (2d) 673 at 687 (C.A.) *per* Martin J.A.: "Where the failure of a witness to mention some circumstance on an earlier occasion when he might have done so, is made the basis for a suggestion that he had invented the story since that occasion, the evidence is admissible that on a still earlier occasion, he did mention that circumstance."

be supported by what is known of the reluctance of victims to complain. It would be ludicrous to suppose that the timing of a complaint would suddenly become relevant because the accused has simply alleged a failure to speak. This stands in considerable contrast to an allegation of some motive for fabrication.[83]

On the other hand, if judges do permit accused persons simply to allege a failure to speak, thus in effect resurrecting the recent complaint rule, it is submitted that attention must be paid to assumptions about when it is "natural" for victims to complain.[84] Again, it is submitted that, in deciding whether a complaint is admissible, it should be understood that many victims of sexual assault find themselves unable or unwilling to complain as quickly as victims of other crimes.[85]

Notwithstanding the ambiguities of the provision, it is concluded that section 246.5 could be interpreted in such a way as to constitute a considerable improvement in our law of evidence. It at least does away with a doctrine based on an across-the-board presumption that complainants fabricate their evidence and it goes some distance toward bringing the law into line with what empirical research tells us about the behaviour of rape victims.

5. CORROBORATION

A complex network of rules gradually developed with respect to the issue of corroboration. Corroboration was required for conviction of some offences, while a warning that conviction was dangerous without corroboration sufficed for others.[86]

---

83 Obviously the accused must be able to suggest that the complainant is lying and indeed this would not be objectionable at all if not in the context of the historical assumption that complainants were lying, and it would then be reasonable to allow prior statements to strengthen credibility.

84 The decision is made by the trial judge who decides on a *voir dire* whether the complaint is admissible as having been made at the first reasonable opportunity. See *R. v. Belliveau* (1978), 25 N.S.R. (2d) 698 (C.A.).

85 For a discussion of whether an objective or subjective test of the first opportunity to complain was used, see S.A. Schiff, *Evidence in the Litigation Process*, Vol. I, (1978), p. 577, See also *R. v. Bodechon*, [1964] 3 C.C.C. 233 (P.E.I. S.C.). The majority held that a complaint made 12 hours later was inadmissible, the complainant having had several opportunities for complaining, but Bill J. dissented on this point, taking into account the complainant's youth, her hysterical condition and the fact that she was in unfamiliar surroundings.

86 See generally A.A. Wakeling, *Corroboration in Canadian Law* (1977).

The following lists show the position as it was prior to the 1976 reforms.[87] Corroboration was required with respect to the following offences:

(1) Section 148—sexual intercourse with a feeble-minded female;
(2) Section 150—incest;
(3) Section 151—seduction of a female between sixteen and eighteen;
(4) Section 152—seduction under promise of marriage;
(5) Section 153—sexual intercourse with a step-daughter or female employee;
(6) Section 154—seduction of female passengers on vessels.[88]

A warning was required with respect to the following offences:

(1) Section 146(1)—sexual intercourse with a female under fourteen;
(2) Section 146(2)—sexual intercourse with a female between fourteen and sixteen;
(3) Section 144—rape;
(4) Section 145—attempted rape;
(5) Section 149—indecent assault on a female.[89]

The only other offence of a similar nature was indecent assault on a male, contained in section 156.[90] No special corroboration rule was legislated with respect to this offence,[91] although, if the victim was a child, the corroboration of children's evidence rules applied. These rules are discussed in the next section of the book, "Children's Evidence."

A major change came in 1976, when section 142, containing the warning provision, was repealed.[92] However, this was followed by a period of uncertainty as to whether an earlier common-law warning rule had been reactivated.[93]

This same period also saw a judicial loosening of the meaning of corroboration which for many years had been governed by the

---

87 When the Criminal Law Amendment Act, S.C. 1974-75-76, c. 93 was passed.
88 Section 139(1) (repealed S.C. 1980-81-82, c. 125, s. 5).
89 Section 42 (repealed S.C. 1974-75-76, c. 93, s. 8).
90 Repealed S.C. 1980-81-82, c. 125, s. 9.
91 There may have been a common-law corroboration rule but this was doubted in *R. v. Cullen*, [1975] 6 W.W.R. 153 (B.C. C.A.).
92 S.C. 1974-75-76, c. 93, s. 8.
93 See Chapter 1, the text accompanying notes 50-1, for a brief review of the case law.

English case of *R. v. Baskerville*.[94] The complainant's testimony had to be confirmed in some material particular by evidence implicating the accused. This caused difficulties generally because in many rape cases the issue was absence of consent and, while there might be an abundance of evidence relating to sexual intercourse, it did not necessarily point unequivocally to non-consensual intercourse. The rule made conviction of accused persons in "gang rape" cases extremely difficult. The Supreme Court of Canada therefore decided on a more flexible approach. In *Warkentin v. R.*[95] the majority of the court[96] stated the view that corroboration was a matter of common sense. The test was whether the evidence was such as would help the jury determine the truth of the matter. There was thus no need to relate corroborative evidence to each accused individually in a "gang rape" situation. The practical impossibility of corroborating each element of the offence in relation to each individual accused was stressed.[97] Dickson J., in dissent, was of the view that corroboration was required on each issue, in this case whether the rape occurred, and as to the identity of those who committed it.

A further leading case on the matter was decided by the Supreme Court on the same day. It was held in *Murphy v. R.*[98] that the complainant's evidence need only be corroborated in some material particular. Spence J., speaking for the majority,[99] stated that there "is no requirement that the whole of [the complainant's] evidence be corroborated. Were that the requirement, there would be no need for even the evidence of the complainant."[100] Thus, the Supreme Court of Canada had clearly moved to a test of corroboration which simply stresses the issue of whether it reinforces the complainant's testimony.[101] Nevertheless, it was

94 [1916] 2 K.B. 658 (C.C.A.).
95 [1977] 2 S.C.R. 355.
96 Comprising de Grandpré, Martland, Judson, Ritchie J.J. and, on this issue, Beetz J., Laskin C.J.C., Spence and Pigeon J.J. concurred in the dissenting judgment of Dickson J.
97 [1977] 2 S.C.R. 355 at 377-8.
98 [1977] 2 S.C.R. 603.
99 Also comprising Martland, Judson, Ritchie, Pigeon, Beetz and de Grandpré J.J. Laskin C.J.C. and Dickson J. dissented in part.
100 Note 98 above at 615.
101 This may well have been part of a general movement away from the onerous intricacies of corroboration law as a whole. See *Vetrovec v. R.*, [1982] 1 S.C.R. 811, in which Dickson J., speaking for the court and providing an interesting contrast to his views in the two rape cases discussed above, held that there was no special rule which automatically applied to accomplice evidence.

still the case that judges, even after this legislative and judicial reform, could still, in their discretion, suggest that juries should look for corroboration with respect to the evidence of a particular complainant. Moreover, corroboration was still required with respect to certain offences, such as incest, listed above.

Parliament has now grasped the bull by the horns, one horn in the new section 246.4 and the other in the repeal of the old section 139(1).[102] Section 246.4 sweeps away any remaining vestiges of a corroboration rule with respect to certain offences. The relevant offences are incest, gross indecency and all the sexual assaults. The section states that "no corroboration is required for a conviction and the judge shall not instruct the jury that it is unsafe to find the accused guilty in the absence of corroboration."

Incest is the subject of the most dramatic change, as the law has moved from a requirement of corroboration to a total rejection of its significance. With respect to sexual assault, this provision prevents a judge exercising his or her discretion to warn in a particular case. Of course ingrained distrust of complainants' evidence cannot be eradicated. A complainant will still have to be believed if a conviction is to be possible in the absence of corroboration. Nevertheless, Parliament has made an unequivocal statement that, in this respect, trials for sexual assault are to be conducted in the same way as other assault trials.

The second step in the reform was to repeal section 139(1) which contained the requirement of corroboration for sexual intercourse with the feeble-minded,[103] incest, seduction of sixteen to eighteen year olds, seduction under promise of marriage, seduction of female passengers and parent or guardian procuring defilement. All of these offences, apart from incest, would have been abolished if the overhaul of all sexual offences in the form of Bill C-53 had completed its journey through Parliament. Nevertheless, the result is to abolish any requirement of corroboration for the immediate future. The position is not so strict here, however, since it is not absolutely forbidden to mention corroboration. Since children are often the victims of the relevant offences, special rules respecting the corroboration of children's evidence will come into play. These are dealt with in the section "Children's Evidence" immediately following.

---

102 Repealed S.C. 1980-81-82, c. 125, s. 5.
103 Also repealed S.C. 1980-81-82, c. 125, s. 8.

6. CHILDREN'S EVIDENCE

Where a child is the victim of a sexual assault, this has been perceived as presenting certain special difficulties for the legal system. The experience of the criminal process can be devastating for a child, especially where the accused is known to the victim. The legal system has developed special rules to deal with the perceived weaknesses in children's evidence, but little attention has been addressed thus far to the question of minimising the trauma for the victim. This issue will be raised in this section, after a discussion of the evidential rules relating to children.

(a) *The Oath*[104]

The general rule is that a witness must swear that he or she will tell the truth before being permitted to give evidence. This presented difficulties with respect to children since they were only allowed to take the oath if they understood its significance.[105] Until the case of *R. v. Bannerman*[106] it was thought that this required an appreciation of both the nature and the consequences of an oath, but since then the only test is whether the child understands the moral obligation of speaking the truth. Some courts still speak in terms of a religious obligation. Thus, in *Budin v. R.*,[107] in which a new trial was ordered on an appeal from a conviction for indecent assault, the court accepted what was felt to be the ordinary meaning of an oath, a solemn appeal to God (or to something sacred) to witness that a statement is true.[108] Jessup J.A. pointed out that the judge's questioning should establish whether "the child believes in God or another Almighty and whether he appreciates that, in giving the oath, ... he is telling the Almighty that what he will say will be the truth".[109] The usual

---

104 For an outline of the present law and proposals for reform, see the *Report of the Federal/Provincial Task Force on Uniform Rules of Evidence* (1982), Chapter 17.
105 See *R. v. Brasier* (1779), 168 E.R. 202. There was no fixed rule about the age at which a child was presumed to understand the nature and consequences of an oath, but fourteen was a rule of thumb. A child under this age was *prima facie* presumed to be incompetent.
106 (1966), 48 C.R. 110 (Man. C.A.); affirmed without reasons (1967), 40 C.R. 76 (S.C.C.).
107 (1981), 20 C.R. (3d) 86 (Ont. C.A.).
108 *Ibid.*, at 91.
109 *Ibid.* The Crown can and should instruct the child in the nature of an oath, as can the judge. See also *R. v. Bannerman*, note 106 above.

procedure, unless the matter of competency is waived, is for the trial judge to conduct a *voir dire* in the presence of the jury, and question the child about such matters as the difference between truth and falsehood.[110]

If the child has a conscientious objection to taking the oath it may be that he or she will be permitted to affirm, thus rendering the evidence of the same effect as that given under oath.[111] It has simply been asserted, however, in *Budin v. R.*,[112] that the right to affirm does not extend to a child of tender years. There seems no reason for this restriction in the meaning of "person" in the relevant statutory provision. A child who is able to understand the moral obligation of speaking the truth may also have sufficiently developed scruples on which to base an objection to the oath. This ought to enhance the ensuing testimony rather than the reverse which would occur if it were relegated to the category of unsworn testimony. However, if the *Budin* test is correct, then a lack of belief in "God or another Almighty" would mean that a child could hardly be found to have a conscientious objection to something he or she does not understand. It is submitted that the test should be the simple one of comprehension of a moral obligation with a choice of taking the oath or affirming. Any other approach could well offend the equality rights in section 15 of the Charter.

If the child is not adjudged competent to take the oath or affirm, then various statutory provisions make it possible for her or him to give unsworn testimony. Section 16 of the Canada Evidence Act[113] states as follows:

> In any legal proceeding where a child of tender years is offered as a witness, and such child does not, in the opinion of the judge, ... understand the nature of an oath, the evidence of such child may be received, though not given upon oath, if, in the opinion of the judge, ... the child is possessed of sufficient intelligence to justify the reception of the evidence, and understands the duty of speaking the truth.[114]

There may be very little difference between the understanding of the moral obligation to speak the truth required for the oath and

---

110 See the *Federal/Provincial Report*, note 104 above, p. 243.

111 See the Canada Evidence Act, R.S.C. 1970, c. E-10, s. 14. Similar provincial provisions, which are not relevant here, can be found set out in the *Federal/Provincial Report*, note 104 above, pp. 236-7.

112 See note 107 above.

113 R.S.C. 1970, c. E-10.

114 Similar provincial provisions can be found set out in the *Federal/Provincial Report*, note 104 above, p. 242.

the understanding of the duty to speak the truth required to satisfy section 16. Thus the provision may not expand receivable evidence to any great extent.

The Canadian Law Reform Commission has proposed the abolition of any special rules of competency with respect to children.[115] "The frailties inherent in the testimony of immature witnesses should affect the weight of the evidence rather than its admissibility."[116]

(b) *Corroboration*

The rules with respect to the corroboration of children's evidence fall into the same two categories of requirement and warning as the general corroboration rules discussed above. With respect to the sworn evidence of a child of tender years, there may be a rule of practice that the judge should warn the jury that it is dangerous to convict without corroboration.[117] Corroboration is required for unsworn evidence of children of tender years, this rule being statutory in origin. Section 586 of the Code states:

> No person shall be convicted of an offence upon the unsworn evidence of a child unless the evidence of the child is corroborated in a material particular by evidence that implicates the accused.[118]

It may well be that these rules reveal the same kind of unsubstantiated distrust of the evidence of children that has been displayed toward that of women complainants. Children are not the only people to have unreliable powers of observation and recollection, so that the case for singling children out cannot be made on this basis. Further, it is a mere assumption rather than an established fact that they are prone to lying and fantasising.[119] It is submitted that these provisions should be subjected to the

---

115 See *Report on Evidence* (1975), Evidence Code, ss. 50-51.

116 *Ibid.*, p. 87.

117 See *Kendall v. R.*, [1962] S.C.R. 469. Judson J. pointed out, at 473, that the "difficulty is fourfold; 1. His capacity of observation. 2. His capacity of recollection. 3. His capacity to understand questions put and frame intelligent answers. 4. His moral responsibility." It is quite possible, however, that the decision in *Vetrovec v. R.*, [1982] 1 S.C.R. 811, will be given a broad interpretation as applying to all rules of practice and not only the accomplice rule.

118 See also the Canada Evidence Act, R.S.C. 1970, c. E-10, s. 16(2).

119 Research does not substantiate the idea that incest reports, for example, are likely to be fantasies. See the sources cited in D.P. Ordway "Parent-Child Incest: Proof at Trial without Testimony in Court by the Victim" (1981), 15 U.

same scrutiny as the sexual assault corroboration rules in general.

A mystery surrounds the interaction of the various corroboration rules. It is not at the moment clear what impact the new provision will have on the special rules relating to children. Section 246.4 abolishes any requirement of, or warning of the need for, corroboration in an incest trial. This must mean that there is no longer any rule of practice *vis-à-vis* sworn evidence of children,[120] but how does it interact with the statutory requirement of corroboration where evidence is unsworn? The same problem exists where the accused is charged with sexual assault of a child of tender years. There seems to be a direct conflict between section 246.4 and section 586. Generally, where two Acts are inconsistent, the later will be held to have impliedly repealed the earlier.[121] This is reinforced by the fact that section 586 contains a general rule while section 264.4 deals specifically with certain offences. The earlier general provision ought, therefore, to yield to the later specific provision. This position is further supported by the repeal of section 139(1), thus making it clear that attention was consciously directed to the removal of a requirement of corroboration in crimes involving children. It would appear, therefore, that section 246.4 should be read as a qualification of section 586.[122] On the other hand, it would be ironic if sexual offences were still singled out for special treatment, but this time in the sense that proof is easier, rather than more difficult. The courts have not yet asserted a power simply to choose the preferred interpretation where two inconsistent provisions exist.

(c) *Trauma for the Child*

Rules relating to competency and corroboration are directed toward the protection of the accused and the prevention of an improper conviction in the criminal justice system. Canadian proposals for reform have not yet addressed the issue of the desirability of protecting the child victim. At present it is essential

---

of Mich. J. of Law Ref. 131 at note 23. See, however, the argument *ibid.*, at 133-8 that the experience of giving evidence may distort the child's testimony and that adults are not experienced in assessing the credibility of children.

120 It is unclear whether this includes all child witnesses or only child victims.

121 See E.A. Driedger, *The Construction of Statutes* (1974), pp. 174 *et seq.*

122 *Cf.* G. Parker, "The 'New' Sexual Offences" (1983), 31 C.R. (3d) 317 at 320 who simply asserts that s. 586 and the Canada Evidence Act, R.S.C. 1970, c. E-10, s. 16(2) remains intact.

in many cases for the victim to give evidence at trial and to be subjected to cross-examination. This may well result in severe trauma and guilt feelings where the accused is known to the victim, especially if a member of the victim's family.[123]

Suggestions for improvement can be found in other jurisdictions. One proposal, based on experience in Israel, is that a special hearing with full cross-examination should be held in a "child courtroom" and a recording used at trial.[124] Ordway suggests that the child should be examined by a person with expertise in both sexual abuse and legal standards. Both sides could ask questions through the expert and call him or her to give evidence at trial. They could also either observe the interview unobtrusively or watch the tapes afterwards. This would minimize embarrassment, guilt and the possibility of false retractions.[125] At the moment, many cases may never be prosecuted because of concern about the resultant harm to the victim.

It is not possible to discuss this issue at length here. However, it is submitted that when Parliament again directs its attention to reform of the law relating to sexual offences against children, it should focus on the need to protect child victims from unnecessary trauma while maintaining adequate due process safeguards for the accused.

7. PAPPAJOHN: ALTERNATIVE DEFENCES

Although *Pappajohn v. R.*[126] has attracted most of its attention for its *obiter dicta* on the defence of mistake of fact, the question actually decided in the case is of importance too, since it relates to the ability to raise alternative defences in the interests of the accused.

Clearly the accused can only offer one version of the facts. He could not, for example, suggest at one and the same time that no

---

123 See J. Goldstein, A. Freud and A. Solnit, *Before the Best Interests of the Child* (1979), p. 64. "[T]he harm done by the inquiry may be more than that caused by not intruding." See also Ordway, note 119 above.

124 D Libai, "The Protection of the Child Victim of a Sexual Offense in the Criminal Justice System" (1969), 15 Wayne L.R. 977. See also D. Reifen, "Protection of Children Involved in Sexual Offences: A New Method of Investigation in Israel" (1959), 49 J. Crim. L.C. & P.S. 222.

125 See note 119 above, at 139-42. There follows a full discussion of the implications for the constitutional rights of the accused.

126 [1980] 2 S.C.R. 120.

sexual activity took place but that if it did it was consensual.[127]
This would undermine his credibility entirely. However, sometimes it is possible that one version of the facts could be interpreted in two different legal ways, as where the accused asserts
that the complainant was either consenting or he mistakenly
believed she was. This was what the accused tried to do in
Pappajohn. The trial judge refused, however, to leave the mistake
of fact interpretation to the jury, a refusal that was ultimately
upheld by a five to two majority of the Supreme Court of Canada.
What does *Pappajohn* tell us about when the presentation of these
alternatives is or is not permissible?

There was in fact very little disagreement (except in the
result) between the judgment of McIntyre J. for the majority, and
Dickson J. for the dissenting minority. Both were agreed that the
defences of consent and mistaken belief in consent were sometimes compatible and sometimes not.[128] Both were agreed that
there must be some evidence to convey an "air of reality" to the
defence before it must be left to the jury.[129] Where they differed
was on the question of whether there was such evidence in the
case before them. The facts were that the accused and the
complainant had been drinking together while discussing
business. They had then gone to the house of the accused where,
according to him, consensual sexual activity, albeit with some
token objection on her part, took place. According to her, she was
raped several times while terrified and hysterical, and then fled

---

127 Although it is possible that the accused could, under the old rape law, argue
that penetration did not take place and that the sexual activity that did take
place was consensual. In addition, conflicting versions of the facts could
emerge from the defence evidence as a whole. See the discussion of the
impeachment of one's own witness by independent contradictory evidence in
A.W. Bryant, "The Common Law Rule Against Impeaching One's Own
Witness" (1982), 32 U. of T.L.J. 412 at 431-3. See the Canada Evidence Act,
R.S.C. 1970, c. E-10, s. 9(1), which suggests that a party may only call evidence
to contradict his own witness when the witness is adverse. The courts have
not paid any attention to what has been called a "great blunder." *Greenough
v. Eccles* (1859), 141 E.R. 315 at 323, *per* Cockburn C.J. See, *e.g.*, *Cariboo
Observer Ltd. v. Carson Truck Lines Ltd.* (1961), 37 W.W.R. 209.
128 *Per* Dickson J., (1980), 111 D.L.R. (3d) 1 at 21 "Nor is a defence of honest belief
necessarily inconsistent with a defence of consent." *Per* McIntyre J. at 34: "To
require the putting of the alternative defence of mistaken belief or consent,
there must be . . . some evidence beyond the mere assertion of belief. . . ." For
another case where the defences were held to be incompatible see *Trottier v. R.*
(1981), 21 C.R. (3d) 330 (B.C. C.A.).
129 *Ibid., per* Dickson J., at 21, and McIntyre J. at 31.

PAPPAJOHN: ALTERNATIVE DEFENCES 165

naked from the house at the first opportunity. Their versions of events, therefore, dramatically conflicted on the issue of consent.

There was some evidence, however, which it was open to the jury to accept while believing the version offered by the complainant. She did not suffer any serious injury, nor was her clothing damaged. Rather it was hung up or folded rather neatly. Her necklace and keys were found in the living-room, which could be seen as some support for the accused's version that they engaged in some initial consensual foreplay there before proceeding to the bedroom. It was this evidence that Dickson J. felt conferred some air of reality on the mistake of fact argument. In contrast, the majority view was that the "evidence must appear from or be supported by sources other than the appellant in order to give it any air of reality."[130]

This majority view is novel, since it appears to deny the status of the accused's evidence under oath. The result of this approach would be that an accused could swear that he honestly believed the complainant was consenting, be believed by the jury, and would still have to be convicted, in the absence of evidence from any other source. Apart from being unsupported by authority, this seems a much more serious and practical limitation on the mistake of fact defence than a requirement of reasonableness, which the majority rejected.[131]

The other novel suggestion in the majority judgment is that only evidence "believed" by the jury can convey an air of reality to the mistake of fact defence.[132] Orthodox doctrine suggests that the test is whether the evidence is capable of raising a reasonable doubt in the minds of the jury. In any event, this would appear to be the source of the legislative formula contained in section 244(4) and discussed more fully elsewhere.[133]

Returning to the need for evidence other than the accused's to convey an air of reality, that evidence could arguably have been found in the folded clothes and necklace in the living-room. This was simply rejected as being relevant only to consent.[134] It, however, satisfied Dickson J.'s requirement of an air of reality,

---

130 *Ibid., per* McIntyre J., at 34-5.
131 *Ibid.*, at 35. It could also be viewed as a serious incursion on the function of the jury.
132 *Ibid., per* McIntyre J., at 31.
133 See Chapter 4, text accompanying note 133.
134 Note 126 above, *per* McIntyre J., at 34.

although he did not subscribe to the extraneous evidence requirement.

It is suggested, with respect, that the view of the majority in
Pappajohn is a departure from precedent on this requirement, but
that the result is nevertheless defensible. This is so since that
evidence could hardly be the basis of a reasonable doubt about
mistake of fact *when combined with acceptance of the complainant's version of events.* Could any reasonable jury doubt that a
man would be aware of the absence of consent, where, even though
a woman had removed her necklace in the living-room, she was
subsequently hysterical and resisted his advances? In other
words, in rejecting the accused's version of events with respect to
consent, the evidence referred to by Dickson J. as the basis for a
mistake of fact argument could not give the argument an air of
reality because it had to be seen in combination with the complainant's story. In order for this evidence to raise any reasonable
doubt, it had to be seen in combination with the accused's version.
This evidence would have to be rejected along with the assertion
of consent.

It is submitted, in light of *Pappajohn*, that the test of whether
the defences of consent and mistake of fact should be put to the
jury is whether the jury, *having rejected the consent defence,*
could still harbour a reasonable doubt based on the remaining
evidence *in toto.*[135] Perhaps this is what the majority meant: the
mistake of fact defence cannot be based on the accused's evidence
with respect to consent, such evidence having already been rejected as not raising a reasonable doubt.

A situation where alternative defences are possible was
suggested by Lambert J.A. in his dissenting judgment in *Trottier
v. R.*[136] He pointed out that the victim may have submitted
because of fear (as opposed to threats) of bodily harm.[137] Thus,
while she would not have been consenting, it would be possible for
the accused to believe she was, being unaware of her fear. It is

---

135   For a case where the defences were compatible see *R. v. Plummer* (1975), 31
      C.R.N.S. 220 (Ont. C.A.). Plummer had already raped the victim. Brown found
      her naked and had intercourse with her. Even if her version of events were
      accepted, it was still possible to find that he had a mistaken belief in consent
      because of his lack of knowledge of previous threats leading to her
      submission. A new trial was ordered as mistake of fact had not been
      considered.

136   Note 128 above.

137   See the new section 244(3)(b) on fear of the application of force.

submitted that, in this type of case, alternative defences would be appropriate. Obviously such cases will be rare.

8. PUBLICITY

A number of interests are at stake here. The accused and the complainant share an interest in a minimum of publicity. They also share a conflicting interest in a public trial if it is assumed that public scrutiny contributes to a fair trial. The complainant and accused may otherwise both be vulnerable to abuse of power. There is undoubtedly a public interest in knowledge of the workings of our criminal justice system. This is true both in the sense that there is legitimate public concern about the process[138] since it embodies the most naked exercise of power by the state over the individual, and in the sense that we are all potential complainants and accused persons. It is no doubt trite to say that a balance must be struck between these various interests, a balance which now has constitutional significance. The accused has a right to a "fair and public hearing" under section 11(d) of the Charter, while freedom of the press is ensconced in section 2(b).[139]

These provisions may well have an impact on a number of sections in the Code relating to publicity, unless section 1 of the Charter, permitting such reasonable limits as can be demonstrably justified in a free and democratic society, comes to the rescue.

The usual sections giving the judge discretionary power to minimise publicity apply. Thus he or she may exclude members of the public from the courtroom both during the trial[140] and the preliminary inquiry.[141] The judge may also, on application by the accused, ban publication of the evidence taken at a preliminary inquiry[142] until the trial is ended.

Special provisions relate to trials for incest, gross indecency and all the sexual assault offences. First, if an order excluding

---

138 For an historical analysis of the nature of this interest, see *Richmond Newspapers, Inc. v. Virginia*, 448 U.S. 555 (1980).

139 See generally M.D. Lepofsky, "Section 2(b) of the Charter and Media Coverage of Criminal Court Proceedings" (1983), 34 C.R. (3d) 63.

140 Section 442(1). Under s. 441, with respect to accused persons under 16 years, a trial without publicity is mandatory.

141 Section 465(1)(j).

142 Section 467.

members of the public is denied, a reason must be given.[143] Secondly, the judge is obliged, on application by the complainant or prosecutor, to make an order protecting the identity of the complainant.[144] Thirdly, the judge must inform the complainant of her right to make such an application.[145] The hearing to determine the admissibility of evidence of the past sexual conduct of the complainant must be held *in camera*[146] and there is a prohibition on publication of the details of this hearing.[147]

The result of all this is that the judge has the discretion to protect the privacy of the complainant or accused or both. However, neither the accused nor the complainant has the right to insist on either a closed or open trial. The complainant in certain cases has a right to anonymity.[148] It is conceivable that a judge might not consider anonymity adequate protection and close the trial against the accused's wishes. In this case, the constitutional argument would arise with respect to the right to a public trial. Similarly, a newspaper charged with an offence under section 246.6(5) or with failure to comply with a non-publication order under section 442(4) could make the constitutional freedom of the press argument.

It is not possible here to discuss fully the constitutional implications of publicity, but some guidance can be obtained from American cases on public trials of persons charged with sexual assault. It was stressed in *State v. Shepphard*,[149] for example, that the state must show a compelling need to deny the accused his right to a public trial. There should not be automatic closure in such cases. Rather there must be a "demonstrated need to protect a witness from a substantial threat of indignity which might induce reluctance to testify about a lurid or heinous sexual assault."[150] Thus a closed trial was justified in a case involving

---

143 Section 442(2).
144 Section 442(3). If the existence of such a non-publication order is disclosed to a jury the judge shall explain that it does not relate to the complainant's credibility. *R. v. Tierney* (1982), 31 C.R. (3d) 66 (Ont. C.A.). Why might anyone have thought that it did?
145 Section 442(3.1).
146 Section 246.6(3).
147 Section 246.6(4). See the text accompanying notes 36-45 above.
148 This no longer extends to s. 146(1) offences. See the Criminal Law Amendment Act, S.C. 1980-81-82, c. 125. s. 25.
149 438 A.2d 125 (1980, Conn.).
150 *Ibid.*, at 127.

multiple rapes by several accused[151] and in a case involving an eight-year-old rape victim.[152] The order itself should be limited to the need for closure.[153]

---

151 *U.S. ex. rel. Latimore v. Sielaff*, 561 F. 2d. 691 (7th Cir., 1977).
152 *Geise v. U.S.*, 262 F. 2d. 151 (9th Cir., 1958).
153 See note 149 above, at 128.

Chapter 8

Sentencing

The law and practice of sentencing is highly significant for a number of reasons. Many accused persons plead guilty. The sentencing process is therefore their main contact with the judicial part of the criminal justice process. On a practical level, after the exercise of police and prosecutorial discretion, sentencing decisions will reveal the most about the reality of the law on sexual assault.[1] In contrast to information about the exercise of pre-trial discretion, information about the range of sentences will be readily available. The sentences which judges impose have the power to convey revealing judgments about the perceived seriousness of particular harms.

Extreme examples can be found in a recent book entitled *The Aftermath of Rape*.[2] The authors refer to the American history of differing punishment for the rape of white women on the one hand (especially where the rapist was black) and slaves on the other. Frequently there was a mandatory death penalty for blacks but not for whites.[3] The authors also quote from the Law of Alfred the Great.[4]

> [If a man] seizes by the breast a young woman . . . and lies with her, he shall pay 60 shillings compensation . . . if another man has previously lain with her, then the compensation shall be half this sum.[5]

Although the new sexual assault offences and the remaining offences against children contain maximum sentences, judges determine what is appropriate within the permitted range. As-

---

1 Thus a maximum sentence can fade into insignificance when one examines the range of sentences actually imposed for particular crimes.

2 T.W. McCahill, L.C. Meyer and A.M. Fischman (1979).

3 *E.g.*, in Georgia, if a white man raped a slave or a non-white free person, the punishment was a fine or imprisonment at the discretion of the court. *Ibid.* p. 202.

4 C. 892 A.D. *Ibid.*

5 F.L. Attenborough, trans., *The Laws of the Earliest English Kings* (1922), p. 256.

suming that it is possible to draw any conclusions about judicial views of bad and not so bad rapes, indecent assaults, etc., Parliament has not indicated in the latest reform that any of these judicial views are to be abandoned. The Criminal Law Amendment Act has made little attempt to control the exercise of discretion at this end of the criminal justice process. It is safe to conclude, therefore, that existing cases will give a reasonably reliable guide to judicial views as to what will be relevant factors in the future. If there has been any labelling of more or less serious sexual attacks and more or less legitimate victims, and if such labelling has influenced sentences imposed, there seems no reason to suppose that any dramatic change will occur. Likewise, assumptions about what causes the most trauma to victims will continue to be made, unless judges are influenced by the research that is available on the consequences of sexual assault.

This chapter focuses on rape and indecent assault as being most revealing about possible trends in sentencing for sexual assault. Brief reference will also be made to sentencing trends *vis-à-vis* offences against children and other vulnerable people.

The new maxima are compared to the old relevant maximum sentences in the following tables.[6]

Indecent assault on a female	5 years	Sexual assault	10 years
Indecent assault on a male; Attempted rape	10 years	Sexual assault with a weapon, etc.	14 years
Rape	Life imprisonment	Aggravated sexual assault	Life imprisonment

---

6 It is not intended here to review the range of sentences available, as there is nothing distinctive about sexual assault. See generally, C.C. Ruby, *Sentencing*, 2nd ed. (1980), and P. Nadin-Davis, *Sentencing in Canada* (1982). No new initiatives have been taken by Parliament with respect to treatment or the varieties of sentence. But see R.S. Brown, "The Castration Alternative" (1977), 19 Can. J. of Crim. and Corr. 157. However, it would have been surprising if Parliament had begun to reform the law of sentencing in a piecemeal manner. Clearly it needs general attention. See K. Jobson, "Reforming Sentencing Laws: A Canadian Perspective" in B.A. Grosman, ed., *New Directions in Sentencing* (1980). See also the proposals for reform contained in Bill C-19, first reading, February 7, 1984, Part XX.

A number of consequences flow from these changes. The most serious form of sexual attack is still punishable by life imprisonment. However, one substantive aspect of seriousness in the past was penetration of the vagina by the penis. Any other type of sexual attack had a ceiling of five years, in the case of a female victim, and ten in the case of a man. The removal of this limitation is an improvement, in the sense that the change in substantive law has removed an unjustifiable limitation on judicial sentencing discretion.

In contrast, a ceiling of ten or fourteen years is imposed where a relatively less violent attack, which would have been labelled rape in the past, takes place. This is, to a great extent, a change on paper only, since sentences rarely approach those limits. It is difficult to generalise about the range of sentences for the repealed offences. Ruby suggests that sentences for rape normally varied from between one and twelve years.[7] A one-year sentence was imposed in *R. v. Shonias*,[8] in which some injury was inflicted but the parties knew each other. An example of a twelve-year sentence can be found in *R. v. Oliver*[9] involving a psychopath. In this case the court pointed out that it would be appropriate to have the accused declared a dangerous sexual offender.

In contrast to Ruby, Nadin-Davis[10] indicates a range of between three and eight years.[11] A number of cases point to a low range. In *Colbert v. A.G. Can.*[12] the accused had attacked the victim in a cemetery, threatening to shoot her if she did not stop screaming. A sentence of fourteen years was reduced to eight on appeal, the Quebec Court of Appeal indicating that a normal sentence should fall between four and seven years and a longer sentence should be imposed only in exceptional cases. The Nova Scotia Supreme Court (Appeal Division) has gone even further, indicating that a six-year sentence was appropriate only if there were grave aggravating circumstances.[13] In *Green v. R.*,[14] four

---

7 See C.C. Ruby, *ibid.*, p. 440.

8 (1974), 21 C.C.C. (2d) 301 (Ont. C.A.).

9 (1977), 39 C.R.N.S. 345 (Ont. C.A.).

10 *Sentencing in Canada* (1982), pp. 234 *et seq.*

11 He gives examples of cases falling outside this normal range. On the high side is *R. v. Bell* (1973), 28 C.R.N.S. 55 (N.S. C.A.), and on the low, *R. v. Rose* (1979), 5 Man. R. (2d) 211 (Co. Ct.).

12 (1981), 24 C.R. (3d) 77 (Que. C.A.).

13 *Amero v. R.* (1978), 3 C.R. (3d) S-45, at S-49-50. However, the same court has referred to a class of "horror rapes" such as in *R.v. Pontello* (1977), 38 C.C.C. (2d) 262 (Ont. C.A.) where a heavier sentence should be imposed. See *R. v. Oliver*

years was reduced to two and a half. The offender had abducted a pregnant woman in the street and kept her naked in the snow at knife-point for one and a half hours while he tried many times to have intercourse. The sentence was reduced to assist rehabilitation.

A sentence of more than seven or eight years should probably be regarded as highly unusual. However, it should also be noted that rapists were occasionally sentenced to imprisonment for life. Such sentences were often associated with some kind of mental or psychopathic disorder so that the protection of the public became a primary concern.[15] It was stated in *R. v. Hill*:[16]

> When an accused has been convicted of a serious crime in itself calling for a substantial sentence and when he suffers from some mental or personality disorder rendering him a danger to the community but not subjecting him to confinement in a mental institution and when it is uncertain when, if ever, the accused will be cured of his affliction, in my opinion the appropriate sentence is one of life.[17]

An accused may also be imprisoned for an indefinite period, where he satisfies the criteria for being a dangerous offender.[18]

Ruby[19] draws a distinction between offenders who suffer from

(1979), 34 N.S.R. (2d) 631 (C.A.). Interestingly, the case of *R. v. Simmons* (1973), 13 C.C.C. (2d) 65 (Ont. C.A.) was mentioned as *not* being in this class. There the victim had been raped 8 times in all by 3 men, but she had been drinking heavily with the men prior to being raped.

14 (1982), 26 C.R. (3d) 285 (Ont. C.A.).

15 The terminology chosen can be very revealing. See, *e.g.*, the remark of Hugessen A.C.J.S.C., in *R. v. Archontakis* (1980), 24 C.R. (3d) 63 at 66 (Que. S.C.) that "[o]ur wives and our daughters [not women and girls] must be able to walk about on the streets...."

16 (1974), 15 C.C.C. (2d) 145 (Ont. C.A.) (affirmed [1977] 1 S.C.R. 827).

17 *Ibid.*, at 147, *per* Jessup J.A. for the court. See also *R. v. Haig* (1974), 26 C.R.N.S. 247 (Ont. C.A.), life sentence upheld where no guarantee of cure; and *R. v. Pontello*, note 13 above. *Cf. R. v. Jones*, [1971] 2 O.R. 549 (C.A.) in which life was reduced to 12 years, even though the psychiatric report indicated the appellant was potentially dangerous and was poorly suited for any form of treatment. The court pointed out that sentences of 6-10 years were being imposed for vicious cases of rape, so a life sentence was out of line in this situation.

18 See ss. 688-695.1. See generally C. Greenland, "Dangerous Sexual Offenders in Canada" (1972), 14 Can. J. of Crim. and Corr. 44; R. Stortini, "Preventive Detention of Dangerous Sexual Offenders" (1975), 17 Cr. L.Q. 416; and Nadin-Davis, note 10 above, at 410-20. It has been held in the U.S. that similar legislation is constitutional as a life sentence is not disproportionate where actual or threatened violence was used. *State v. Beck*, 286 S.E. 2d 234 (1981, West Virginia App.).

19 *Sentencing*, 2nd ed. (1980).

a personality disorder or sexual psychopaths (who may receive life sentences) and others. This raises an interesting question. It is clear that at least some rapists act out of a deep-seated hostility to women.[20] If hatred of women were regarded as a "mental or personality disorder" within the *Hill* doctrine, then it would appear that such sentences ought to be relatively common. It is not unknown for such a view to be expressed. In *R. v. Pontello*[21] a life sentence was upheld on appeal. The offender was a respected person in the community, married, with a job. Psychiatric evidence indicated that he had a very high degree of hostility toward women and constituted a continuing danger to them. This stands in contrast to the vast majority of cases, however, where attention was focused on the circumstances of the offence and little or no inquiry was made into the motivation of the offender. It is possible, therefore, that rapists who acted out of hatred of women were given a sentence in the normal range, to be released without treatment in a given number of years.

What other factors have been chosen as relevant to the sentencing decision, and what do they reveal about judicial views on the relative seriousness of different rapes? The aggravating factors were obvious and included the use or threat of violence,[22] accompanying indecent or unusual acts,[23] the number of people involved in the attack[24] as well as whether the accused was the leader,[25] the length of time the victim was held,[26] whether there was an element of breach of trust[27] as well as factors that are always relevant such as the criminal record, if any, and whether the offender gave a false alibi. Nadin-Davis suggests that the courts

---

[20] Professor Marshall in his paper "The Classification of Sexual Aggressives and the Associated Demographic, Social, Developmental and Psychological Features" in S.N. Verdun-Jones and A.A. Keltner, eds., *Sexual Aggression and the Law* (1983), at 7, refers to research indicating that "rapists are hostile toward women, ... that they have a need to humiliate their victims ... and that an angered man is more sexually excited by the prospect of raping a woman than is a nonangered man."

[21] Note 13 above.

[22] See, *e.g., R. v. Turner*, [1971] 1 O.R. 83 (C.A.); *R. v. Dubien* (1982), 27 C.R. (3d) 378 (Ont. C.A.).

[23] See *Dubien, ibid.; R. v. Willaert*, [1953] O.R. 282 (C.A.); and *Pontello*, note 13 above.

[24] See *Willaert, ibid.*; and *R. v. Bell* (1973), 6 N.S.R. (2d) 351 (C.A.).

[25] In *R. v. Bell, ibid.*, the leader of a gang rape received 12 years. See also *R. v. Lévesque* (1980), 19 C.R. (3d) 43 (Que. S.C.).

[26] See *R. v. Thornton* (1980), 42 N.S.R. (2d) 647 (C.A.).

[27] See *R. v. Savard* (1979), 11 C.R. (3d) 309 (Que. C.A.).

have failed to take into account the effects on the victim.[28] It seems
clear, however, that the above aggravating factors (as well as the
mitigating ones, to follow) were based on assumptions about harm
to victims in general, even if the court did not inquire into the effect
on a particular victim. The question of whether these assumptions
are warranted will be returned to when all relevant factors have
been mentioned.

Mitigating factors have been less obvious and more controversial. They included the age of the accused and an indication that
rehabilitation was possible.[29] They could also include the moral
standards and behaviour of the victim, although the cases are not
consistent in this regard. In *R. v. Simmons*[30] six years was reduced
to four, emphasis being placed on the victim's character. She had
been drinking with three men, who took her to a deserted place, held
her down and raped her eight times in all. Brooke J.A. pointed out
that she was "married and separated and living in a common law
relationship.... She admitted to having relations with men with
whom she met at bars and with whom she would dance."[31] This can
be contrasted with *R. v. Savard.*[32]

> ... [I do not] attach any significance to her particular lifestyle (concubinage
> with another taxi driver), for that in no way affects her right to be protected
> from assaults of this kind.[33]

A recent case applying a notion of contributory negligence
attracted public attention. In *R. v. Brown*,[34] eight years was cut in
half on appeal, McGillivray C.J.A. stating:

> ... it would not have been surprising to that young woman that something
> might well happen to her going up to the man's apartment between 2:00 and
> 3:00 in the morning, having been drinking beer all evening, with the expressed
> intention of smoking marijuana and drinking more beer. [W]e think it is a very

---

28 *Sentencing in Canada* (1982), p. 237, though he makes reference to *R. v.
Sweitzer*, [1982] 5 W.W.R. 552 (Alta. C.A.) (reversed [1982] 1 S.C.R. 949); and *R. v.
Selamio* (1979), 23 A.R. 403 (N.W.T. S.C.).

29 See *R. v. Turner*, note 22 above, and *Green v. R.* (1982), 26 C.R. (3d) 285 (Ont. C.A.).

30 (1973), 13 C.C.C. (2d) 165 (Ont. C.A.).

31 *Ibid.*, at 70. See C. Jones and E. Aronson, "Attribution of Fault to a Rape Victim
as a Function of Respectability of the Victim" (1973), 26 J. of Personality and
Soc. Psych. 415.

32 (1979), 11 C.R. (3d) 309 (Que. C.A.).

33 *Ibid.*, at 311 *per* Kaufman J.A., for the court. One wonders how this evidence was
admitted in both *Savard* and *Oliver*.

34 (1983), 34 C.R. (3d) 191 (Alta. C.A.).

different situation from the rapist who breaks into somebody's home and attacks them or picks somebody off the street.[35]

There are, therefore, at least some judges who think it is less serious sexually to assault someone who is utilising her freedom to drink and visit others late at night. What was also revealed here and in other cases was the view that it is less serious to assault a friend or acquaintance than a stranger, in spite of the breach of trust factor. This may become even more significant now that prosecutions are possible for marital sexual assault.

The cases on indecent assault may be of even more assistance than those on rape as the former resembles sexual assault in that many types of behaviour can be involved. Nadin-Davis[36] suggests that the offences against females could be divided into three types. First, there was infringement of sexual privacy, as in *R. v. Konzelman.*[37] The facts were that the offender, acting on a bet with his drinking companions, grabbed a woman from behind and shook her breasts. A conditional discharge was granted. The assaults in the second category involved sexual interference akin to attempted rape where sentences ranged from six months to two years, aggravating factors being similar to those for rape.[38] Lastly, there were assaults on children.[39] One basic question which the courts will now have to confront will be the relevance of vaginal penetration. It is clear that this is to be no longer of substantive significance; the degree of violence is the main aggravating factor according to Parliament. However, in the past sentences have been considerably lower for indecent assault, not involving penetration, than for rape, and judges may resist change. On the one hand, treating penetration as a factor would bring rape in by the back door. On the other hand, subjecting a victim to the risk of pregnancy is something that may well be viewed by many people as an aggravating factor in a sexual attack. It is submitted that the courts should avoid anything which might lead to the continuation of detailed examination of the witness as to whether penetration

---

35 *Ibid.*, at 191-2.

36 Note 28 above, pp. 239-42.

37 (1980), 5 Man. R. (2d) 165 (C.A.).

38 He states that probation with compulsory psychiatric treatment is common, as in *R. v.Sabean* (1979), 35 N.S.R. (2d) 35 (C.A.).

39 Touchers may receive treatment as in *R. v. D.*, [1972] 1 O.R. 405 (C.A.). Repeaters can get 3-6 months and probation, *R. v. Deihl* (1972), 5 N.S.R. (2d) 21 (C.A.). Incarceration may be longer if there is an element of perversion, *R. v. Mochan* (1978), 23 N.B.R. (2d) 90 (C.A.).

actually took place or not. This is supported by research indicating that touching short of penetration can be as devastating to the victim as penetration itself.[40]

Sentences for indecent assaults on males were also influenced by the age of the victim, assaults on children obviously being viewed as much more serious than attacks on adults.[41] Within the scope allowed by the maximum of ten years, a wide spectrum could be observed ranging from horseplay involving the grabbing of genitals, for example,[42] to homosexual rape.[43] Other aggravating factors resembled those of rape, such as the violence used, the length of the victim's confinement and an element of breach of trust.[44] It was not a mitigating factor that the assault took place in a setting, such as prison, where such assaults occur from time to time.[45]

At the time of writing, cases on the new sexual assault offences are very few and, in any event, it will take a long time for discernible patterns to emerge. In *R. v. Williams*[46] a total sentence of seven years was imposed for two sexual assaults, one causing bodily harm to a sixty-year-old victim. Sexual intercourse had been attempted, with considerable violence. This seems to be in line with previous rape cases, and points in the direction of emphasis being placed on the degree of violence rather than whether or not actual sexual intercourse took place.

Life imprisonment was reduced to fourteen years in *R. v. Connors*,[47] a case of aggravated sexual assault. This seems to be

---

40 T.W. McCahill, L.C. Meyer and A.M. Fischman, *The Aftermath of Rape* (1979), p. 67.

41 See *R.v. Solem* (1979), 1 Sask. R. 181 (C.A.); *R. v. Marple* (1973), 6 N.S.R. (2d) 389 (C.A.). Here four men attacked the private parts of the 19-year-old victim. A sentence of one day's imprisonment plus a $500 fine was upheld, the court pointing out that he was not hurt physically or mentally. *Cf. R. v. Hopkins* (1977), 23 N.S.R. (2d) 550 (C.A.), where the accused showed a 13-year-old boy his penis and pulled down his pants. A sentence of one year's imprisonment was upheld. The Alberta Court of Appeal has pointed out that persons who attack children must have substantial sentences to deter others: *R. v. Zdep* (1981), 21 C.R. (3d) 283.

42 See Nadin-Davis, *Sentencing in Canada* (1982), p. 244.

43 In *Young v. R.* (1980), 27 C.R. (3d) 85 (B.C. C.A.), 7 years was imposed for a series of attacks on young boys.

44 *E.g.*, the accused was a Cub Scout Master in *R. v. Webster* (1978), 20 C.L.Q. 430 (Ont. C.A.).

45 *R. v. Hennessy* (1968), 66 W.W.R. 383 (Man. C.A.).

46 (1983), 60 N.S.R. (2d) 29 (C.A.).

47 (1983), 60 N.S.R. (2d) 219 (C.A.).

on the heavy side, especially in view of the fact that the victim was only slightly wounded. However, she was only seven years old and was confined by the offender for twelve hours while he forced her to commit various sexual acts. The offender also had a previous conviction for indecent assault of a child. The age of the victim and the length of confinement were obviously serious aggravating factors here, so that again this could be characterized as a continuation of past sentencing policy.

To the extent that prediction is possible, it would appear that judges will take the following factors into account when passing sentence: the age of the victim, the extent of the violence, the nature of the attack, the length of the confinement and the relationship of trust, if any, between the offender and the victim. At least some judges will also take into account their opinion on whether the victim contributed to the attack. This last factor is highly questionable since it involves a political judgment that sexual assault laws do not offer the same protection to all women, *in their own right*, as to those conforming to traditional expectations of the virtuous woman.

Are any of the other factors questionable? What little research there has been leads one to question assumptions about age. In *The Aftermath of Rape*,[48] the authors produce data from the Philadelphia Sexual Assault Victim Study, which indicate that, at least in the short run, adult victims of sexual assault are more likely to face adjustment problems than adolescents or children. Various factors could account for this. A woman may not have the same support system as a younger victim and may worry about the effect on her marriage. The assault may affect her sense of maturity and control over her environment. She may have more permanence in her life and thus may not be able to imagine an escape from her surroundings. However, the authors are careful to state that it is not possible to draw conclusions about long-term effects, as children may suffer adjustment problems as they enter adult life.[49] This may be particularly true where the offender is a family member, as in incest, and one of the very people who would normally be a source of support to the victim in adjusting to the fact that she has been assaulted. Further research is desirable, but the courts should not necessarily assume that the older the victim, the less she will be traumatized by sexual assault.

---

48 T.W. McCahill, L.C. Meyer and A.M. Fischman (1979).
49 See also J.S. Peters, "Child Rape: Defusing the Psychological Time Bomb" (1973), 9 Hospital Physician 46.

A similar point can be made with respect to the nature of the attack. Judges have been influenced by the severity and the range of acts inflicted on the victim. However, it is possible that the more the attack resembles non-assaultive affectionate behaviour, the more the victim's future experience of sexuality and affection may be affected.[50]

The third factor which perhaps should be questioned is the relationship between the offender and the victim. Where the victim is a child this is likely to aggravate the sentence or at least not mitigate it. It seems much more likely to be a mitigating factor with respect to adult victims. The data generated by the Philadelphia Sexual Assault Victim Study suggests that the victim is most traumatized by being assaulted by a casual acquaintance. An attack by a stranger may lead to distrust of all strangers, and contact with them can be minimised. It is possible to treat an attack by a close family member in isolation. However, it is difficult to avoid acquaintances, and the victim lacks the information about them that would help her particularise her feelings about a family member.[51] The very cases which judges may treat as less serious, for example sexual assault by a date, may well involve severe feelings of insecurity and distrust on the part of the victim.

It is concluded that, in determining sentences, judges should think in terms of what is most threatening and damaging to victims, mostly women, rather than in terms of what is most threatening to themselves as husbands and fathers—for example, the random attack of a "respectable" woman or girl accompanied by acts of sexual perversion.

It is concluded that Canadian research is needed on the victim's experience of harm and the difficulties of adjustment so that judges can take this type of data into account in deciding upon the factors which relate to the seriousness of sexual assault. This is not the whole picture, of course, since judges must be influenced by factors pertaining to the offender and also by the fact that Parliament has indicated that violence must be treated as a significant aggravating factor.

---

50 "When a rape incident contains several ambiguous elements, it becomes more difficult for the rape victim to mentally segregate the rape from her every day life. . . . '[F]ondling and caressing' and 'contact without penetration' are significantly associated with changes in sleeping patterns, increased nightmares, fear of being home alone, worsened heterosexual relationships. . . ." Note 48 above, p. 67.

51 *Ibid.*, pp. 67-9.

The remaining offences against children and other vulnerable people were outside the scope of the sentencing reform, so that sentences are more predictable than with sexual assault. The maximum for intercourse with females under fourteen is the most serious, being life.[52] The vast amount of judicial discretion is underlined by the fact that the moral guilt involved in such offences can vary enormously. This was pointed at in *R. v. Taylor*.[53]

> What does not seem to have been appreciated by the public is the wide spectrum of guilt. ... At one end of the spectrum is the youth who stands in the dock, maybe 16, 17 or 18, who has had what starts off as a virtuous friendship with a girl under the age of 16. That virtuous friendship has ended with them having sexual intercourse with one another. At the other end of the spectrum is the man in a supervisory capacity, a schoolmaster or social worker, who sets out deliberately to seduce a girl under the age of 16 who is in his charge.[54]

For a youth, a warning may be an appropriate sentence,[55] in contrast to imprisonment for an older man, the courts stressing the elements of exploitation and breach of trust.[56] The range of sentences is therefore very wide, from cases where young people have been engaging in sexual experimentation[57] to sentences of periods from eighteen months to six years in step-father type cases. It is not unknown, however, for the maximum to be imposed.[58]

---

52 This maximum, together with the imposition of absolute liability in s. 146(1), makes the offence vulnerable to constitutional challenge under s. 7 of the Charter. In *Ref. Re S. 94(2) of the Motor Vehicle Act* (1983), 33 C.R. (3d) 22 (B.C. C.A.), an absolute liability offence was declared unconstitutional because of a mandatory period of imprisonment. However, in *R. v. Stevens* (1983), 3 C.C.C. (3d) 198, the Ontario Court of Appeal held that s. 7 did not invalidate s. 146(1), assuming that it gave the courts power to assess the constitutionality of the substantive content of offences.

53 [1977] 1 W.L.R. 612 at 615 (C.A.) quoted by the Ontario Court of Appeal in *R. v. Belanger* (1979), 8 C.R. (3d) S-10. See also *R. v. B.* (1982), 23 Alta. L.R. (2d) 131 (C.A.).

54 *Ibid.*, at 615.

55 In *Belanger*, note 53 above, 3 years imprisonment was changed to one year of probation for a naive and immature 17-year-old.

56 *E.g.*, in *R v. Farmer* (1978), 30 N.S.R. (2d) 79 (C.A.), a period of 3 years imprisonment was imposed on a 28-year-old who had intercourse with his 13-year-old step-daughter, the court stating that potential danger to the accused in the penetentiary should not be treated as a mitigating factor. *Quaere* whether it is morally justifiable for the state to expose the offender to the risk of assault in condemning his assault?

57 *R. v. St. Onge* (1977), 17 N.B.R. (2d) 99 (C.A.), and *R. v. Kirby* (1976), 24 Nfld. & P.E.I. R. 260 (Nfld. Prov. Ct.).

58 *R. v. Head* (1970), 1 C.C.C. (2d) 436 (Sask. C.A.). A life sentence was not disturbed where the accused, with a previous conviction for indecent assault, had raped a

Where the victim is between fourteen and sixteen, a similar approach is taken,[59] although the main difference is that the really serious offences against very young children are excluded. On the other hand, since the offender will only have been convicted if "more to blame," the victim being of previously chaste character, this offence is confined to cases very similar to rape. Nevertheless, the maximum here is only five years,[60] providing a stark contrast, at least on paper, to life imprisonment for a section 146(1) offence.

Sentences for incest rarely approach the maximum of fourteen years.[61] The few cases that there are tend to fall in the two to four year range.[62] Aggravating circumstances, such as a previous conviction,[63] can result in a heavier sentence. In contrast, imprisonment is not always imposed. For example, intercourse with an older daughter not living at home has been treated much less seriously than intercourse with a younger dependant child.[64]

There are too few cases on the remaining offences of seduction and intercourse with a step-daughter or employee to make any generalisations or predictions with respect to sentencing.

The above outline has been very brief, but a full analysis of sentencing law in the context of sexual assault will not be possible for several years. Uncertainty has also been created by the fact that, at the time of writing, Parliament is considering an extensive legislative statement and reform of the general law of sentencing, as well as other aspects of the criminal law.[65] The sentences envisaged include imprisonment, probation, restitution, fines, forfeiture and community service orders. The principle is adopted that a sentence should be the least onerous appropriate in the circumstances.[66] Thus, a new section 645(3)(f) would read:

6-year-old girl. Psychiatric evidence pointed to a likelihood that he would repeat the offence. The protection of the public was regarded as essential.

59 Nadin-Davis, *Sentencing in Canada* (1982), p. 239, suggests "some parallelism" in the sentencing practices.

60 Section 146(2). In *Train v. R.* (1959), 31 C.R. 139 (N.B. C.A.) 2 years was lowered to 15 months, partly because of "certain circumstances leading up to the offence."

61 Section 150(2).

62 An example in the father-daughter situation is *R. v. Richardson* (1973), 6 N.S.R. (2d) 130 (C.A.): 3 years.

63 *R. v. Moore* (1979), 30 N.S.R. (2d) 638 (C.A.). A suspended sentence and probation was raised to 5 years, although the court noted that usually sentences ranged from 2-4 years. See also *R. v. Wyatt*, [1944] 2 W.W.R. 168 (B.C. C.A.).

64 Probation and treatment were ordered in *R. v. Truax* (1979), 22 C.L.Q. 157 (Ont. C.A.). where an older daughter was not living at home.

65 See Bill C-19, which was given its first reading on 7 February, 1984, Part XX.

66 Bill C-19, s. 199 (s. 645 (3)(f) in the Criminal Code as amended).

[A] term of imprisonment should be imposed only
   (i) to protect the public from a violent or dangerous offender,
   (ii) where a less restrictive alternative would not adequately protect the public or the integrity of the administration of justice or sufficiently reflect the gravity of the offence or the repetitive nature of the criminal conduct of the offender.

These provisions would give ample scope for the imposition of sentences of imprisonment for sexual assault, except where minor assaults are concerned, for example, a touching of a sexual nature in the workplace. Conversely, they would leave the door open for decisions denying the gravity of the offence or the dangerousness of the offender, as in cases of sexual assault by an acquaintance or spouse. However, this possibility is the inevitable concomitant of any system based on judicial discretion,[67] so that would not be a new development.

What would be new is that specific reference would have to be made, in a pre-sentence report, to an interview with the victim. Such an interview would have to be conducted where "practicable," section 648(1) stating:

Unless otherwise specified by the court in a particular case, a pre-sentence report shall contain ...
   (f) the results of an interview with any victim of the offence, including any information concerning any harm done to, or loss suffered by, the victim, in cases where it is applicable and practicable to conduct such an interview.

This should have the advantage of providing the judge with information about the victim in all sexual assault cases where a pre-sentence report is deemed desirable, rather than this being a matter of chance, as it presently is. The judge would thus have more complete information on which to assess the sentence. As well the consultation with the victim may have beneficial effects with respect to her perception of the criminal justice system.

---

67 The new s. 645(2) would state this principle in legislative form.

Index

Printed in Canada